COME HOME, AMERICA

COME HOME, AMERICA

THE RISE AND FALL
(AND REDEEMING PROMISE)
OF OUR COUNTRY

WILLIAM GREIDER

New York Times best-selling author of **Who Will Tell the People**

RODALE

Printed in the United States of America
Rodale Inc. makes every effort to use acid-free ∞, recycled paper ☉.

Book design by Anthony Serge

Library of Congress Cataloging-in-Publication Data

Greider, William.
    Come home, America : the rise and fall (and redeeming promise) of our country /
William Greider.
        p.   cm.
    Includes bibliographical references and index.
    ISBN-13: 978–1–59486–816–0   hardcover
    ISBN-10: 1–59486–816–6   hardcover
    1. United States—Economic policy—2001—Citizen participation.
    2. United States—Social conditions—21st century.   3. Conservatism—United
States—History—20th century.   I. Title.
    HC106.83.G74   2009
    330.973—dc22   2008052292

Distributed to the trade by Macmillan

2   4   6   8   10   9   7   5   3   1   hardcover

We inspire and enable people to improve their lives and the world around them
For more of our products visit **rodalestore.com** or call 800-848-4735

For Lawrence Goodwyn and Lee Halprin
Two wise and generous teachers

CONTENTS

CHAPTER ONE

FAIR WARNING

I have some hard things to say about our country. Beyond recession and financial crisis, we are in much deeper trouble than many people suppose or the authorities want to acknowledge. Because I think Americans always deal better with adversity if they have a clear understanding of what they are confronting, this book will address the gloomy circumstances and rough passage I see ahead for the American people.

Everything around us is changing, and Americans must change, too. First, we must be honest with ourselves, face the hard facts, and put aside some comforting myths. Then, we must find the nerve to take responsibility again for our country and democracy. Taking responsibility means having the courage to step up and reclaim our power as citizens. We have to relearn what many in earlier generations knew: how to assert our own ideas and values on what the future should look like, how to make ourselves heard amid the empty noise of politics, how to avow our convictions as aggressively as necessary to alter the course of history.

Americans will get through this. Our country has been through far worse in the past. We can emerge from it in promising new ways, not necessarily richer, but wiser and joined more closely together as a people, more able to realize fulfilling lives. If we do the hard work. If we change.

★   ★   ★   ★   ★

We live in a country where telling the hard truth with clarity has become taboo. Its implications are too alarming. Any politician who says aloud what some of

1

them know or feel in their guts is vilified as defeatist or unpatriotic. Many are clueless, of course, and others are too scared to raise forbidden subjects. I understand their silence and I do not forgive them.

This book is about harsh truths that were mostly not addressed during the long and intensely reported campaign for the presidency. A few marginal candidates did challenge the orthodox version of American greatness, but their also-ran status ensured they would not be widely heard. Most politicians looked the other way and stuck to familiar themes of patriotic optimism. The news media did not help much, either, by generally adhering to conventional thinking and ignoring dissenting opinions. Under these circumstances, citizens are more or less on their own, and remarkably, they do often find their way to the truth about things. In these very difficult times, I hope this book will help them.

Our newly elected president's victory and inauguration have stirred the national spirit—a new president always renews our optimism—but during the campaign Barack Obama did not stray far from the accepted assumptions about the American condition. He promised big changes on many important issues and, like most Americans, I hope for his success.

But the ominous historical circumstances moving against the nation pose adversities that dwarf any single leader. One damaging myth Americans ought to abandon is the naive notion that the celebrity power of the presidency can somehow solve our problems. That faith has been disappointed again and again in recent decades. First, the new leader is built up with miraculous powers, then cast down when he fails to prevail.

Blaming politicians is a healthy American pastime and I intend to do a lot of it, but I want to suggest a more complicated perspective. Politicians are human. That is, they are fallible, prone to folly and error, subject to all of life's usual confusions. I have spent my adult life around government and politics, working as a reporter and dealing closely with the people who have power and make the decisions that govern the nation. Many are earnest and fun to be around. Some rise to noble stature and are courageous and wise even when their causes do not prevail. Many politicians are spear carriers and merely follow routines. Others are corrupted by power and go for the money. They are a mixed lot, but so are we all.

Knowing this about them and knowing the obstacles they face within the deformed political system, I feel a measure of sympathy, especially for the conscientious few who struggle heroically to make the governing system function as it should, serving the general welfare as servants of the people. I do not blame them when their efforts fall short.

The political behavior I do not forgive is failing to give people fair warning. This is the very least we should expect from a system that describes the American people as "sovereign" citizens and proclaims the United States a "self-governing" democracy. Those who govern ought to tell people what's coming so they at least have a chance to get out of the way.

Modern politicians routinely evade that obligation on matters large and small. I have frequently observed the silence that comes over Washington when Congress, the White House, or one of the federal agencies enacts a measure that will deliver a damaging blow to many citizens. The insiders know what's ahead and may even have participated in making it happen. Yet they do not share the bad news with the public in a timely manner.

Evasion is merely one symptom of the deep decay in America's representative democracy. The political system functions well enough for some purposes and some interests, but it does not honor its democratic obligations—usually, it doesn't even try. A wide gulf has opened between the governing and the governed. I once described this poisoned relationship as "mutual contempt." Americans in general are blunt about their disgust with the political order. But people in power don't think so much of ordinary citizens, either. They don't express this openly for obvious reasons, but their contempt is reflected in their behavior.

More than 15 years ago, I wrote a book—*Who Will Tell the People*—that explored the bleak reality of representative democracy. It helped ordinary citizens understand why their representative system has lost much of its meaning and how democratic principles are routinely betrayed in everyday practice. The book was not warmly received by governing elites. By governing elites, I mean more than the elected officials. The term is meant to include the deep ranks of influentials in and out of the government who exert disproportionate influence on the decision-making—the policy makers and professional experts and party functionaries, the lobbyists and lawyers and the financial and business sectors they represent, the academic thinkers and major media. These opinion leaders did not much like how my book depicted them.[1]

The deformities in our democracy, they complained, were not caused by Washington, but by the people. Office holders are compelled to take evasive actions, they explained, to fend off lazy and inattentive constituents, voters who randomly act on irrational impulses and make impossible demands. Blame them, not us. Democracy "works," I was assured, by giving the people the screwed-up government they deserve.

The governing classes' sour view of the governed still prevails. The democratic condition has not improved but deteriorated further. So has the public's regard for the system. Democracy is broken and most Americans seem to know it. Even in Washington, this is no longer news.

★　★　★　★　★

I start with the failing democracy because it is the soggy mattress thrown over everything else this book will discuss. The immobilized political system that allows powerful interests to exercise virtual veto power over major reforms is not a new condition. But the stakes of failure and paralysis are much higher today because the country is on far more dangerous ground. The public yearns for the enormous changes that are required on many fronts. Yet the status quo is stuck, deformed by the concentration of power and unwilling to respond with anything more than limited gestures.

Electing a new president and shifting control to a different party can help, of course, and a new political opening has arrived. Republicans are in disarray; Democrats are hesitantly taking up some of the larger issues. But I am not going to dwell on the combat between the two major parties or on the failures of George W. Bush's presidency. Bush is gone, but the larger predicament still threatens the nation.

On the whole, it has bipartisan origins. Both political parties are implicated in the country's darkening prospects, both are reluctant to come clean about momentous mistakes. Despite important differences between them, Republicans and Democrats largely overlap in their ideological convictions and governing strategies. Neither party has been willing to face its own culpability or abandon policies that are deeply destructive to the national well-being. Yet the 2008 elections could eventually be seen as a historic turning point. In spite of the stark circumstances, Barack Obama provided fresh evidence for the redeeming promise of our nation and persuaded an energetic majority to believe that Americans can still remake the country anew. I believe this, too. I shudder at the alternative.

★ ★ ★ ★ ★

This is what the politicians and policy elites don't want to talk about. I don't see a nice way to put it. America as "number one" is over. The United States is headed for a fall, a great comeuppance that will impose wrenching changes on our society and deliver humiliating blows to our national pride. As a nation, we will still be very wealthy and awesomely powerful, but the country's preeminent economic strength is steadily deteriorating, as is its ability to dominate other nations through persuasion or military force. America's worldly power, wealth, and status are all rapidly diminishing in historic dimensions. The long and triumphant era during which America led the world and largely got its way is approaching an end.

It's easy enough to see why political candidates and the collaborating elites cannot bring themselves to talk honestly about this, much less to propose plausible alternatives that might replace the failing status quo. They dare not even admit that American power is faltering. In spite of their reluctance to speak of this honestly, I have a sense that many Americans—perhaps most of them—know this is happening. Americans feel at least a great, shuddering shadow is hovering over American life and hard circumstances are converging on the country like walls closing in around us. A lot of people know it because the consequences are evident in their daily lives. This will not be the "worst of times" in American history—the nation is too rich for that—but it may feel that way to many families. The pain and loss will be distributed widely throughout society, but very unevenly. Some deeply rooted convictions will be upended, starting with the enduring faith in onward-and-upward prosperity. That self-confident assumption is already faltering. For many, it has already failed.

Given the deep forces at work, we hardly have a choice about how to react. The country *has* to change because, like it or not, the country is going to be changed by events and adverse forces that will not yield to our can-do optimism.

The rest of the world appears to recognize the United States' weakening position, even if American governing elites do not. Other nations, large and small, friendly and unfriendly, are discreetly preparing for the transition by rearranging the distribution of power among themselves in various ways and without seeking approval from Washington. These developments alarm US policy makers and add to their sense of the potential danger in the world. But, as Iraq has demonstrated, war making is not a reliable solution to all the country faces.

History, in any case, is not going to wait for the American political system to wake up and get its act together. The longer this nation ignores the new realities or imagines it can overpower them with blunt force, the more difficult and dangerous this transformation will likely become.

Other great powers have experienced similar humbling passages in history, and some learned with sorrow that stubborn denial can lead to tragic outcomes (think of the blood-soaked history of European nations battling to dominate each other). A nation blinded by the arrogance of its own power may eventually wind up embittered and divided, lunging after delusional solutions and searching for scapegoats to blame. The national character can curdle in the process and people may try irrationally to strike back at history. I won't dwell on the darker possibilities because they are avoidable—if a country faces reality and responds maturely to new circumstances. For Americans, this will be the great test of character.

The first proposition in this book is the hard reckoning ahead. I will explain the complexities behind it as concisely as I can. My goal is clarity. I will examine how we got into this situation, and how we might get out.

But there are two other propositions at the heart of this book, less certain but far more hopeful. I want readers to see that, despite the adversities we face, promising possibilities also lie ahead. Past the loss and humiliation, America has the chance to become a new and better place. Once relieved of the burdens of worldly dominion, we will find ourselves free to redevelop the interior landscape of our own country—how we want to live, what kind of society we want to become. A renewed America can emerge more fulfilling and equitable, a society that liberates its citizens—all of us—to pursue life, liberty, and happiness in more satisfying and self-directed ways. We can get closer to our deepest human yearnings and imagine life in full, beyond the relentless imperatives of greater material wealth.

America the Possible—that is my second proposition. I will describe ways in which it might be created through politics, social action, and plausible reformation of the economic system and society.

The third proposition may be the most difficult for readers to envision. Some will find it implausible. It is something only the people can do: Rescue the country and redeem ourselves. The country can reinvent itself—it has before—but only if ordinary Americans find their bearings and reclaim their voices and unrealized power. That is, become *citizens* in the fuller meaning of the word. I am convinced that only the unruly energies of engaged citizens can break through the encrusted status quo and force deep changes in government and society. Political parties, presidents, and governing elites cannot do this. They are too comfortable, too complacent and self-protective, too embedded in the defunct assumptions inherited from past glories. If the people do not do this, it will not be done.

A wise friend, a retired professor named Lee Halprin, listened to me go on this way about my hope for democratic revival. Then he interrupted with a question: "Why do you think this is possible?" I had to pause and think. "The history, I guess," I said. "This is how it has always happened."

From the birth of our nation, it was always ordinary people, pushing from the bottom against an entrenched status quo, that led to the most momentous changes in American life. Usually humble and powerless, these common citizens struggled to win better lives and to fulfill the noble vision expressed in the nation's founding documents. Progress was always hard-won and regularly frustrated. It took years, sometimes even decades, to succeed. Think of the abolition of slavery and the modern civil rights movement, or the rights of citizenship won by women and the still-active campaigns that seek to broadly ensure economic justice.

Conventional history tells these stories differently, as the triumphs of great leaders who moved the country forward and the genius of the founders who wrote the sacred texts of our democracy. But it was ordinary people who gave meaning to those noble words. The presidents who championed great reforms were responding to people—plain citizens who reached for power, motivated by their own deep values and convictions. This is the life force that has always driven America to higher ground and gradually redefined our meaning of progress. Frequently, people failed and their aspirations passed to future generations. When the people prevailed, it changed the country.

Our moment in history, I suggest, demands something similar of ordinary citizens. The United States is not a finished story, still far from being the "more perfect union" envisioned by the founders. These new circumstances have reopened questions that governing elites had assumed were long settled by the nation's great wealth and accumulated power. The people on the whole, however, feel the tension wrought by promises betrayed and ideals not yet realized.

The question is whether people will do anything about it. Are we too content and comfortable to speak up, too bullied and manipulated by mass-market politics to disturb the existing order?

I believe that ordinary Americans today have the same creative qualities as pioneers of our past—the deep beliefs and yearnings, the capacity to mobilize the idealistic values within them and break free of the cynicism around them. Those who grasp the urgency of our situation can light the way for others. In mutual endeavors, people teach each other, pick their own leaders, and argue out their own declarations of purpose. Democracy is hard work, but it is also exhilarating. People can discover within themselves strengths they didn't know they had.

This generation of Americans, I am convinced, confronts a great turning point in the national story, unlike any that occurred before. For better or worse, the fractured moment we face is different from what previous generations confronted. The United States, after all, is not a newly formed, developing nation struggling for survival and basic material comforts. Nor is it a robust, young industrial economy suddenly flattened by worldwide depression. The United States today is fabulously wealthy, awesomely well armed, and abundant in goods and pleasures and power, yet profoundly troubled in new ways.

The distinctive challenge for this era is coming to terms with our once exalted status, facing up to tough questions and some long-unresolved contradictions. How will American society fare if it finds itself facing a common routine of less rather than more? If that comes about, what might replace the economic imperatives that have organized American life with machinelike efficiency? For that matter, we may want to ask ourselves whether the great accumulations of wealth and power actually deliver the "good life" and for whom. Or whether our awesome military power makes us feel more secure or more fearful.

Our burden is different from those of the distant past because we are not starting with a clean slate. We have to examine what is and imagine how we might change it—governing institutions, political and social routines, the laws and economic relationships we inherited. This is a little like renovating an old house that is well loved but neglected; the process is more difficult than building a new house. How might our country look after we get through these adverse circumstances?

We have a chance to dream. I think we have an obligation.

"'The dogmas of the quiet past are inadequate to the stormy present,'" Abraham Lincoln once declared. "'The occasion is piled high with difficulty, and we must rise with the occasion. As our case is new, so we must think anew, and act anew. We must disenthrall ourselves and then we shall save our country.'"[2]

His words are from 1862, when the Civil War was in its second year and already more terrible than expected. I think we are in a roughly similar place, without a great war to focus our energies. The "stormy present" has begun and it will become harsher and more confusing. But if we think anew, we can save the country.

Come home, America. Instead of trying to run the world, let us tend our own wounded society. Let go of inflated claims to global dominance. Instead, redeem the fundamental values and sacred principles of the national inheritance. Do not resign from the world. Rejoin it on more practical and promising terms.

CHAPTER TWO

THE OTHER AMERICA

Like most Americans, I was born to optimism. I inherited from my parents a reflexive faith in a bright future, and events in my own life confirmed it.

My sense of the country is grounded in my personal experience of World War II. I was a small boy at the time, and for me the war was glorious. Nobody in my family was killed or wounded. My mother assured me at the outset that America was going to win.

Friends shared the good feelings of wartime. Even little children participated in the "war effort." We stamped tin cans flat for scrap metal drives and helped our parents tend neighborhood victory gardens. We watched the fighting at the front in the newsreels at Saturday movie matinees.

Small boys memorized the silhouettes of enemy warplanes—they were printed on cereal boxes—and scanned the skies over Ohio for German Messerschmitts and Japanese Zeros. At school, we pasted little stamps in our war bond savings booklets—twenty-five cents every Monday—to help Uncle Sam win the war.

I remember the day the war ended—August 15, 1945. My family was at my grandmother's farm in western Pennsylvania, an old-fashioned country home that did not have electricity or a telephone. We had a portable radio, but the battery was dead. We heard the news announced by the towboats hauling coal and steel up and down the Monongahela River a few miles away. All day long, a chorus of shrill whistles declared victory. The war was over, we had won.

That evening, we drove into the mill town on the river and found a spontaneous celebration swarming through the streets. People hugged and danced and sang. An Italian mother carrying the American flag marched through the crowd on Main Street, her son beside her banging on a kitchen pot for a drum and her daughter playing the clarinet in an impromptu replica of the *Spirit of '76*. A sailor came stumbling out of a bar and swooned in the arms of his friends. I assumed it was patriotic delirium.

The Scotch-Irish farmers—my mother's people—mingled in the streets with the Italians, Bohemians, and Irish who worked in the mines and steel mills. These people—Protestants and Catholics—normally did not mix in those days, but that night, they congratulated one another in a fraternal mood. The feeling was that "my people are as good as your people."

I came away from this with an expansive, joyful confidence in the country: We Americans accomplish great things when we pull together. That's what I absorbed as a child, and what Americans told themselves at the moment of victory. I still believe it. The French called it "fraternity." The labor movement called it "solidarity." I guess I thought it was simply being American at its best.

Later on, of course, I learned the more complicated facts of American history involving bitter abuses and conflicts, and about the long struggle to overcome the nation's failures and evil contradictions. Strangely enough, that knowledge deepened my confidence in the country, my sense of its forward motion. It is not that Americans are uniquely virtuous and wise. We definitely are not. We get things terribly wrong and ignore intolerable transgressions. Our saving grace lies in the hope for the self-correction a functioning democracy can achieve when people make themselves heard.

In my own lifetime, the story played out most dramatically in the civil rights movement. It's still a shock to look back at the society that existed then. Laws and terror enforced a cruel racial caste system. The raw injustices imposed upon black Americans were accepted by most white people, myself included, as normal, "just the way things are." Civil rights agitators forced us to see the immoral reality of white supremacy and to react. The old America was delegitimized—defeated—and a new America began to emerge, though it is not yet complete.

I don't mean to romanticize Americans. Like any other people, we harbor good stuff within us, but also foul qualities that go against our proclaimed values and lead to destructive errors. The human condition is not perfectible. But democracy can alter social arrangements and economic circumstances in ways that help people uncover their better selves.

★   ★   ★   ★

I believe in our possibilities, but somewhere along the way, I developed a different way of thinking positively. I have a lot of confidence in the potential of ordinary Americans, but not so much in the system that governs them. Most people, I have found, do the best they can given their circumstances. They sometimes get little help when they need it.

I feel as though I know Americans in a special way because I have spent my adult life tramping around this country as a reporter. I heard the stories of people who dwell in the bleakest circumstances—urban ghettos and Indian reservations. I also interviewed many of the powerful people who run things, from statesmen and politicians to business managers, financial executives, and influential opinion leaders.

Americans turn out to be gorgeously diverse and often eccentric in appealing ways—decent and serious about life, inventive and practical, good humored and disposed to generosity. Most people, including powerful people, want to be understood and are astonishingly open with an inquiring stranger.

America has its full share of greed-crazed scoundrels and egomaniacs. But Americans are not the clownish, dim-witted public depicted on TV. They are not addled sheep manipulated by political propaganda or herded along by commercial advertising.

Up close and personal, Americans are much more than that. They are also less than they could be.

They could be citizens in the full meaning of the word, the sovereign citizens lauded in the founding documents who participate in the decisions that govern their lives and pursue "happiness" in their own ways. We are not yet there as a society—not even close.

Americans seem to know this, if their bleak opinions on politics and government are any indication. In recent years, they have turned uncharacteristically pessimistic about the country, notwithstanding the "good news" regularly announced by experts. Some 80 percent of the populace thinks the country is on the "wrong track," but you don't have to rely on polls to find that out. You can hear the same grave assessment in casual conversations anywhere in the country, including the living rooms of the affluent. People are fearful American life will not be better for their children, and may even be a lot worse.

The onward-and-upward story line that has always been part of American life is in doubt. The people are on to something their leaders do not want to face. In plain and simple terms, I am a reporter—not an expert or puffed-up insider—and that is how I want to talk over Americans' apprehensions about our future.

One crippling divide in American public life is the great gulf between the authority of the governing experts and the rest of us. That separation is far more damaging than the much-lamented partisan conflict between Democrats and Republicans. Many Americans, and probably most, are effectively disenfranchised—cut out of the democratic process. Government is complex and the experts speak the language. Most citizens do not. And most have neither the time nor the desire to become policy wonks. The language barrier also surrounds economics and other dense subjects blanketing public issues. It makes most citizens speechless.

In theory, the political system could learn to translate this complexity and make itself understood. In my opinion, if average Americans can operate the remote control for a complicated home entertainment system (I can't), then they can grasp the essential logic behind most government policies. Political parties used to do this for people by educating them about the big issues and connecting them to decision making in our representative democracy. But speaking clearly to everyone is time-consuming. The governing classes often find it is more convenient not to be understood.

It is worse than that. The governing authorities, even many successful politicians, begin with a snide presumption that people are like children and can't handle the hard facts. The complexities of public issues are dumbed down to a crude form of baby talk that skips the real content of what's being decided. Voters, it is true, often react with misguided tantrums, but they are provoked by the condescension. People know when they are not being told the whole story.

Ordinary folks are at a natural disadvantage, but we are not helpless. We can begin to regain our footing by first taking ourselves seriously, by learning to listen to our own thoughts and private feelings, even if the system does not. Democracy begins within the self by thinking and saying what we truly feel and believe, even if only among our family members and close friends. The chemistry of how people find the courage to engage the larger reality is an elusive subject and we will return to it later. But it starts with people asking themselves gut-level questions.

What keeps you up at night? What are the private dreams you may be too shy to share outside the family? Think about the children. Talk about the grandparents, where they came from and whether their lives were fulfilling. About what makes you feel good about being an American. What makes you sad or angry. This is the raw material for thinking like a citizen. If you had the power to change the country for the better, where would you start?

People can acquire power, but it will not be conferred on them. They have to fight for it. They have to discover it within themselves. I believe they can. Do you remember Ronald Reagan's famous declaration when he was inaugurated back in 1981? "Government is not the solution to our problem. Government is the problem."

I want to turn his thought around and declare: "The people are not the problem. The people are the solution."

Some of my friends regard my optimism as delusional. My readers are sometimes exasperated by it. Over the years, I have written books and articles that critically examined the maldistribution of power in this country—the deformed principles and economic inequities that are embedded both in the government and in the private sector that also governs our lives.

These analyses are filled with bleak facts about how things really work behind closed doors. Readers now and then have asked me, "How can you be so optimistic? Your book left me totally depressed."

It's a reasonable question. Actually, it describes the tension that has stalked me for years. I live with my personal, private understanding of America—the country I know and love—colliding with the very powerful nation of the same name. I criticize and rebuke the official America. I give pep talks to the other one. It is this other America—the place that is still forming, still rich in possibilities—that keeps my optimism aloft.

An authentic democracy would learn how to listen respectfully and incorporate this private knowledge of citizens into the processes of public decision making. I am convinced by the nature of our current troubles that this country will not get through the hard passage ahead—equably and wisely—unless people of ordinary status are somehow engaged in the public debate and stand up for their ideas of what America should become.

CHAPTER THREE

THE WALLS CLOSING IN

We Americans have many outstanding qualities but, let's face it, humility is not one of them. On nearly any occasion, we will noisily celebrate our country as the best of all possible nations. At the Olympics, people from other countries cringe when the Yanks launch into their overbearing chant, "U-S-A, U-S-A, U-S-A." After the deep trauma that followed 9/11, Americans were shocked to learn that some people in the world were not-so-secretly relishing our pain.

Why do they hate us? After 9/11, leading newspaper columnists provided comforting answers. They hate us because we are so good. Because the United States is fabulously rich, yet also free and democratic. Because we are the preeminent military power yet also well intentioned and generous, innocently championing freedom for others. Many Americans liked this explanation—hatred as a form of flattery—and felt a sense of virtuous martyrdom. If any public figure suggested we were responsible for some bad things that happened to others, the unpatriotic notion was shouted down.

The mass culture, in fact, marinates Americans in self-congratulation and triumphalism. We hear the same message from everywhere around us—politics, movies, talk radio, commercial advertising. Our action heroes battle against alien fiends and always triumph. The America-centric news media publish "foreign news" stories that are mainly about us, about what we are doing in the world and how other nations are reacting to us.

Scholars promote the national egotism with books that extol America as an indispensable goliath that performs the thankless task of governing the world for the benefit of all. Boilerplate political rhetoric encourages the same self-pity. Misunderstood, America selflessly labors to help others become more like us.

In our time, I fear, Americans are going to learn humility the hard way, blow by blow. Both at home and in the world at large, a convergence of deep historical forces is bearing down on us. Some are natural in the sense that no one planned these adverse outcomes, they resulted simply from the world's changing over time, most notably with the end of the cold war (US capitalism won). Other great wounds are self-inflicted.

Our dominance has turned into our great vulnerability. The economic and political foundations of America's prosperity and global power are rapidly crumbling. The US military, notwithstanding its extraordinary capabilities, can no longer enforce the American writ, even in small, disorganized countries or among once deferential allies who are no longer intimidated by American power.

The presumption that we get to run things for everyone else is perversely undermining the overall well-being of our own people. Abroad, the maximum leader has lost its rationale and viability. At home, the American dream is breaking up.

These are among the taboo propositions in the upper realms of politics and policy. With rare exceptions, elected politicians discuss them only to fervently deny their existence. Such talk is derided as "declinist," un-American pessimism. Pessimists are losers. Americans are winners.

Nevertheless, it is in our self-interest to put the substance of our predicament on the table and examine the hard facts. Five major elements are driving the deterioration of American prospects.

1. Globalization's net negative consequences for the country. The global trading system the United States launched and led for six decades has become a losing proposition for the nation, though not for everyone, obviously. People attached to the upper tiers of multinational corporations and finance capital prosper fabulously from the status quo. So do highly educated professionals and others whose occupations are not subject to global wage pressures. But the national economy as a whole is losing, including working people in the broad middle class and below.

The US economic engine is running on empty, borrowing vast sums of capital from abroad every year to stay afloat. We borrow to pay for the privilege of consuming more than we produce—that is, living beyond our means. A very wealthy nation can do this for quite a long while, but not forever. When the reckoning arrives, sooner or later, suddenly or gradually, Americans in general will experience a steep falloff in their living standards. The event will confirm the nation's weakened condition for all to see.

To appreciate what's underway, think of the overall national economy as behaving much like millions of families do. They keep going deeper into debt, trying to sustain their threatened way of life. Their incomes do not keep up with their living standards and so they find themselves borrowing to pay the mortgage or other monthly bills. The collective US economy—government, households, businesses—is doing the same, and on an awesome scale.

The nation as a whole is sliding into a dangerous debtor's dependency, borrowing more and more each year from other nations to pay for the lifestyle it can no longer afford. In 2007, foreign borrowing totaled nearly $800 billion, roughly 7 percent of the gross domestic product, what economists call the current accounts deficit. For many years, the trend resembled slow bleeding. However, during the last decade, the debt has been a hemorrhage. The United States has accumulated more than $5 trillion in indebtedness to foreign creditors over the last fifteen years.

It is important to know that this is not the federal debt that results from the often-discussed deficits in Washington budgets. This is much larger and more ominous. The bleeding I am describing results from the global trading system and America's swollen trade deficits. Every year, the United States buys more goods from other nations than it sells to them—about 80 percent more—and to pay for this gap, the United States borrows from the rest of the world an amount gradually approaching $1 trillion a year.

A central explanation for the enormous US trade imbalance is that so much US manufacturing has been transferred to other economies, making the US base of production relatively weak. Americans now buy from other countries much more of what we used to produce (and we borrow to do so). As one Asian economist observed with only mild exaggeration, "'The U.S. has little to sell back to China but Boeing and beef.'"[1] America is in a deep hole, with its wealth gradually draining away and its long-term prosperity undermined.

To sharpen the dilemma further, our principal creditors are also our major trading rivals, led by China and Japan. They lend us hundreds of billions of dollars so we can keep buying more of their stuff. They will continue to treat us generously until they decide the United States is no longer a good risk. Or when American consumers are tapped out.

The historic meaning of this situation is ominous because the swelling capital indebtedness leads eventually to political dependency or financial ruin, and possibly to both. No other wealthy nation has ever experienced such an extreme level of profligacy or survived as a great power when it had to rely on money borrowed from lesser nations to stay afloat. Great Britain lost its "greatness" a century ago for this very reason. The United States is far more powerful, but it will not be exempt from the laws of compounding debt.

2. Militarism and its dominance of US foreign policy. America's military power remains truly awesome and spans the globe, but its uses have been expanded far beyond the original idea of national defense. The military now attempts to direct other nations' politics by "projecting power"—deploying troops and forward bases to distant places where no obvious enemy exists. Meanwhile, in Iraq and Afghanistan, Americans are learning once again—the hard way—that military force is not necessarily a reliable tool for modifying other people's behavior. They tend to resent the presence of conquering armies, and they resist.

Given the world's shifting circumstances, the US military institution is itself becoming a perverse threat to peace. The global reach of American deployments and strategies for seeking out new enemies are magnifying the risks for Americans rather than reducing them. Once the war in Iraq has been ended, other wars are likely to follow, and the military establishment is preparing to fight them. The US military strategy, which has bipartisan blessing, amounts to sticking out our chin around the world to see if anyone will take a punch.

While citizens remain focused on the "preemptive war" in the Middle East, the Pentagon is proceeding to deploy still more forward bases and personnel in nonthreatening nations (critics have counted as many as seven hundred overseas bases). The military plans to expand army and marine ground troops by ninety thousand, presumably to achieve better results in future conflicts. Military leaders insist that Pentagon budgets cannot shrink after Iraq, but instead must grow larger to cover all contingencies.

To what end are we mobilizing? The logic of this "defense" seems clearly aggressive, but despite recent failures, both political parties have given the military institution an open field of play. Some new alliances and deployments are designed to encircle Russia and China—both identified as potential threats of the future. No one seems to have noticed a bizarre contradiction: US war planning

is targeting our major Asian creditor and its fast-rising economy, which US multinationals are vigorously helping to develop.

To prepare for a major war against China or Russia, the Pentagon is going
forward with advanced weapons systems originally designed during the cold war.
These new planes and ships are extraordinarily expensive and arguably obsolete
in strategic terms, but there is very little political resistance to projects that have
long been planned by the arms manufacturers.

Meanwhile, terrorism has been grandiosely redefined as the new cold war.
Bases are being established in Muslim countries and, more ominously, the military is inserting thousands of special forces into obscure and very poor countries
where terrorists are thought to pose a potential problem. These intrusions are in
some cases by consent, in others clandestine. The soldiers undertake civil actions
to improve conditions for the local societies, but they also kill or try to assassinate with selective bombing people who are suspected of having dangerous
intentions.

The Pentagon has dubbed all this "the Long War." The preparations assume
a generation of military conflict in large and small wars to be America's new
obligation in protecting a peaceable world. Indeed, the US government is laying
down potential trip wires for these wars anywhere and everywhere. The strategy
is very costly and largely secretive. It may very well prove to be self-fulfilling.

**3. The triumph of the free-market ideology and its destruction of an
equitable society.** For the last thirty years, conservative reforms like the deregulation of industries and finance and regressive tax cuts gradually eviscerated the
government's protective mantle. Families were exposed to the harsh edge of market forces. Businesses and banks were freed to innovate and maximize returns,
but also to discard their long-standing obligations to workers and society. The
federal government essentially switched sides in the enduring contest between
capital and labor.

The reigning conservative order, one could say, mainly produced more billionaires and debt while leaving a broad wake of social dislocation and insecurity. The purchasing power of industrial wages has been stagnant for thirty years,
while profits and productivity have boomed. A striking consensus has formed
among the political elites of both parties and, until very recently, no one of prom-
inence was willing to question the reign of the markets.

One million households in the uppermost tier—the top 1 percent—now collectively earn the same amount as the 60 million families who make up the lower two-thirds of the income ladder. Major corporations destabilized middle-class security by walking away from the unwritten social contract they had once embraced. Health care, pensions, job security, and other elements of worker protection were gutted or revoked by right-wing reformers in Washington. This is partly why so many families are caught in the debtor's trap and spiraling downward.

But the conservative order has essentially failed as an economic system and its advocates are now in political disarray. It failed for practical reasons as well as its ideological contradictions. The size of government and of federal subsidies for financial and business interests did not get smaller. Instead, conservative economics merely withdrew the assurances business had previously given people, whether they were workers or those in need. The "market friendly" regime failed because it did not lead to the widely shared prosperity its sponsors promised would appear once they got government out of the way.

In another era, this economic deterioration would have led to a rapid shift in politics and the governing agenda, but it is not clear whether Democrats are ready to pursue significant changes. For three decades, most Democrats gradually retreated before the rightward march in economic policy or collaborated actively in making market forces dominant over government interventions. The social stresses resulting from the gross and growing economic inequality were occasionally lamented, but even when they held Congress or the White House, Democrats were largely silent on the wage question.

The disparities could become politically explosive if a sharp adjustment in the US economy's debt-supported consumption occurs and families have no choice but to accept falling living standards. Many already are. The pain and loss will not be equitably distributed. The least among us will suffer the most, followed by many millions in the broad middle. Those at the very top will suffer hardly at all. Social injustice compounds desperation and anger. The politics of class conflict—supposedly extinguished by the prosperity that followed World War II—is making a comeback as America's enormous middle class is gradually being dismantled.

4. The ecological crisis and the coming scarcity of oil. Coping with both of these threats requires a profound industrial transformation—the thorough redesign and retooling of virtually every product and production process.

Everything from packaging to buildings and transportation systems must be redesigned, and everything from eliminating wasted fuel and other resources to recovering spent industrial materials and using them again in production will have to be instituted. The first impact this reformation will have is to raise the price of nearly everything. Material pleasures that are commonplace in American life will have to undergo wrenching examination or changes, and some will be eliminated. The carefree mass-consumption society that we have known since World War II is essentially done for.

The United States is not alone in facing these challenges, but we are particularly vulnerable, first because our society consumes more than any other nation and is wasteful on a bloated scale, and second because the United States lags far behind other advanced nations in developing ways to cope with the well-understood imperatives. Global warming is the greatest and most obvious danger, but it is compounded by the overall destruction of nature as industrial capitalism steadily encroaches upon and undermines the finite capacities of the land, air, water, and ecosystems needed to support all life on earth. The industrial transformation that is now required must also simultaneously invent a system for producing alternative fuels that can replace hydrocarbons. The price of scarce oil recently exploded, then collapsed, and is sure to explode again.

The good news, we can say, is that these fundamental changes are technologically possible and potentially life enhancing. Indeed, the transition can proceed on positive terms by creating new industries and jobs, improving the design and durability of goods, and saving by improving efficiency rather than expanding our careless excesses.

At first, however, there will be no escaping the current predicament's implications for greater social injustice if the costs of transformation are pushed upon those least able to afford it. In a country already fractured by economic inequality, with millions of families struggling to hang on with inadequate incomes, doing "the right thing" about global warming or energy alternatives might simply worsen the pain by making it impossible for working people to afford everyday products they now can manage. That dilemma is one of the reasons the political order has been so reluctant to face up to the problems. As the tragedy of Hurricane Katrina illustrated, the United States has a huge backlog of neglected public works the political system has ignored.[2]

5. Our decayed democracy and the paralysis of reform. The political factor trumps all the others. Major policy shifts that could begin to address these large wounds have been effectively stymied. The same business and financial interests that profit robustly from the status quo stand in the way. Representative democracy has been captured and deformed by these interests, and the voters are distanced from those in power. Both parties collude to insulate themselves from voter retribution.

Not long ago, I heard a health care expert, Bruce Vladek, recount the failure to institute health care reform during the Clinton administration. The American people, he pointed out, are overwhelmingly in favor of strong federal intervention to reform the health care system. A majority of the public has wanted this for decades.

"It doesn't matter what the American people think," Vladek told attendees at a policy conference in New York. Policy on the issue, he explained, is controlled by four or five business sectors led by the insurance and pharmaceutical industries. Reform can happen, but only on their terms. George W. Bush was able to secure a major reform—Medicare prescription drug benefits—because he let the pharmaceutical and insurance lobbyists write the legislation. Not surprisingly, their version of reform provided them with billions in added income.

Similar barriers stand in the way of virtually all the major imperatives I have described. Each of the five threatening elements involves an epic political struggle and requires difficult-to-achieve reversals. In fact, three adverse forces are now interacting in vicious crosscurrents that add confusion to Washington's usual risk avoidance: Rising oil prices, which make it more difficult for politicians to enact the industrial changes needed to curb global warming, have been pushed upward by the costly military venture in Iraq, which has also deepened our dependence on foreign borrowing. Was the war in Iraq really designed not to combat terrorism, but to ensure US domination of Middle East oil? Only a transformed political system will have the courage to sort out these and other contradictions. Washington, I fear, will not find its nerve unless citizens rise up and force them to get serious about resolving the country's deepening dilemmas.

A new president could not reasonably be expected to sort all this out by himself or in a single term, though he can begin by talking more honestly about the dimensions of what we face. He will need more than earnest good intentions. I fear that there will be no significant changes unless the broad ranks of citizens engage directly in the fight.

I have put forward a lot of heavy questions for readers to sort through, but I intend to proceed in digestible ways. The next chapter focuses more closely on our historical moment and suggests how our inherited legacy of America's greatness may have led governing elites into misguided folly and still blinds some to our threatening circumstances. Chapter 5 then takes up substantive concerns, starting with the frightening financial crisis that has sown alarm and confusion in both Washington and Wall Street.

Subsequent chapters take up the large adversities I have enumerated—the negative impact of globalization, heightened dangers of militarism, the collapse of the conservative dogma, and the paralysis of politics that prevents us from achieving desperately needed reforms to deal with the twin threats of ecology and energy. Then I turn to America the Possible and a brightening vision of what the country can become. A series of chapters lends a guiding hand—helping citizens think creatively about developing a new and better country, how they can reclaim their power as citizens and fulfill the democratic promise beyond anything Americans achieved in the past.

Bad things—some of them by now unavoidable—are going to happen, and bad things have already started to happen, including the financial crisis enveloping Wall Street and threatening to collapse more financial firms, not to mention the US economy. This event is an ominous alarm bell signifying the deep rot in the American system. Investors in both Asia and Europe took enormous losses because they parked their surplus wealth in US financial markets. The shock of discovering Wall Street's propensity for fanciful valuation adds to the growing disillusionment about US power elsewhere in the world. It increases the potential for a dreadful economic reckoning when our foreign creditors decide to back away and put their capital in safer places.

If that occurs, the pressures on everyday Americans will intensify in new ways. If economic recovery becomes even harder to achieve, how will folks pay their bills or stay ahead on their credit cards? Or for that matter, how will they hold on to their homes? I am not trying to spread more gloom. These questions have already arisen for many struggling families. The gnawing preoccupation of the middle class is the fear of falling.

Billionaire investor Warren Buffett warned several years ago that if the country does not reduce its trade deficit and stop borrowing so heavily from abroad, it will wind up as a "sharecropper's society." Americans, he explained, will find themselves working longer and longer hours each year simply to make payments on last year's borrowing. Yet, if debt-soaked consumers are no longer able to take on more debt, what will keep the economy going? For that matter, what will keep the entire global trading system going, since it has come to depend upon the United States as the "buyer of last resort" for its expanding production capacities? Buffett's warning was ignored.

As these forces play out, I foresee a deep collision occurring between governing elites and the broad ranks of ordinary citizens, a bitter flourishing of class conflict. The elite influentials, both public and private, talk about the need for greater fiscal discipline in American society, but what they have in mind is cutting benefits for people, not for the powerful interests or wealth holders. They promote schemes to break old promises and shrink the federal "entitlements" that protect people—Medicare, Medicaid, and Social Security. This would free up money to pay for an expanded military and other obligations that have not been met. People at large, already anxious about their futures, oppose this solution for obvious reasons. Given our economic circumstances, people need expanded social guarantees to help them get through this hard passage.

Establishment influentials are educating the political community, including the new administration, about how the federal entitlements can be "reformed" without arousing the public's ire. An alliance of economists from leading think tanks and corporate front groups has suggested that Democrats and Republicans together can work out a grand "bipartisan compromise." If the political parties hold hands and act together, neither party can be blamed by injured citizens. The press takes little interest in this alliance since it involves no fight between the two major parties. Perhaps a blue-ribbon commission of "wise men" can be assembled to work out the compromise's details.

This is a standard approach in Washington, and it is always portrayed as statesmanship. Among ordinary folks, it should be understood for what it is. When official America talks of "bipartisan compromise," it usually means the people are about to get screwed.

CHAPTER FOUR

THE "WINNER'S COMPLEX"

With rare exceptions, political leaders and opinion makers avoid gloomy portents and remain true to the idea of an invincible America. For every symptom of disorder, they have an answer that usually involves changing policy on obscure economic variables. *The country is working fine on the whole,* they explain, *though it's not without its problems. All that's needed is to adjust a few dials. Changing the macroeconomic policy or reorganizing the fighting force will do the trick. We need more savings, less debt. They're all manageable problems.*

The governing class inherited this confident spirit from their predecessors who oversaw the long and triumphant era that followed World War II, beginning at the glorious moment of victory I remember fondly from my childhood. America Triumphant remains the bright, shining beacon of who we are as a nation.

George W. Bush took the faith in American superiority to bellicose extremes with disastrous consequences. But the attitude is not really subject to partisan differences since both political parties embrace the same understanding, though with varying shades of intensity. After the disastrous invasion of Iraq, politicians and policy thinkers argued about whether "mistakes" were made, but very few were willing to oppose the assumption that the United States has the right to invade another country based only on our own justifications.

Listen to Madeleine Albright, Bill Clinton's secretary of state, expressing self-righteous self-confidence more than a decade ago: "If we have to use force, it is because we are America. We are the indispensable nation. We stand tall. We see further into the future."

During the campaign for the 2008 election, every major presidential candidate stepped forward to affirm the faith, like Christians reciting the Apostles' Creed. Barack Obama, for example, took the oath with these words:

"I reject the notion that the American moment has passed. I dismiss the cynics who say that this new century cannot be another when, in the words of President Franklin Roosevelt, we lead the world in battling immediate evils and promoting the ultimate good. I still believe that America is the last, best hope of Earth. We just have to show the world why this is so. . . . The American moment has not passed. The American moment is here. And like generations before us, we will seize that moment and begin the world anew."[1]

This strand of patriotic culture is potent because important events in our history have confirmed it. The idea that the country is good, strong, and well intentioned derives from triumphant experiences that stretched across more than half a century.

When people like me come along and suggest that our claim on sole world leadership is no longer valid and may be dangerous for the country, it sounds to many like heresy, maybe even treason. But I and others like me are arguing from the perspective of a different American tradition—a self-critical and tough-minded tradition that could be called patriotic realism.

The history is important to our sense of self-regard. When America took charge of world affairs in the post–World War II years, our motives were always self-interested, of course, but also deeply progressive. The United States set out to remake the world in ways that would prevent another horrendous bloodletting like the war from occurring. Instead of punishing the vanquished enemies, as the Allied victors did after World War I, America became the leader and architect of a new international order. It founded global institutions like the United Nations and World Bank that embraced collective principles to stabilize the peace and encourage general prosperity.

The United States served as supervisor and benefactor in reconstructing the collapsed economies of Europe and Asia. Its stewardship restarted global trade and launched the globalization of commerce and investment that continues today. America's mighty armed forces and arsenal were not dismantled. They instead became the protectors and enforcers for the world.

American capitalism took on its ideological rival, Soviet state communism, and eventually won. In the cold war, both sides employed power in brutal ways, engaging in surrogate wars over the real estate of third-party nations.

I am deliberately leaving out the darker, unsanctioned version of this history—though I largely agree with it—because that interpretation is excluded from the triumphalist view. We don't need to reargue the cold war with its pointless and dangerous arms race, the Central Intelligence Agency's clandestine manipulations, or McCarthyism's suppression of nonconformist speech and thought.

Those injuries and injustices have troubled Americans again and again. But they did not appreciably alter the nation's sense of itself as uniquely good and great. This inherited mind-set still presides powerfully, and it also fogs our minds. The largest obstacle to fundamental change may be our American triumphalism.

Leader, architect, supervisor, benefactor, protector, and enforcer—the United States still claims to fill those muscular roles around the world. But over the intervening decades, the nation's progressive commitments have evolved into something quite different. America's governing elites came to embrace a self-centered understanding of their unchallenged power. They awarded privileged status to certain economic interests and ignored others. They adopted inflated expectations of what their stewardship would accomplish.

When the cold war ended in 1989, the door was briefly opened for a reconsideration of America's unilateral role. But Washington instead enlarged its conception of the American position. George H. W. Bush went to war for a virtuous reason—liberating Kuwait—and announced that this would birth a "new world order." Bill Clinton, after some hesitation, sent "humanitarian" military forces into the Balkans and kept the peace in Iraq by periodically bombing that country.

George W. Bush expanded on the supremacy premise. He claimed for America the open-ended right to wage "preemptive war." It would always be done with good intentions and endorsed by Congress, he promised, but critics charged that it was still waging aggressive war without a demonstrated provocation. That concept deeply alarmed old allies and also appeared to violate the Geneva Conventions ratified by the United States and other nations after World War II. But Bush's political opponents at home still have not renounced the concept of preemptive war.

Most notably, official America decided we really are indispensable. That's always a dangerous assertion for a country that styles itself a great power. In history, it has often been the reason for "powers" becoming no longer "great."

In America's case, I would credit the attitude to late-stage arrogance. Why do old allies refuse to follow our lead? They must be cowards, the reasoning goes. Why do distant nationalities hate us? They must be crazed with envy. This sort of befuddlement is evident in our actions in Iraq and elsewhere. It illustrates how the overweening pride of power can blind otherwise rational people to realism and reason.

What should be obvious—though the influential elites won't acknowledge it—is that our nation no longer has the capacity or the right to supervise and police or reorder the lives of all humanity, regardless of whether our intentions are good and our motives genuine. It is simply too much. We cannot handle it. We have to let go.

The United States fails at implementing various strategies and loses influence for many reasons. But at the heart of the matter is the kind of mythic self-delusion that the Greeks and Shakespeare understood. Washington is trying to command the tides of history. Alas, the tides do not obey.

The economic model of self-correcting markets, for instance, reassures the authorities even when markets fail to correct. A trade deficit is dismissed as an unimportant side effect of free trade, and even a hidden blessing that allows Americans to get cheap goods from China and to borrow and spend freely. Failed wars are explained away as policy mistakes, not the failure of military power itself.

These are the standard views of well-informed men and women who regard themselves as hardheaded experts and practical-minded realists because they are, after all, running things for the rest of us. Some critics like to call them the ruling class, but I avoid using that term because it confers upon them more power and wisdom than they possess. These people are not so much pragmatic as they are crackpot realists, a handle coined in 1958 by sociologist C. Wright Mills to refer to the higher authorities and opinion makers who peddle their preposterous certitudes.

We are governed now by many expressions of crackpot thinking. For example, the US military is assigned not only to conquer and control other societies, but also to reform them. Soldiers are sent abroad like missionaries with guns to teach democracy to the inhabitants of one village at a time. Some critics call this imperialism, but if that's so, it is a goofy version of an empire.

US manufacturing has on a large scale been relocated to poorer nations where people who make the goods get much lower wages, making products cheaper. The millions of Americans who lose their high-wage jobs to outsourcing are told they can find something else to do. If their incomes decline, they can always borrow money.

Washington led in the creation of the World Trade Organization (WTO), a prototype for world government that has elaborate powers to supervise global commerce and investment. The WTO enforces rules that protect capital investors and corporations, but it has no rules protecting workers and communities, that is, people. The so-called Washington Consensus—a stern dogma imposed on developing countries that borrow from the World Bank and International Monetary Fund (IMF)—preaches that national governments must not try to protect their people from the harsh side effects of capital and commerce.

America's representative democracy, meanwhile, is offered as the model the world should follow, despite the democratic breakdown that Americans well know is in progress.

★　★　★　★　★

The American center is not holding. Various geopolitical pressures are tugging it this way and that. Rival powers are distancing themselves from the throne in Washington and creating new power centers by clustering together nations whose interests are different from ours. We can already glimpse the outlines of this historic transformation.

Influential nations that were part of the old Western alliance did not sign up for the American invasion of Iraq, they actively tried to prevent it. Their judgment was dramatically confirmed by subsequent events. Predictable deference to US leadership is no longer assured, even from our best friends.

Meanwhile, major oil-producing and oil-consuming nations have begun meeting occasionally in Shanghai to discuss the shape of world oil markets, among other matters. Could this gathering form a new kind of OPEC? An "oil club" anchored by China and Russia, with Iran and Venezuela also at the table? Their objective is not clear. The United States was not invited.

When Europe launched its unified currency, the euro, its success created a potential alternative to the US dollar as the world's reserve currency, which provides a safe storehouse where nations can park their wealth. Every so often, Russia proposes trading its oil in euros instead of dollars, and other nations are flirting with the same idea. Conditions are yet not ripe, but this is another important marker of the eclipsing of US economic power.

In early 2007, Europe's twenty-four stock markets reached capitalization of $15.7 trillion, surpassing the girth of the US markets for the first time since before World War I. Since 2003, European shares have outperformed America's stock shares, rising in value by 160 percent compared to 71 percent in the United States.[2]

The financial realm experts expect Shanghai to eventually emerge as the new Wall Street. Finance capital follows the money, goes wherever new wealth is accumulating. That is why the largest US financial firms—Goldman Sachs, Citigroup, and others—are rushing to find banking partners in China so they too can participate in the "good times" that are coming.

These and other indicators are like straws in the wind, showing the smart money which way the wind is blowing. None of these movements is decisive by itself—not yet, anyway. But on important fronts, the deepening trend is to shift away from the old centers of power, Washington and New York.

If Americans want to come to terms with this new reality, they might start by dropping their condescension toward the countries of Europe and Asia. Could those rival nations know things that America does not? They certainly know more about us than we know about them.

When I was traveling in a dozen foreign countries researching my book on the global economy, *One World, Ready or Not*, I was struck by how often people said that, yes, they admired Americans enormously, but they did not want their growing prosperity to foster an economic system like that in the United States.

Elsewhere in the world, US convictions about what constitutes sound economics or a desirable society are not always shared and emulated. Thanks to global communications, people know about our slums and racial separation. They are familiar with the extremes of great wealth and enduring poverty in this very wealthy country.

These observations may sound discordant to most Americans. After all, we are told repeatedly by politicians and the mass media that our country is the "city on a hill" admired and envied by others. Americans need to set aside the triumphalism and study the rest of the world more closely.

The advanced economies of Europe and Asia do not adhere to the economic policy prescriptions of Washington or Wall Street. Japan, Germany, France, and most other successful industrial nations pursue their national interest in the global economy quite differently than the United States does. They also get very different results—including less economic inequality—because their systems shield citizens and society from the harsher effects of market capitalism.

This distinction, in my view, is the most damning refutation of the American orthodoxy. The pressures of globalization and low-wage competition from poor nations are buffeting every wealthy nation, and every nation is compelled to deal with these forces and make concessions. Yet Western European countries do not have America's horrendous trade deficits, capital imbalances, or brutal social inequalities. Typically, their mature economies manage to produce steady-state trade surpluses. Japan enjoys especially large trade surpluses year after year, even when its economy is depressed.

Workers in these countries, including Asian tigers like South Korea, fill advanced production jobs that pay high wages, but they do not suffer the wage depression or rising poverty familiar to Americans. Industrial wages in most other leading economies matched or surpassed US wage levels more than a decade ago and most have held their ground since. Despite US cheerleaders' claims, Europe has nearly closed the gap between its constituent countries and the United States in prime-age employment levels, excluding the youngest workers.

In Europe, being jobless does not mean being destitute. Recession does not mean losing your home. Many workers are able to retire in their mid-fifties. Families and individuals are kept whole by the welfare state, which guarantees them health care, pensions, and other social protections that are rapidly unraveling for workers in wealthy America. Japan's system of social welfare is uniquely based within the country's private companies and its manufacturing multinationals play a central role in sustaining the social fabric.

How can this be possible, given the brutal competitive forces of globalization? It is essentially a political choice. Asian and European political systems are grounded in cultures that put higher value on social comity than on individual fortune seeking. Those societies have an egalitarian cultural tradition much stronger than America's and it is embedded in their governing systems.

Europeans sometimes mount vigorous protests, with swarms of marchers stopping commerce to defend and enforce these social guarantees when political parties waver under pressure from financial or industrial interests. People pour into the streets in noisy demonstrations, sometimes shutting everything down with a general strike. American citizens are told to write their congressperson to register their discontent.

In other advanced economies, governments strategically manage multinational corporations to uphold a broader conception of the "national interest." With protective laws, political leverage, and social consent, they make sure their societies get more equitable results—that is, that they retain the good jobs and high-value production.

Like the United States, these countries are also compelled by economic pressures to send production offshore and move jobs to low-wage markets. Unlike the United States, they strive to keep their core manufacturing and the best value-added jobs at home. In arcane ways, these countries informally protect their domestic markets and producers from being overwhelmed by cheaper imports. They defend labor more reliably and they regulate corporations more rigorously.

Meanwhile, American politics defines "national interest" much more narrowly. Under both Democrats and Republicans, the US government first and foremost promotes and defends the fortunes of America's multinational corporations and financial firms. If the multinationals are winning in the global competition, then it is assumed that America is winning. That assumption is clearly wrong. The opposite has been occurring for some years now.

These older societies, especially Japan and Germany, possess something Americans typically lack—historical memory. They remember what can happen when utopian ideologies are in the saddle. They experienced the social destruction and moral debauchery that arose when an extreme idea imposed its will. Whole sectors of society were first marginalized and then decimated. Civilized values were destroyed, along with the order of law and individual freedom. It was called fascism. In time, it led to the human catastrophe of World War II.

More than a decade ago, Japan tried to explain its different approach to American leaders. The "East Asian miracle" by which Japan and its neighbors gained economic strength was not based on unfettered free-market capitalism. It drew upon the region's deep cultural traditions that emphasize economic cooperation between private enterprises and society and broadly sharing the rising prosperity. In this system, nobody expects to get extremely rich, and nobody, not even rural peasants, expects to get thrown over the side.

The Americans didn't get it. The Asian model sounded retrograde and collusive to them. It offended market principles. American ideology sought a different goal and frankly favored capital over labor—profits over wages, shareholders over workers and communities. That approach's collateral damage to society was essentially brushed aside as inconsequential.

The American approach pushes to maximize economic growth first and then to worry about any injustices and social injuries the growth caused. In this way, the United States usually does achieve higher growth rates than many other advanced economies, but the social cleanup that should follow never seems to get done.

"Growth before justice" is how writer Lew Daly characterizes the American system. Addressing social inequalities or environmental effects after the fact is always more difficult and costly than preventing them beforehand. The same industrial interests that profit handsomely from laissez-faire economics inevitably object to spending the money repairs require and may even exercise their veto power. This helps explain why the United States lags well behind those other countries in supporting social well-being and sound environmental values.

To put it bluntly, America is no longer "number one" in many important ways that matter to people. It hasn't been for quite a long time. We might find out much about ourselves by looking more honestly at the experiences of other people in the world. We can put aside patriotic pride and inquire into the facts.

Mikhail Gorbachev, former president of the Soviet Union and one of the wise statesmen of our time, has been trying—gently but persistently—to coax American leaders out of their self-centeredness. The United States, he suggested, "'should get rid of this disease which I call the winner's complex.

"'The victory complex is even worse than the inferiority complex,'" Gorbachev explained. He does not specifically say it is the "arrogance of power," but I think that is what he means. US influence in the world can still flourish, Gorbachev said, but "'leadership should be done not by domination, not by becoming a policeman in the world, but by being a partner.'"[3]

This book is not a treatise about grand strategies, but some elements of the necessary fundamental change should be obvious. The United States should resolve to shrink the footprint of its military power and reexamine the purpose of its burgeoning arsenal. This would open the way for new power-sharing arrangements among nations and compel the redistribution of the costs and responsibilities of maintaining world order.

If that were done, nations would have a practical incentive for reordering and strengthening the international institutions that were created half a century ago, starting with the United Nations. The World Bank and IMF have both lost their original visions and effectiveness. In addition, the global trading system needs a new financial institution to maintain stability and equity among rich and poor nations. There's a long list of promising opportunities.

American power essentially has a choice. It can dig in and continue to resist change on all fronts, or it can back off a bit and accept the role of an important advocate for international reform. That would allow the United States to rediscover the progressive spirit that was its hallmark half a century ago. What the United States can no longer do is pretend that it runs the world.

Roughly speaking, that is what I mean by the title *Come Home, America*. I borrowed the phrase from South Dakota senator George McGovern, who used it as the slogan for his failed presidential campaign in 1972. Senator McGovern told me he borrowed it from a sermon given by the Rev. Martin Luther King Jr. a year before his death. Both men opposed the war in Vietnam, but their larger purpose was summoning Americans back to their country's inherited ideals and principles.

"America has strayed to the far country of racism and militarism," King warned in 1967. "A home that all too many Americans left was solidly constructed idealistically; its pillars were solidly grounded in the insights of our Judeo-Christian heritage. All men are made in the image of God. All men are brothers. All men are created equal. . . .

"But America's strayed away, and this unnatural excursion has brought only confusion and bewilderment. . . . It is time for all people of conscience to call upon America to come back home. Come home, America."[4]

Martin Luther King was murdered. George McGovern was famously buried in a landslide defeat. The evocative phrase lives on in American politics, but usually as a backhanded rebuke. Anyone who expresses the idea is derided as an "isolationist" or "protectionist," a "defeatist" who no longer believes in the country and thinks America is "in decline." Those labels crudely slander McGovern and King because both men were profoundly internationalist in their perspectives (so am I).

I want to put "coming home" back into common usage and coax people to consider a different kind of patriotism that may be right for our troubled circumstances. I have no doubt that most Americans—if given a choice—would choose to focus on America first. This is not because people are isolationist or want to withdraw from the world, but because people know things are going wrong and concentrating on our own problems sounds like a sensible priority.

It was never America's destiny to run the world. That was not why waves of immigrants came to our shores. They came to be free, to make a better life for their people. Our global preeminence and power grew out of America's successes and accumulated strengths, not the other way around. Our global posturing is now actively undermining what made the nation strong and successful in the first place, including the constitutional principles often corrupted by US efforts to prevail over other nations.

Turning inward will make it easier to balance our relations with the rest of the world. Instead of dominating others, we can learn to live with differences. Instead of attacking foreign governments that deviate from the US model, America can once again advocate for self-determination by all nations. For better or worse, people should choose their own governing systems, just as we have.

"Decline" is the wrong word to describe America's situation. We are not Imperial Britain or Napoleonic France. We are not conquering Romans or Greeks. Despite the imperial pretensions evident in high places, the United States has been rather inept at empire building. It makes a lot of citizens uncomfortable or angry. The governing classes dare not speak openly about having imperial aspirations since that would contradict our democratic values. Americans are always patriotic, but they have little tolerance for patriotic sacrifice undertaken on behalf of wrongful causes.

I think a better word for what's facing America is "maturity." Remember, this country of ours is still quite young as nations go—only 230 years or so—and we are still developing in many ways. Despite our wealth and power, we are not yet a finished nation.

Think of America at this point as a muscular teenager, full of talent, adolescent energy, and youth's over-reaching impulses. This is a critical stage in human development, and for our nation it could go either way. Some nations that acted like willful children when they were young formed balanced societies when they became adults. Other nations have never really grown up.

The question, I think, is whether we—the people who proudly call ourselves Americans—can mature as a society. The country can develop a deeper sense of what matters most in life and what doesn't. It can shed some self-destructive reflexes and acquire a wiser sense of national self-interest that is anchored in the nation's ideals. Wisdom tempers egotism. This is true for both people and nations.

Or, the United States can plunge ahead self-indulgently, repeating destructive habits, acting out reckless ambitions, and getting into deeper trouble. We all know children who, for whatever reason, got older but never found themselves. This is possible for nations too, especially ones that refuse to reconcile themselves to new realities.

I am betting we will grow into our maturity and hoping that lots of Americans agree. This book proceeds on that framework. I describe the adversities we face and how we got here and then discuss how we might recover and develop a more rewarding society for all, a society that is still rich, still strong and capable, and still striving to fulfill a more promising destiny.

Can we redeem the goodness of the country we know and love? Or are we going to fritter it away in adolescent excesses? Must we abandon the original promise, or should we fight for it? Governing elites are not going to decide this for us. How could they?

CHAPTER FIVE

THE POLITICS OF
"HARD MONEY"

The panicky crisis that enveloped the US financial system in the early months of 2008 put the country on the brink of a historic catastrophe—the kind that can collapse the economy and destroy illusions that have ruled for a generation. Wall Street's financial crisis is an ominous warning for the country, one that gives greater immediacy to everything I want to say in this book. The United States is in a ditch and the ditch just got a lot deeper. Americans have at last been given fair warning, though not by their political leaders. As I write this, nobody knows whether this crisis will develop into a full-blown calamity—a depression like that in the 1930s. I fervently hope not. The titans of high finance might need the humbling a climactic reckoning would deliver, but the lives of many millions down below would be devastated.

I start with Wall Street because the financial crisis and its economic consequences are at the forefront of our thoughts and reflect the basic disorders of our era. In many ways, the power of bankers and their fraudulent illusions were fundamental causes in the unhinging of the US economy and the deforming of our representative democracy.

When major financial houses were tottering and the Federal Reserve rushed to save them with emergency loans of hundreds of billions of dollars, I called an old friend and longtime source who works in the upper reaches of the financial system. He is an expert in banking and politics who has a talent for looking over the horizon at the shape of things to come. What he sees usually puts him well ahead of conventional opinion. He tracks global affairs for a major hedge fund and looks for the deeper trends that will influence investment decisions months or years down the road.

"We are witnessing the crack of history," he told me. Even if the worst is avoided, he explained, the United States will be profoundly altered by this financial crisis because it intersects with every other weakness and vulnerability now confronting the nation: the massive indebtedness piled up by the perennial US trade deficits, the burdens of war making, the need to divert capital to deal with global warming, the pressing necessity of converting to a postpetroleum economy. My friend had visited the offices of several congresspeople to explain the full implications of the crisis and offer suggestions. "The degree to which people are thinking about these problems is not very impressive," he told me.

He skipped over immediate questions—Which bank might fail next? Will the Fed's bailout succeed?—and went to the heart of the matter. The United States has lost a massive amount of capital, thanks to the Wall Street debacle. No one can yet say how much. Jan Kregel, a senior scholar at the Levy Economics Institute of Bard College, an economics think tank, estimated total credit losses among borrowers, creditors, and banks to be as high as $900 billion. Others say it is twice that. To return to a well-functioning economy, this lost capital must be replenished, not only to shore up damaged banks and financial firms but also to ensure the availability of adequate capital and credit flows to the real economy of production and consumption.[1]

"The Chinese will need to bail us out," my friend surmised. China and other leading Asian economies, along with oil-rich Arab nations, accumulated vast surpluses of capital—trillions of dollars in wealth reserves—during the last decade while the US economy was steadily losing strength. Foreign wealth, he explained, has to be recycled back into the US economy essentially to recapitalize the injured financial system and corporations that depend upon financing to function. Wall Street firms, as I write this, are scrambling to raise new capital, and authorities are still nervously watching several big names, Citigroup among them. The bailout, my friend explained, may take several forms. Foreign investors and especially foreign governments could place huge deposits with US banks or buy up to the 10 percent legal limit on foreign ownership of stock shares in US companies. They also could invest indirectly in crippled companies through private-equity funds or lend their capital directly to the US government by buying

Treasury bonds. Probably, foreign creditors will do all of these. Washington, he suggested, could create a US recovery fund—something like the Reconstruction Finance Corporation of the 1930s—that would borrow foreign investment capital and relend it to damaged American enterprises, essentially recapitalizing the US economy.

The experience will at best be awkward and humiliating for Americans. No one in authority is likely to admit that a "bailout" by China or any other foreign power will be needed, but that is the probable outcome, and it means we will descend still further into debtor dependency on economic rivals and foreign creditors will gain greater influence over US decision making. American pride may be injured and the fear of foreigners aggravated, but the alternative is a lot less attractive. Without foreign capital to assist us, the climb back will be slow and much harder on everyone, including the foreign producers who count on the wide-open US market to sell their goods.

The financial crisis is not a "perfect storm," as many Wall Street players want to believe. That popular term suggests a freak convergence of natural forces that no one could have predicted, and it is a clever way to shrug off blame and assure everyone that normal life will resume as though nothing has changed. But the origins of this disaster were visible for several years. Numerous critics (myself included) sounded the alarm. But the skeptics were outside the circle of respectable authorities and therefore Washington and Wall Street ignored us.

"Normal life" is not going to resume. It can't. The events constituting Wall Street's sudden debacle shattered the economic framework the US system has functioned within for roughly a generation. The exposure of Wall Street's falsified valuations scrambled the business plans of tens of thousands of companies, not to mention millions of households. The context for US prosperity was easily available credit accompanied by growing debt underwritten by the generosity of our foreign creditors. Those assurances, as business negotiators like to say, are off the table.

Wall Street got in trouble because it was selling bad "financial paper" to investors—financial instruments that were inflated in value and falsely advertised. The volume of the most famous of these rotten assets—bonds that bundled the so-called subprime mortgages into marketable securities—mushroomed as the bubble in housing prices grew. The mortgage securities were sold to banks and investors around the world, including pension funds and local governments, as safe and sound investments claimed to be virtually risk free with the triple-A grades private rating agencies gave them.

The fantasy collapsed when the housing bubble burst and home prices started falling. Millions of home owners, most of modest means, were stuck with overvalued mortgages charging usurious interest rates they could not afford and that left them headed for default. The brokerages, banks, and mortgage companies had already collected their profits up front by taking inflated fees on the dubious transactions. Any remaining risk, bankers assumed, had been dumped on others, principally unwitting investors and hapless home owners. The bankers were mistaken.

As the word spread among nervous investors, the specter of huge losses caused a full-scale panic. Institutions holding these poisoned US assets tried to flee but discovered that nobody was gullible enough to buy them. In fact, nobody could say what the "paper" was really worth. Other credit markets seized up as investors wondered what else Wall Street was hiding from its customers.

Quite a lot, as it turned out. Some of the biggest names—Citigroup, Bear Stearns, Merrill Lynch, Morgan Stanley—were themselves holding a lot of this bad paper, often conveniently hidden off the balance sheet in so-called special purpose entities, an accounting fiction legalized by financial deregulation during the Clinton administration. The sleight of hand banks used to conceal their portfolios of damaged assets was not so different from the phony bookkeeping that brought down Enron and other fraudulent corporations.

The exposure of these hidden assets terrified bankers, who lend many billions of dollars every day to other Wall Street firms to finance their lending and investing. The "run" on Wall Street that followed was not composed of panicky small depositors. It was big banks and major investors "calling" their loans to brokerages, demanding repayment from fellow club members. The best minds in Wall Street, one could say, were brought down by their own accounting gimmicks—the innovations they had sold to Washington lawmakers as "modernization."

When shareholders started dumping stocks of Fannie Mae, the quasi-public financial institution that had originated many of the inflated mortgage securities, we saw a rescue drama that will be repeated many times over. The feds came forward with even larger assurances, hoping to restore "investor confidence." But in spite of the Federal Reserve's protective efforts, more financial firms are going to fail, shrink in size, or be compelled to merge with other firms or sell themselves to foreign owners. Wall Street will still be Wall Street, but it will be a lot less cocky and overbearing. These events, taken together, have led the nation to a significant watershed—the deflation of Wall Street. By "deflation" I mean the financial system will get smaller and less powerful in both political influence and domination of the economy and American life in general.

This crisis, unlike some previous episodes, cannot be explained away by blaming a few bad actors or random bad luck. This time, Wall Street has been disgraced because it failed on its own terms. What blew up was the new "financial architecture" that bankers and brokers had devised in the name of allocating capital more efficiently and giving financial markets greater "transparency." Those boasts sound like wicked jokes in the aftermath of Wall Street's debacle.

Shrinkage is bad news for deal makers used to getting multimillion-dollar bonuses, but it may contain good news for the rest of us. Compliant politicians who for many years deferred to Wall Street's ambitions and collaborated by dismantling the old system of financial regulation are now anxious to be seen as born-again reformers. They haven't turned against their old patrons—not yet— but they are scrambling to do something for the folks, such as enacting emergency relief measures for the millions of stranded home owners facing foreclosure. Liberal interventions in the marketplace seem much less radical when the Federal Reserve is bailing out the largest financial players wholesale. Congressional loyalties will be tested more severely in the debate over reimposing regulatory controls on the financial system. Congress has to literally repeal many of the lenient measures it enacted to benefit Wall Street, as well as the draconian bankruptcy law that put a tighter noose around debt-soaked consumers.

Regardless of what unfolds in US politics, the rest of the world also participated in Wall Street's losses and will not soon forget them. From small towns in Norway to Germany's largest bank, it may be a long while before foreign lenders and investors believe again in US "transparency" or defer to its fanciful "innovations." Before the breakdown, the US financial system was already losing customers as investment capital gravitated to the rising financial markets in Europe and Asia, partly because foreigners resented the sky-high fees and commissions charged by US financiers.

But the wealth of US finance is subsiding for fundamental economic reasons, not simply because of disenchanted customers or discredited accounting.

For twenty-five years, Wall Street enjoyed an unprecedented hyperinflation of US financial assets—ever-rising valuations for stocks, bonds, loan paper, and other credit instruments. Financial wealth grew much faster than the real economy, where average wage incomes have long been stagnant or falling.

Wall Street's spectacular run-up broke from historic patterns because year after year, the financial system's valuations and profits departed from the underlying economy upon which financial assets are presumably based. Normally, financial markets may run ahead of the real economy for a while, typically during an economic recovery, but sooner or later the historic relationship is reestablished and the two realms grow roughly in step. This era was dramatically different. The financial system achieved its own lofty altitude and most who profited didn't bother to look back to ponder why everyday economic activity wasn't keeping up.

The triumph of capital is reflected in the extraordinary flight of the Dow Jones Industrial Average. The Dow, which tracks the stocks of thirty very large companies, was a little below 800 in August 1982, when an explosive rally began the era that became known as the "super bull market." Twenty-five years later, the Dow was at 14,100. In spite of the stock market crash in 1987 and the severe meltdown of stock prices in 2000 and 2001, the Dow reached its peak in October 2007, just before the financial crisis struck.

This contrast expresses our nation's basic disorder: The Dow's value was multiplied seventeen times while the US economy grew only five times larger. Standard & Poor's 500, a broader index including five hundred stocks, grew nine times during the twenty-five-year period, nearly double the real economy's growth. Other types of financial transactions were also enhanced because debt and investment agreements typically use stock prices as benchmarks for judging credit worthiness and corporate performance. A rising share price means easier terms for borrowing, as well as bigger bonuses for the CEO.

This long-running gap between the financial sector and the rest of the economy underscored that something was fundamentally out of sync, that the basic relationship between Wall Street and the real economy of producers and consumers had been fundamentally altered. Financial prices may run ahead for a time, but not for a full generation or to such extravagant extremes. To put it bluntly, this is where a lot of the new billionaires came from. But it was also the source of the intensifying disorders that warped economic circumstances for average Americans. The ever-rising stock prices put excruciating pressures on companies and managers to achieve higher returns on capital and keep their stock prices rising. That meant extracting more from workers and other costs, often by moving production to poor countries with cheaper workers and weaker law enforcement.

The owners of capital are in essence claiming a larger and larger share of the economy's overall returns—squeezing the orange to get more juice for themselves while leaving other participants parched and cheated. In the early 1980s, the financial industry's profits were about 10 percent of all corporate profits. By 2007, at a time when corporate profits were booming generally, the financial sector was claiming 40 percent. The value of all US financial assets used to average a bit more than four times the gross domestic product. By 2007, financial assets were ten times the GDP.[2]

The great inflation of our era was not the inflation in prices for consumer goods and services, but the explosive inflation of financial wealth. The question is why. How did it happen that finance and capital triumphed over nearly everything else in our time? And where does the blame lie for this fundamental disorder?

At the risk of disappointing some readers, I am not going to line up a bunch of villains and make them the "bad guys," though there are plenty of candidates. It may be satisfying to demonize a few leading actors for what went wrong, but focusing on the greed of selected rogues glosses over the deeper political forces at work. If we are to restore what is lost—an equitable balance in American economic life—understanding the system, the why and how of what happened to the country, is an essential step.

Leave aside Wall Street's greed and reckless overreaching. Instead, I start with the federal government. Not the government of elected politicians, though Congress and presidents played supporting roles, but the appointed governors of the Federal Reserve, the central bank that manages money and credit.

It was mainly the Federal Reserve—sheltered from public scrutiny and protected from political accountability—that engineered America's great shift in fortunes. The Fed "hardened" the value of money and wealth with its successful campaign to suppress price inflation. Then it proceeded to encourage or passively allow the scandalous financial behavior that followed—wealth being concentrated in the financial sector, the growing inequalities among Americans, deregulation and the creation of dominating megabanks, and recurrent frauds and financial bubbles followed repeatedly by government bailouts of banks and financial firms.

The Federal Reserve's policy essentially tilted the normal economic balance hard in one direction, then held it there for a generation. It favored wealth over wage income, creditors over debtors, capital over labor, financial investors over producers. It was as though the tectonic plates beneath American democracy and commerce were forced into a new alignment that favored the few over the many.

My indictment may sound extreme and unfamiliar since few in public life talk about the United States' central bank in terms of the deeper consequences its policy decisions have. Both the press and the politicians defer to the mystique of the Fed. They tend to regard it reverentially as a technocratic and apolitical governing institution composed of gnomish economists who decide arcane issues too complex for the rest of us to understand. This deference enhances the central bank's power. The overall ignorance allows the Fed to act without being held accountable for its one-sided judgments or grave errors.

In 1987, I wrote a book—*Secrets of the Temple: How the Federal Reserve Runs the Country*—that demystified this obscure institution and described the high drama involved in making monetary policy (the book, I am proud to note, was on the bookshelf in Alan Greenspan's office when he was Fed chairman). The final chapter, called "The Triumph of Money," detailed the great shift in political power the Fed had engineered. Washington politics, I wrote, would thereafter be trumped by the Federal Reserve and the values of Wall Street. That sounded radical at the time, but I now think that I understated the case. I did not grasp then that the Fed would hold on to its political dominance for another twenty years.

★ ★ ★ ★ ★

The Federal Reserve—largely unchallenged by the elected government but cheered on by Wall Street—has abused its powers as a governing institution. By favoring wealth and wealth holders over the broader interests of Americans year after year, the central bank's policy decisions proved to be deeply unfair and antidemocratic, and also irresponsible. By persisting in its narrow-minded "hard money" approach, the Fed ultimately destabilized the overall US economy, amplifying the adverse effects of globalization. Eventually, the central bank led the country into our present mess, flirting with the full catastrophe.

Yet respectable opinion, especially from those in Wall Street, now proposes giving the Federal Reserve still more governing power. The Fed would be assigned the role of a "supercop" authorized to supervise all of the largest financial houses, not just commercial banks, and provide them with emergency bailouts if necessary to avert another crisis. This is backward—it gives a larger safety net to the very financial interests that have so damaged the country, rewarding the governing institution that failed spectacularly to do its public duty.

Along with Wall Street, the Federal Reserve was the principal coauthor of the financial disaster. By going to extremes, by favoring one sector of society over the others, the Fed revealed itself to be an untrustworthy agent of the public interest. The central bank cannot possibly lead reforms when it has to be reformed itself.

★　★　★　★　★

In the nineteenth century, the "money question" was a continuing political preoccupation of ordinary citizens. Even uneducated, impoverished farmers in the humblest circumstances understood the centrality of money and credit in their lives. They knew why bankers and working people were on opposite sides of money issues. When the Federal Reserve was created in 1913, it was billed as the "great compromise" that would take the "money question" out of politics. Wall Street banking ceded its formal control of money to Washington, but financial wealth still was protected from the raw, unruly masses who might demand the "easy money" of lower interest rates and booming economic growth. The veil of the Federal Reserve obscured the politics, but financial special interest advocates remained very close to the new institution, hovering around the central bank and constantly lobbying to influence its decisions. Citizens lost their voice in the money debate and were ignored. The historic oddity is that sophisticated modern Americans (including most elected representatives) do not grasp the political implications that barefoot farmers understood more than a hundred years ago.

The Federal Reserve is positioned on the fault line between the interest of mere voters and the reckless excesses of the banking industry. Maintaining stable valuation of money is always the divisive central issue because inflation tends to undermine the value of accumulated wealth while slyly helping the debtor class cope with debt. Over generations, the Fed tried to keep a tolerable balance. Its mandate from Congress tells it to pursue both full employment and a low rate of inflation, supporting the real economy while also protecting the purchasing power of money and wealth. These goals frequently come into conflict, but the central bank has a formal obligation to do both.

The trauma of inflation in the 1970s triggered a change in the Fed's role. Price inflation was rising out of control during that stagnant decade, fueled by OPEC's increasing oil prices and the economy's overheating by the war in Vietnam. The Federal Reserve floundered badly and was accused in conservative circles of failing to do its job. The effects of an inflation rate approaching double digits were especially hard on the capital and financial markets, but they also induced a frenzy of buying as people rushed to make purchases before prices went up again.

In the fall of 1979, the Federal Reserve launched its counteroffensive with the monetary equivalent of George W. Bush's "shock and awe." Paul Volcker, the Fed chairman newly appointed by President Jimmy Carter, threw out the usual rules and slammed on the brakes, sending interest rates soaring, shutting down credit, and abruptly stopping economic growth. This started a wrenching two-year recession in which unemployment peaked at 11 percent. It also doomed Carter's reelection in 1980. But political reactions were surprisingly muted. If the Fed was going to induce the pain to stop inflation, let the Fed have the glory and take the blame.

By taking forceful action, the central bank effectively took control of government economic policy, pushing aside Congress and the White House by imposing a unilateral solution. The Fed led its own single-minded campaign to break the back of rising inflation and stabilize the value of money. The central bank had traditionally been a kind of silent partner in managing the national economy. It set monetary policy while elected politicians managed the more visible budget issues of fiscal policy, government spending, and taxation.

Volcker's tough intervention against the inflationary disorders effectively preempted the politicians, and he basically ignored their complaints. The Fed's abrupt tightening of credit initially created confusion in financial markets, but it had the full and fervent support of Wall Street as well as of many citizens alarmed by rising prices.

Economists call the process that ensued "disinflation"—steadily ratcheting down the rate of inflation—but in olden times people spoke of it as enforcing "hard money" policy—making the value and purchasing power of money stronger. If inflation rises 5 percent, a dollar is worth only ninety-five cents. Disinflation reverses the process, making a dollar worth more than a dollar. The consequences of this move have been central to everything that has followed. "Hardening" the value of money may modestly benefit average consumers, but the true winners are people with vast accumulations of financial wealth. As the Federal Reserve drove the inflation rate lower and lower, eventually getting it close to zero, disinflation was a great gift to the wealthy, one that kept on giving.

Virtually every financial asset, especially stocks and bonds, became more valuable as inflation declined, adding percentage points to financial returns and stimulating greater optimism and higher prices in the financial markets. Many market players probably did not understand this, but instead simply thought they were getting richer because they were brilliant investors. In any case, the hardening of money sustained the "super bull market" and helped drive the price of financial assets higher and higher year after year.

Think of purchasing $1,000 in stock shares with money that is losing value every year due to rampant inflation. Even if the stock is a good investment, you will still lose real value when you sell the shares a few years later because you'll be paid back in dollars that are worth even less. The Fed reversed the trade-off. As money hardened in value, investors began collecting bonuses—the unseen dividends from disinflation—because when they sold their stock shares they were paid in dollars that were worth substantially more than the dollars they had originally spent. As the disinflation continued, investors collected bigger bonuses, depending on how long they had held the financial assets. This naturally made them feel more enthusiastic about investing.

Debtors, on the other hand, experienced the opposite consequences (though most likely didn't see the connection to monetary policy). A home owner who borrowed money to buy a house would see his or her indebtedness and housing costs in real terms steadily reduced by inflation. The monthly mortgage payments became a declining share of living expenses, while the asset—the house—steadily grew in market value. Home ownership created a nest egg for retirement.

The Federal Reserve's victory over inflation essentially reversed the benefits. A new home owner typically would have to pay off the mortgage with steadily hardening dollars. Newfangled mortgages tended to conceal this from home buyers, initially giving them low interest rates that subsequently ballooned. Instead of declining over time, their housing costs steadily rose, and many found themselves unable to keep up with the higher payments. Since incomes were stagnating, families fell behind and turned to borrowing on their credit cards or equity lines to pay the bills. The bankers felt good. They were collecting more income from housing. Home owners felt nervous. They were spending their savings.

In August 1982, Volcker finally relented on his recessionary policy and abruptly reduced interest rates, signaling that the Fed would at last allow the economy to recover. The long recession had claimed many victims, but by then major banks were also being threatened by defaulting borrowers. The news of Volcker's shift touched off an explosive stock market rally in Wall Street. It was the beginning of the fabulous run-up of financial prices that would last for twenty-five years.

The Federal Reserve had won its great battle against inflation—it fell substantially during the 1982 recession—but the Fed continued its war once the economy was recovering. By its estimate, inflation was still too high—bouncing around 4 to 5 percent—and Wall Street's so-called bond-market vigilantes who lobbied for tight credit demanded that the Fed keep rates higher to dispel the "inflationary expectations" of investors. So the Federal Reserve kept the pressure on, holding interest rates higher than normal to restrain economic growth, thereby further reducing price inflation while the economy was expanding.

The "hard money" policy was sustained in a way that might have shocked many Americans if they had known about it. The Federal Reserve suppressed inflation by targeting the wages of working people. It prevented their incomes from rising even though, in a healthy economy, wages would normally rise consistently. Nobody in authority ever acknowledged this strategy in a straightforward way, but the reality was well understood by economists and financial investors. By holding back the natural energies of the economic recovery, this monetary policy kept labor markets slack and the unemployment rate higher as a result, at around 6 percent. That made it very difficult for industrial workers, union and nonunion, to demand higher wages. If the economy had been allowed to grow faster, more jobs would have been created, unemployment would have fallen, and workers would have gained bargaining power.

But the conservative Federal Reserve regarded rising wages as an inflationary threat and worked deliberately to prevent it. Throughout the 1980s and most of the 1990s, the Fed protected its victory over inflation by keeping its foot on the brake and tapping it occasionally to make sure the economy did not get too healthy. That is, the federal government—represented by the central bank—ensured that the broad ranks of working people would not share in the "good times."

Paul Volcker used to carry in his pocket a card setting out the latest wage settlements in contracts negotiated by unions. When politicians urged him to let up and lower interest rates, the Fed chairman would cite recent wage agreements as evidence that he must hold tight. Monetary economists devised a theory to justify the antiwage policy. They claimed inflation would return if the Fed let the economy progress to below a so-called natural rate of unemployment. The theory was bogus; it was subsequently disproved by real-world experience when unemployment fell to 4 percent in the late 1990s, yet no inflation appeared.

The Federal Reserve, in other words, has played a central role in suppressing wages during the last three decades, a policy that was powerfully reinforced by globalization and the migration of US jobs to low-wage economies. Was this in the public interest? The question was not discussed in polite circles. The presumption among the governing elites, including the most influential newspapers, is that everyone shares a common interest in subduing inflation and therefore wage suppression is required. Wall Street celebrated the central bank's success in restraining economic growth by dubbing it the "Goldilocks economy"—not too hot, not too cold, but just right. It may have seemed just right to financial investors. For working people, it was way too cold.

Volcker's hard-nosed posture inflamed Republicans in the Reagan White House because it put the central bank on a collision course with the administration's economic policy—"a game of chicken" between monetary and fiscal policy, as some economists called it. Ronald Reagan's huge budget deficits were highly stimulative and would have driven faster economic growth. But the Federal Reserve blocked the way by keeping interest rates too high. Volcker warned that he would not relent until the elected government first reduced its budget deficits. He rejected the private pleas of Republican senators and economists.

The Reagan White House could not budge Volcker and eventually replaced him with the more politically reliable Alan Greenspan. Democrats, meanwhile, sided with Volcker and the Fed, even though the central bank was hurting working people and organized labor, an important Democratic constituency. The party of the working class was moving rightward, recasting itself as the party of "fiscal responsibility."

The Federal Reserve changed significantly when Greenspan succeeded Volcker in 1987. Greenspan continued to enforce the policy of disinflation and was, if anything, even more dogmatic about driving the inflation rate as close to zero as possible. He often took precautionary moves that subdued the economy when no price inflation was visible. In print, I wickedly referred to him "the one-eyed chairman" because he could see inflation in the real economy even when it wasn't there, but he was blind to the runaway price inflation in stock markets.[3]

In fact, the Fed under its new chairman became an active contributor to the great financial inflation that led to Wall Street's subsequent disorders. Unlike his predecessor, Greenspan deliberately backed away from the central bank's regulatory obligations, failed to discipline banks for predatory lending and other abuses, and aggressively promoted the repealing of regulatory restraints on bank behavior. Volcker, in contrast, was a career regulator who was deeply skeptical of bankers and financial markets. He knew their fads and follies. Volcker bailed out bankers when their excesses got them in trouble, but he believed in exerting strong supervision and regulatory discipline to curb the market's occasional delusions. Greenspan was an ideologue who sincerely believed that a freely running marketplace possessed superior wisdom.

The new Fed chairman set out to liberate finance from government. His most audacious initiative was the Federal Reserve's single-handed maneuvering to legalize the new all-purpose megabank that would concentrate financial power in a handful of very large institutions. Greenspan preempted Congress on this issue by unilaterally approving what was still prohibited by law. Citibank became the financial conglomerate called Citicorp. Hard lessons learned during the crisis of the 1930s were discarded as obsolete. Democrats and Republicans collaborated in repealing or gutting prudential safeguards enacted in the New Deal.

For three decades, Wall Street bankers had lobbied to reunite commercial banking with investment banking to create all-purpose financial firms. The two realms had been separated after the stock market crash of 1929 because fraudulent self-dealing by Wall Street's major banks fed the stock market mania that led to the crash. Preaching financial modernization, Greenspan restored the system that had failed some seventy years before. Once the Fed unilaterally authorized Citicorp to merge banking, investment, and insurance into one bank, Congress went along. The megabanks claimed to have "fire walls" that would prevent a recurrence of the old conflict-of-interest scandals. In reality, these banking conglomerates were equipped with trapdoors and accounting gimmicks that allowed the bankers to hide their debts and troubled assets. The financial gimmicks blew up in the subprime mortgage crisis of 2008.

Instead of playing the role of skeptical regulator, the Federal Reserve became a cheerleader. In the 1990s, as money's value was further hardened and stock prices soared still higher, Greenspan began to embrace "new economy" themes that supposedly justified the sky-high valuations. The United States was said to have entered a new era in which technologies and rising productivity made possible a golden vista for the future. Lots of people believed it.

The rising stock prices and pressures from Wall Street financiers applied strong pressures on corporations by pushing their management to toughen up and extract greater profits in the name of boosting "shareholder value." As firms competed on share prices and CEO compensation packages, employees suffered the consequences. Boosting profits meant tightening work rules, cutting benefits, holding down wages, and shipping more US production overseas to find cheaper workers. The old social contract between major corporations and their employees was dumped.

In Wall Street, meanwhile, financial players began to talk about the "Greenspan" put. A "put" is a commodity option contract that promises the shares will be bought at a certain price within a set period of time. The traders felt that "Greenspan" had implicitly given them a put—an assurance that the Fed would come to their rescue whatever happened, be it falling stock prices or financial crisis. The Fed, they assumed, would always be there for them. The financial sector's belief that it had its own special safety net in Washington was naturally a factor in traders bidding stock prices still higher. The self-congratulatory rhetoric of the 1990s that made every man a brilliant investor sounded a lot like the overconfident optimism that led to the 1929 crash.

Yet, unbeknownst to the general public, the Federal Reserve governors were already worrying that they had inadvertently permitted a stock market bubble to develop. By the fall of 1996, they were privately expressing alarm. If stock prices kept soaring beyond reality, there could be a damaging unwinding when the bubble popped. Several Fed governors urged the chairman to intervene by tightening the regulatory limits on stock market borrowing—the margin leverage investors use to make larger purchases.

"I recognize that there is a stock market bubble problem at this point," Greenspan told his colleagues in a private meeting of the governing board. But the chairman refused to raise margin requirements. "I guarantee you that if you want to get rid of the bubble, whatever it is, that will do it," he conceded. He was afraid, he said, of what else might happen. Given his ideological convictions, Greenspan did not have the inclination to discipline the financial assets or free market. This failure to use the Fed's powers in a timely fashion proved to be a fateful error, one in a series that led literally to an unhinging of the overall economy.[4]

At about the same time, the Federal Reserve faced another climactic challenge. After nearly two decades of deliberately restraining the real economy in order to drive the inflation rate lower and lower, the central bank had entered dangerous territory by the mid-1990s. The Fed had ratcheted down inflation from double digits to below 2 percent, and it was headed lower still. If the Fed persisted, the US economy would soon get to zero inflation. Then it would be flirting with a larger catastrophe—a general deflation consisting of falling prices, wages, and output. Debtors and working people would be devastated by a full-blown contraction, as would healthy enterprises and the overall economy.

To avoid this, the Federal Reserve executed a sharp turn in policy, taking its foot off the brake and allowing the real economy to follow its natural energy to expand faster. The central bank did not advertise the threat of deflation, but instead claimed that revised calculations of productivity permitted it to ease its policy of control. For the first time in fifteen years, Americans began to experience the glow of a vibrant, free-running economy. Unemployment fell to 4 percent. Wage incomes started rising smartly, even for the working poor. It was "good times" for everyone.

The Clinton administration took credit for the booming economy, but more sophisticated observers understood that it was the handiwork of the Fed. Contrary to the Federal Reserve's long-held theory, price inflation did not occur under these prosperous conditions. Prices remained steady as jobs multiplied, wages rose, and the real economy flourished.

The good times did not last for long. The central bank had failed to confront the stock market bubble, and it was rising to dangerous heights. The reenergized economy and relaxed interest rates reinforced stock buyers' giddy optimism and financial valuations rose to exaggerated extremes. The Dow passed 10,000 in late March 1999 and 11,000 a month later, then went higher. Some deluded analysts even predicted it would hit 35,000.

The Federal Reserve belatedly took action to stop the stock market mania. But it did not act by tamping down the financial markets. Instead, the central bank once again targeted the real economy and used its powers to cripple the growth in production and employment. Claiming to see renewed risks of inflation in goods and services, Fed officials started a new campaign in 1999 to tighten credit and slow things down. The central bank pushed short-term interest rates higher than long-term rates, an unnatural condition that produces recession if it persists. Savvy Fed watchers at financial firms assumed the central bank's real intention was to subdue the runaway inflation in stock prices—to slow down the economy so the financial frenzy would gradually subside. The Fed chairman denied this, but close associates confirmed that popping the bubble was his objective.[5]

The Federal Reserve lost its gamble on both fronts. The bubble did not simply moderate, it melted away. The real economy did not simply slow down, it slid into recession. The short-lived boom was over. Stock prices suffered a severe decline, with some $6 trillion in value disappearing from investors' accounts. The twin blows to finance and economic growth triggered a new threat—a renewed danger of deflation. The sudden disappearance of so much financial wealth would make it difficult to stimulate a normal economic recovery, and the price levels were still hovering near zero. Japan had suffered a similar collapse of its huge financial bubble a decade earlier and was still struggling to overcome a deflationary depression characterized by falling prices and a faltering economy that could not regain its momentum.

To escape the same fate, the US central bank went to extremes again, this time by shifting hard in the direction of "easy money." The Fed cut interest rates swiftly and drastically—nearly to zero—hoping this would stimulate the borrowing and buying needed to revive economic activity while the Bush administration cut taxes for upper income brackets. It worked, but in a perverse manner. The stock market, buoyed by the low interest rates, recovered its optimism and started climbing again toward a new record, reached in 2007 when the Dow hit its peak of 14,100. The economy had ostensibly recovered, but the benefits did not extend to most working people. While governing circles celebrated robust growth, workers experienced a kind of low-grade depression, with declining incomes and a steadily eroding supply of industrial jobs.

The Fed's extremely low interest rates, meanwhile, set in motion a new financial bubble. This time, the runaway prices were in housing and other interest-sensitive assets. With very cheap money available, people borrowed more to buy homes, and the increased demand ran up housing prices. Some monetary analysts thought the housing bubble was the Fed's deliberate strategy for recovery; others thought it was a mistake, another fateful error. Either way, it was a false recovery based on a great abnormality—the exaggerated borrowing and buying made possible by the near-zero interest rates engineered by the Federal Reserve. Like stock prices, the price inflation in the housing market was very difficult to reverse once it had gotten started. The Fed first denied there was a housing bubble, then tried to restore order by repeatedly raising interest rates in small increments. The gradualism had no effect until the bubble popped—and revealed the mess in Wall Street.

The Federal Reserve declined, once again, to use its powerful tools as financial regulator. The central bank could have imposed tighter rules on the financial firms, major banks, and investment houses that were pumping out home mortgages in explosive numbers. The financial industry was earning inflated profits from this new line of business, and many firms borrowed heavily themselves to leverage greater activity for greater profit. The bankers and brokers kept the bubble growing, marketing millions of dubious mortgages to people who couldn't afford them and selling securities based on assets doomed to fail. Federal Reserve leaders said they saw no problem.

In the first decade of the twenty-first century, some critics asserted that the US financial sector essentially functioned as the "debt industry." Wall Street and allied firms had turned to managing the nation's explosion of borrowing and indebtedness. Their innovative financial methods convinced leading banks and investment houses that this new line of business was less risky and more lucrative than the slowly plodding functions of old-fashioned investing, like creating new production capacity.

The "debt industry" became increasingly unstable and self-indulgent as it prospered, but the Fed stood by it. Monetary policy had generated a succession of asset bubbles that lent a superficial glow to Wall Street's balance sheets. To sustain the prosperity of finance, monetary policy swung back and forth dramatically, like the tail wagging the dog. To correct one extreme, the Federal Reserve scrambled quickly to the opposite extreme, then back again. When the accumulated excesses led to crisis and failure, the central bank rushed to rescue the endangered Wall Street firms.

When Alan Greenspan retired in 2006, he was celebrated almost universally for his wise stewardship (a few cranky dissenters like me did not join in the toasting). His successor was Ben Bernanke, a monetary economist from Princeton University who shared Greenspan's "hard money" bias. The central bank, Bernanke thought, should pursue an inflation-fighting target as its first priority, before dealing with competing concerns like the real economy. The new chairman was preoccupied, however, with the more immediate challenge of preventing a financial collapse—cleaning up the mess the Federal Reserve had helped to create.

I have detailed the role monetary policy played in creating the current economic conditions because I am reasonably certain that most Americans have never heard this version of events before, not even those who follow the financial news. I can attest that some of the best minds in finance—professionals who invest billions of dollars at very sophisticated levels—share my critical view of the central bank. The Federal Reserve was not the only player responsible for what has unfolded, but it was the principal agent in designing the "hard money" platform and sustaining it for far longer than was good for the nation.

The central bank is not a conspiracy composed of wicked bankers. It is a lawful agency of government that makes important public decisions on behalf of the rest of us. Its decision makers are serious and highly skilled, conscientious professionals. But, like any other aspect of government, the Federal Reserve is not infallible. Citizens should ask themselves why they know so little about the institution and why the deeper economic and political consequences of the Fed's decisions are never discussed. People should ask why they are kept in the dark.

★   ★   ★   ★   ★

The Federal Reserve's first historic disgrace occurred after the crash of 1929 when the Fed failed to counter deflationary forces that contributed to what became known as the Great Depression. The central bank, despite its location in Washington, was still run by bankers, and they resisted the political cries for prompt action. Lowering interest rates, they feared, would undermine "sound money" and, not coincidentally, damage the balance sheets of major banks. For three grueling years, Fed officials hesitated as the American economy unwound, wiping out 40 percent of the US banking system and driving unemployment to a peak of 25 percent.

In the aftermath of the destruction, the Federal Reserve was substantially reformed. Washington consolidated its control of monetary policy and the Fed adopted a more balanced understanding of the broader public interest it was supposed to serve. It still claimed to be "independent" of politics, but it readily deferred to the fiscal policy Congress and the White House set. Fed chairmen tried to coordinate with presidents privately and avoid confrontations.

The modern Federal Reserve once again faces the prospect of historic disgrace. Given its distorted policies and failure to regulate banking interests, the Fed is again ripe for fundamental reform, though few elected politicians have the courage to voice that conclusion. The new Federal Reserve chairman is determined not to commit the same grave errors the central bank made in the 1930s. Bernanke is a scholarly expert on the Fed's Depression-era failure to act, and he has taken unprecedented steps to pump hundreds of billions in federal money into damaged banks and investment brokerages to defuse the danger of another calamitous unwinding. If Bernanke succeeds, the central bank no doubt will be allowed to survive with its present powers and privileges intact, still shielded from the hot breath of democracy.

If Bernanke fails and an important megabank like Citigroup goes under, the consequences will produce a historic shock wave in politics—a "teachable moment" and a rare opportunity for serious reform. Faced with horrendous losses, the nation might be compelled to reexamine this odd governing arrangement, because its inherent democratic contradictions are becoming visible to all. The US government protects certain large interests from the costs of their own recklessness, but prescribes the perils of market competition for everyone else.

The illegitimacy of the present system is reflected in the recent bailouts of major financial houses in what amounts to American-style socialism for selected interests—the largest and wealthiest enterprises in finance. The losses incurred by these Wall Street firms were effectively socialized by the bailouts, meaning that the costs were dumped on society and the taxpayers. The Fed relieved the banks of their rotten assets and transferred them to the balance sheet of an unwitting public. The Federal Reserve, having aided in creating the oversized megabanks and having declined to regulate their behavior rigorously, routinely denies that it regards these banks as "too big to fail." Yet when these institutions are endangered, the Federal Reserve rescues them because, well, they are indeed "too big to fail." If banking behemoths go down, the entire US economy—all of us—may suffer the consequences—or so we are told.

This arrangement is not only unjust and hypocritical, it also actively encourages the kind of reckless behavior the central bank is supposed to prevent. The potential for collusion at the public's expense is enormous. I do not suggest there is corruption at the Fed in the old-fashioned sense, but the central bank has accepted being in a very weak position when it negotiates rescue terms with those it is rescuing. Since the public is not allowed to know all the terms, we cannot judge whether the Fed defended the public interest or simply gave the bankers whatever they said they needed. The bailout process resembles poker night at a gentlemen's club—there's no need to bother taxpayers with the messy details of what happens behind closed doors.

In the 2008 deal making, for instance, the Fed brokered the forced sale of Bear Stearns, a vulnerable brokerage, to JPMorgan Chase, a leading megabank of esteemed reputation. Fed officials emphasized that Bear Stearns shareholders lost nearly everything in what was hardly a sweetheart deal. The bank, which traces its venerable lineage back to J. P. Morgan and John D. Rockefeller, was promoted as acting in a spirit of noblesse oblige. In reality, however, the Bear Stearns deal was designed to save JPMorgan Chase. By selling risk-insuring derivative contracts, that bank had amassed a staggering $91 trillion in potential liabilities, nearly triple the exposure of the next largest bank. If more financial firms began to fail, JPMorgan Chase could be swiftly overwhelmed with claims it could not pay, because its total assets were $1.5 trillion.[6]

In spite of its weak position, the Morgan bankers drove a hard bargain in weekend negotiations with the Federal Reserve. They insisted that the central bank put up another $30 billion to cover all of Bear Stearns's bad assets before JPMorgan Chase CEO Jamie Dimon would sign off on the deal. Fed officials, desperate to announce the Bear Stearns sale before the global financial markets opened on Monday, consented to his terms. "Mr. Dimon took them to school," the *Wall Street Journal* observed.[7] The JPMorgan bankers negotiated a deal to save themselves, virtually risk free. The risk was assigned to the rest of us.

In any other part of the federal government, this kind of self-dealing would be considered scandalous and the press would explore it rigorously. If the Fed were less deferential to banking titans and more vigilant about acting in the pubic interest, it would set harsher terms for saving the private financial sector from its own follies. If firms resisted the terms, the central bank could seize the assets and put a troubled financial house in receivership. Doing so would strip shareholders of their equity stake, but it also would relieve top management of their perks, including those cushy severance contracts that reward fired executives after they have wrecked a firm. The regulators could impose strict new rules on banking operations to force them back from the brink. If financiers resisted such interventions, they could be left to bail themselves out.

The point is, if the financial crisis is truly a national emergency—and I think it is—why does the government act like a supplicant and offer friendly terms to those who caused the crisis? It should instead be disassembling the mammoth financial conglomerates it created, making them smaller for the safety and soundness of the overall system. The federal government has implicit authority to defend the general welfare in times of crisis, and it should use that power aggressively. The central bank itself has explicit legal authority, though it is vaguely defined, to take extraordinary measures to keep the economy going if the banking system fails to function. The Fed can lend money directly to nearly anyone—state and local governments or private enterprises—if it decides this is necessary to save the economic system.

If the nation is lucky and avoids the worst, then I fear the reforms enacted will be timid and shallow—measures that correct some of the obvious excesses without confronting the larger deformities in the central bank or the deep rot in the financial system. The political community seems too intimidated by Wall Street and the Federal Reserve to push for bolder ideas. People are angry enough, but the people still have to learn a lot before they can be forceful advocates for more profound reform. Citizens will have to teach themselves. They cannot count on the media or either political party to honestly explore the deeper contradictions in monetary policy.

If the economic damage is contained, the Federal Reserve may, in fact, be given even greater powers to supervise the financial system. The central bank would thus have an open-ended charter to run the country and intervene wherever it sees a threat to stability—in effect, a blank check for taking care of the biggest financial players. The Fed would then be supervising not just commercial banks and the hybrid megabanks, but also investment houses and related financial firms, including unregulated hedge funds and private-equity firms if they are big enough.

What makes this especially ominous is that many of these specialized investment funds already own and manage regular corporations, so the lines between finance and commerce would be obliterated. The Fed's reach would inevitably be expanded because Wall Street innovators would invent new, unregulated financial entities that required Fed protection. General Electric, for example, is a very large financial house—GE Capital—in addition to a multinational manufacturer. Because of its financial girth, the government might have to make sure it did not fail.

This is dangerous territory—the formation of a corporate state. Enlarging the Fed's powers not only further weakens democratic accountability, it also expands the private club that already enjoys its own exclusive federal safety net and is virtually exempt from serious political oversight. Maybe this is how representative democracy loses meaning—not with the invasions of dictators or foreign hordes, but from within as very large corporate enterprises use their political clout to win privileged protections from government. If the Fed's protective canopy is broadened to protect corporate forms outside of banking, then competing companies will take on the same characteristics to make themselves eligible for the special advantages. Who can compete with that?

The unfinished nature of American democracy—our immaturity as a nation—is reflected in the Federal Reserve's peculiar status and expressed bluntly by the central bank's growing domination of elected representatives. The unaccountable Federal Reserve governs our lives as assuredly as the politicians in Congress or the White House do, but without the inconvenience of facing elections. The Fed is not required to listen to citizens or even provide them with an honest accounting of what it has decided for us. The Federal Reserve consults closely with bankers. It does not give fair warning to the people.

In this manner, citizens are treated like children who are not to be trusted with power or even clear explanations of what the government is doing to them. If citizens had power, we might do something rash. We might charge blindly after ruinous illusions. We might try to take what is not ours. The financial sector, of course, has done all of these things in recent years, yet it is still regarded as the grown-up. The Federal Reserve wants to act as the father figure in this family constellation, a remote authority that is stern, unemotional, willing to punish with a hidden hand. We are asked to believe that Father always acts in our best interest. The sweep of events over the last thirty years ought to make it clear that this is not true.

Perhaps it is time for systemic reform that allows Americans to be treated as grown-ups. A century ago, when the Federal Reserve was created, it was easy to see why bankers and wealth holders were afraid of democracy. By then, the Populist revolt of southern and midwestern farmers was ebbing, but it was still a fresh and frightening memory for governing elites. Socialists were mobilized as a viable third party. The growing labor movement was in a bruising conflict with business.

We live in a different country now, one that is wondrously prosperous in comparison. Roughly half of American families now have capital accounts of their own, albeit usually of modest size. Organized labor manages huge pools of capital in pension funds for its members. The notion that ordinary citizens cannot be trusted to deal responsibly with the "money question" is obsolete, especially when it is the financial titans and the Federal Reserve who have gone to irresponsible extremes.

The simplest way to change things is to make the Federal Reserve an operating component of the executive branch—no longer "independent," but directly answerable to the president and subject to vigorous oversight by Congress. If a governing board is retained to make monetary decisions, it will need new checks and balances, including having a few congressionally appointed politicians as board members to counter the biases of economists and bankers. The political appointees would be allowed—even required—to offer regular commentary and public criticism. The governors do not need to make their decisions in public sessions, but the country needs timely access to the public debate on these important issues in terms that ordinary mortals can understand.

A reformulated banking system could be built around regional banks—twenty or thirty or forty of them—that by definition never become "too big to fail." The existing banking behemoths would be made to shrink in size gradually and accept close supervision in the meantime. Banking and finance could be rechartered to serve the society first—people and business enterprise—with strict prohibitions against usurious lending and other antisocial practices. A society that saves prudently for the future needs trustworthy institutions where people can store their wealth for retirement. Government rules can ensure that mutual funds and other financial agents are not charging exorbitant fees or using people's savings on behalf of other customers with conflicting objectives.

At a minimum, the central bank should be stripped of its role as banking regulator since it has failed utterly to protect the country from the financial system's self-destructive excesses. The Federal Reserve cast itself as Officer Friendly, a pal of major financial players as well as their policeman. That contradictory role does not protect the public interest. A new regulatory agency could take over the Fed's supervisory roles and perhaps be consolidated with other banking regulatory agencies under the Comptroller of the Currency in the Treasury Department.

The existing arrangement is wrong on democratic principles, but it also doesn't work very well as a practical matter. Fundamental changes are needed to demystify the institution and compel elected politicians to take responsibility for the government's monetary decisions. This would empower voters to discipline irresponsible actions at election time. Obviously, such great changes will require education and adaptation on the part of politicians and citizens, not to mention the Fed technocrats who are accustomed to cloistered privacy.

As subsequent chapters detail, the country is headed toward harder times, when economic conflicts and complications will require stark choices and serious reforms. Treating citizens like witless spectators makes it far harder for the country to make sensible choices or even to face the right questions. Most citizens, I believe, are capable of grasping complicated matters *if*—the big if—the complexities are explained in plain English. If ordinary Americans can understand defensive alignments in pro football, they can understand the dynamics of monetary policy. Candidates might see that they can talk to voters without relying on demagogic baby talk.

I am not a utopian. None of this is going to eliminate deceit and evasion in politics or banking and finance. But the idea of democracy rests on the assumption that including more people and diverse viewpoints in deliberations should lead to wiser decisions for the country. We know the present system does not.

CHAPTER SIX

BLINDED BY FAITH

T he United States of America (which has a per capita gross domestic product of $46,000) is ensnared in a perverse symbiosis with China (which has a per capita GDP of $2,400). The richest nation on earth borrows—massively, every year—from this very poor country so Americans can sustain a fabulous standard of living. It is an embarrassment, especially for advocates of globalization, but America's depleted condition makes it necessary. The burgeoning US indebtedness to foreign nations contradicts the familiar claims that free trade among nations is a winning proposition for America. Unlike the typically symbiotic relations between species in nature—think of honeybees pollinating apple trees—the cooperative relationship between China and the United States does not deliver mutual rewards.

The Chinese are willing to freely lend hundreds of billions of dollars to America because we need the money to keep buying China's exported goods. Companies producing in the United States sold some $79 billion in exports of goods and services to China in 2007, but Americans bought more than four times that from China in return, about $330 billion. The lopsided trade enables China to accumulate vast reserves of new wealth and lend much of it back to its US customers. China, along with other major foreign creditors like Japan and the oil-rich Arab states, is America's national credit card.

This recycling of wealth allows US consumers to enjoy cheaper goods and to keep living beyond our means, consuming more than we can competitively produce every year. It also gives China the wherewithal to continue its spectacular transformation into an advanced industrial nation by absorbing manufacturing jobs and now professional services that used to be based in the United States. China gets new factories and wealth. The United States gets outsourced production and an ominous, growing mountain of debt. In the short run, both sides gain something. In the long run, America is a big loser.

China is the source of that "giant sucking sound" Ross Perot talked about back in 1992 when he ran for president (although he thought it would come from Mexico). Between 2001 and 2007, 2.3 million US jobs were lost as the trade deficit with China grew to $260 billion. The nonprofit, nonpartisan Economic Policy Institute has calculated the devastating impact that has had on the American working class, including those who did not lose their jobs. Competition with Chinese workers costs all working people without a college degree—about 100 million people, roughly 70 percent of the workforce—an average $1,400 each in wage income. Of course the same group suffered similar losses from imbalanced trade for many years before China's rise. The average wage of industrial workers, when discounted for inflation, has remained flat since the early 1970s.[1]

It is easy to demonize China, and many Americans do. After all, the Communist mandarins brutally suppress human rights and exploit young rural villagers who leave home to work in the new factories. Furthermore, the US government and US businesses regularly accuse Beijing of various forms of cheating—manipulating its currency for price advantages; blocking foreign products from entering China's market; and ripping off US patent and copyright holders by copying musical works, films, and electronics, for example. The charges have some substance, but not much.

China is merely doing what the global trading system allows it to do. In fact, China is simply following the successful development strategy that Japan pioneered four decades ago and that other Asian tigers like Taiwan, South Korea, and Singapore undertook for their own rapid industrialization. A poor nation rises above poverty not by practicing "free trade," but by leveraging its primary asset— plentiful cheap labor—and managing its national economy in smart, self-interested ways that target the industrial assets of wealthy economies. In the face of criticism of these practices, some Asians point out that the United States targeted Great Britain in much the same way during America's rise to industrial power in the nineteenth century. In those days, Yankees stole English textile-producing technology and built domestic industries by blocking foreign imports.

China is demonized today, but twenty-five years ago, it was Japan. In the 1980s, US leaders loudly accused Japan of instituting policies that caused us to run huge trade deficits and of slyly taking business away from America's advanced industrial sectors. The Japanese apologized occasionally, but they did not back off. In the end, US companies and government capitulated. Starting in the late 1980s, the manufacturers in the major industrial sectors decided, one by one, to embrace the strategy of shifting more US production offshore to take advantage of the low-wage workers available in Asia and elsewhere. Machine tools, computer technologies, auto parts, advanced semiconductors—these and many other industries moved abroad, and more would follow.

South Korea, Taiwan, Singapore, and other nations hoisted themselves up the technological ladder by attracting US multinational corporations to invest capital and technology. China is distinctive only by virtue of its colossal population of 1.3 billion people and its wealth reserves of $1.2 trillion (mainly invested in US debt paper, Treasury bonds, and some private lending).

These once-poor countries are also now among our leading creditors. They share with China the same strong incentive to keep America afloat. If the United States becomes tapped out and can no longer buy what the rest of the world makes, the exporting nations will lose their best customer. That will send the global trading system into deep trouble, leaving it with lots of factories capable of producing far more than the world's other consumers can afford to buy.

No one in the upper realms of US government or industry can claim to be surprised by China's self-interested strategies. Beijing, if anything, has been far more forthright about its intentions than Tokyo and the other Asian tigers were. In the early 1990s, the Chinese government issued a series of policy directives for five strategic industrial sectors and explained how China intended to become a world-class producer and exporter of autos, chemicals, advanced electronics, and other goods. Foreign multinational companies were eager to gain access to China's promising market of domestic consumers. Beijing invited them to compete for entry, but on China's terms.

Foreign companies would be given generous tax breaks and other incentives, but they would be required to relocate some production, both jobs and technology, in China. Furthermore, foreign investors would have to partner with domestic enterprises and help China's infant industries acquire more sophisticated industrial skills. Some nations like Japan were wary at first and held back. American multinationals plunged in with enthusiasm.

Washington officials understood all of this. Corporate ambitions to invest in China were embraced and aggressively promoted by the federal government. In the 1990s, the Clinton administration cleared the way by agreeing to grant China full membership in the global trading system and the World Trade Organization. Bill Clinton at the time predicted win-win results for both countries, including lots of good jobs for Americans. But the reverse happened. China's great leap forward was driving the US trade deficit skyward as Clinton left office, and it has tripled since.

The trade deficit and national debt are the clearest evidence of America's weakened condition. In 2007 alone, the US economy swallowed an overall trade deficit of nearly $731 billion. It was compelled to borrow almost 6 percent of US GDP from abroad. Over the last fifteen years, the United States has accumulated more than $6 trillion in trade-deficit debt, which, by virtue of encompassing the entire economy of households, the business community, and government, is more ominous and far-reaching than debt incurred by the federal government.

When a family or company has to borrow more money than it earns every year to pay its bills, the company or family is understood to be very unhealthy financially. The same gauge applies to a national economy. The US trend is ominous because it has been going on for many years, although it has usually been ignored or blamed on peculiar circumstances. The change in the country's fortunes represents an extraordinary shift of power: Twenty years ago the United States was the creditor nation, lending its surplus capital to the rest of the world. Now we are the borrower nation, busily digging ourselves a deeper hole.

The deterioration of America's economic strength has been difficult for many to grasp because it is happening like a slow-motion mudslide. The commonly discussed economic statistics do not reflect it, and influential opinion leaders seldom talk about it with any candor. News media outlets treat trade deficits as unimportant and report the telling statistics deep in the financial pages.

Yet the United States is in the midst of a profound and frightening industrial transformation tantamount to an aging person gradually losing weight and muscle. Economists prescribe various remedies to conceal the wasting, but in fact it continues, driven by fundamentals of global industrialization the economists do not recognize. The United States is like a family awaiting notice that its credit cards are maxed out. Imagine the impact it would have on Americans' lifestyles if the country had to abruptly reduce consumption by 6 percent—roughly the amount supported by foreign borrowing. Someone ought to tell the Pentagon that in such circumstances it seems unwise to pick a fight with our biggest banker.

How could this have happened to us, the nation with incomparable advantages, the richest and arguably most inventive society? We were the only great industrial power left unscathed after World War II. The United States was the broad-shouldered giant that set out to rebuild the global economy when nobody else could do it. Fifty years ago, the United States' economic power permitted us to reorganize and take charge of the world. Now we are a stumbling Goliath.

In the victor's role, America shouldered the burdens of leadership to pursue both self-interested intentions and a progressive vision. Leaders understood that our muscular economy could not prosper if the rest of the world remained in ruins. So the United States adopted a broadly generous agenda, and other countries joined in. Don't punish the losers, as had been done after World War I, the policy said. Instead, help them recover and rebuild. Don't let old colonialist powers reclaim their dominion over poor countries. Create new institutions—the World Bank and the International Monetary Fund—to rebuild the international trading system and keep it stable and fair. Make the US dollar the reliable anchor for the world's other currencies. Use the United Nations to mediate rivalries and sustain the peace among nations.

The cold war struggle—capitalism versus communism—raised the stakes of power and split the industrialized world into two competing realms with scores of underdeveloped nations in between. The United States fused global development assistance with its strategy for containing the Soviet Union. Military spending and overseas deployments of American forces stimulated the economies of struggling nations, rewarding Japan, Germany, and other allies with money and jobs. US multinational corporations became the engine for dispersing the American system worldwide, relocating low-skill production of consumer goods like shirts and shoes to poorer nations to jump-start their industrial development.

On the whole, the process worked. Poor nations gained, and some became wealthy competitors of the United States. Others at least became less poor. Third world countries observed the contrast in the economies of the Soviet Union and the United States and, one by one, those who had a choice chose the American side of the argument. The global expansion of trade and investment was being transformed, meanwhile, by great technological breakthroughs in an industrial revolution driven by semiconductors, computers, digital communications, and other life-enhancing inventions. Most of these wondrous things were invented in America. So how did it happen that the United States, progenitor of such great advancements, wound up in its deep hole?

The short, simple explanation, I regret to say, is national arrogance. The glory days of World War II and its triumphant aftermath brought on presumptions of singular American greatness—really, American superiority—that were profoundly flawed. It was widely assumed that, whatever the circumstances, the United States would prevail because we were inherently better than other peoples of the world—more principled, more productive, and, of course, more powerful. Weren't World War II and the fabulous postwar prosperity proof of American supremacy?

Not everyone subscribed to these inflated convictions, of course, but the nation itself used them as a subtext for governing the world. If push came to shove, the United States would have its way. This great fallacy—resulting from the human conceit of overweening pride—is still believed by the people in charge, if not the broad population. The nation is learning, slowly and painfully, how wrong it was. People from everywhere in the world are capable.

The United States' approach to globalization was also informed by companion fallacies derived from the assumption of superiority. Though never stated explicitly, they were clearly visible in US policies and actions. One fallacy was the belief that, deep down, everyone else in the world wanted to be like us. No matter what other governments might say, the US economy was considered the obvious model for success, and sooner or later other nations would have to follow it. We would tolerate foreign deviations from this model for a while because we assumed that ultimately the American system would prevail.

A second fallacy was that US economic prowess could not be surpassed. After all, the reasoning went, American science and engineering were leading the technological revolution. If other nations ascended the industrial ladder, their success was not a threat: Americans would simply climb higher. We would get more education, become even more skillful and productive, and invent new stuff to sell the world.

A third fallacy was aggressively preached and even pushed on other nations. The US system of capitalism—which tolerates less governmental intrusion and places more power in the hands of private enterprise and capital—was depicted as the only legitimate version of capitalism, superior to all others. The American approach gives its own multinational corporations as much freedom and influence as possible and assumes that these companies embody the national interest and will do all they can to advance it. This US perspective has been embedded in numerous trade agreements and World Trade Organization rules governing global trade. The WTO protects the interests of capital and corporations; it has nothing to say about defending workers and societies against capitalism's depredations.

These strands of American belief fused together to form the dogmatic ideology that rules American politics. This orthodox doctrine of corporate-led globalization is deeply embedded in respectable thought and embraced by both political parties. The belief system is so powerful, and its adherents so devout, that I sometimes think of it as "the church of free trade." Yet US market doctrine has never fully convinced other advanced nations, and many have ignored important aspects from the outset. Poorer countries that were too weak to resist at first are now openly revolting against the stern dictates that Washington pompously labels the "Washington Consensus."

America's governing elites seem blinded by faith. They are true believers who are, not coincidentally, also under the influence of the nation's most powerful business and financial interests. You can see why they might believe in this ideology. Young and old alike, they have been running the world for two generations—or at least they thought they were. Whatever setbacks it faces, the United States somehow has always seemed to come out okay. Despite the deepening US predicament, very few politicians are willing to suggest departing from the orthodoxy for fear they will be scorned as reactionary protectionists. Major media outlets play the role of enforcers, punishing dissenters who stray from the faith and express unsanctioned ideas. The political debates are exceedingly simpleminded and revolve around the orthodoxy's favorite bromide— "more trade good, no trade bad"—as if that were our only choice.

Globalization has claimed the high moral ground in American politics for another, more substantial reason: It represents progress. The rise of global trade offers the historic promise of reshaping the relations between rich and poor nations in positive ways. The process that advocates envision enables impoverished nations, aided by trade and foreign capital, to lift themselves up by gaining at least a foothold on the economic ladder. There is much truth in that assumption, and as a result, critics of globalization are often accused of being narrow-minded and indifferent to world poverty.

But the dogma does not tell the whole truth. We are in the midst of an industrial revolution and, like previous technological upheavals in history, it is both progressive and brutally reactionary. Its retrograde force enriches some by injuring and destroying many others, exploiting the powerless low-wage workers at one end of the global system as it robs industrial workers at the other end of their livelihoods and hard-earned place in society. Every industrial revolution of the past has tolerated the same moral contradiction—creativity and shocking injustice, side by side. In the industrial revolution of the late eighteenth and early nineteenth centuries, children worked in coal mines and "dark Satanic mills," as poet William Blake characterized their workplaces. Now, new billionaires live in princely splendor while great masses of their fellow citizens are cast aside and ruined.

Every previous technological revolution has been followed by political storms created by protest movements and new ideologies that arose to confront injustice and restore injured societies or to overthrow capitalism. Today, in the United States and around the world, we are seeing the early stages of similar reform movements—popular rebellions against the human and environmental destruction that flow unchecked from free-market globalization. In this sense, capitalists and corporations are the reactionaries resisting the future. The US government, for the most part, is their ally.

There is something else the proponents of the established dogma did not explain to Americans: Their own country would become a loser. The national economy would experience severe erosion in exchange for globalization's advances, and so would the finances of many ordinary Americans. For many years, the authorities have vehemently denied this possibility and promised the opposite. But people figured it out for themselves.

★   ★   ★   ★   ★

Americans have developed what I call an "extreme consensus" on the subject of globalization. According to pollster Daniel Yankelovich, the public reached a tipping point several years ago, when 87 percent expressed concern about the outsourcing of US jobs. Polling firm Lake Research Partners found there to be a similar consensus about globalization's impact on wages. In 2006, some 81 percent of Americans agreed with the statement: "No matter what you hear about the economy, working families are falling behind." Half of the population (51 percent) believes the next generation—today's children—will be worse off in economic terms than they are.

When people talk about this in everyday conversation, they say things like "I don't see how the country can go on like this" and "We are going to be okay, but I worry about what it's going to be like for the kids." People don't claim to know all the economic facts and theories, but they can see what's happening around them. The lost jobs, the closed factories, the middle-aged men working behind the counter at Starbucks. What keeps people up at night is wondering how to pay the bills and worrying about what will come next. Most Americans are not opposed to the idea of global trade, and they accept the inevitability of globalization. What they are against is the unaddressed consequences globalization will have for their own country.

The governing powers, with few exceptions, do not share the public's sense of urgency. In 2005, the Pew Research Center compared the public's concerns with the opinions expressed by "American influentials" in various sectors—government, politics, foreign affairs, news media, and others. The public believed overwhelmingly (84 percent) that "protecting the jobs of American workers" should be the government's "top priority" and considered that to be as important as fighting terrorism. The influentials did not think so. Of those in the news media, only 29 percent agreed. Among academics and scholars at think tanks, only 16 percent agreed. The only group that more or less agreed with the people was religious leaders (55 percent). Opinion leaders overwhelmingly regard new trade agreements as good for the country. Less than half of the public agrees.[2]

Though the church of free trade retains its hold on its adherents in the upper reaches of the power structure, it has lost most of its parishioners. Opinion leaders insist that the people are simply mistaken. A continuing stream of editorials, opinion columns, and even news stories appears in leading publications to explain things and clear up the people's confusion about globalization. If you happen to read any of these articles, note how few mention the trade deficits or numerous other facts that contradict the sermons' messages. More elected politicians are becoming globalization skeptics—dissenters now make up vigorous minority blocs in both parties, especially among House Democrats—but political leaders are sticking with the true faith.

As is probably obvious, I am a heretic myself. Observing the progress and politics of globalization over more than three decades convinced me long ago that the people essentially have got it right. They do not necessarily know how globalization works or what to do about it. They may not know where to direct their anger. But the public's visceral conclusion that something is deeply wrong with the establishment's story is abundantly confirmed by disturbing facts that are seldom reported in the local newspaper. The trade deficits are one symptom of our troubles, not the cause. To see what drives these deficits, you have to look closer. I will cite a few examples.

China now runs a substantial trade surplus in advanced technology products every year with the United States. These are not shirts, shoes, and consumer electronics, but manufacturing devices of the highest complexity and importance associated with famous American brands like Microsoft, Intel, and Motorola. China's advanced technology surplus has tripled since 2003, reaching $65 billion in 2007. The reversal in roles is impressive: The inventive nation that spawned our high-tech era is buying more high-tech stuff from ancient China than it sells to it. The stereotype of China as a backward nation no longer holds true. Microsoft and Google—two of our largest US high-tech firms—have established important new research centers in China, staffed by Chinese engineers, and they will participate directly in China's rise to industrial sophistication.

Mexico is now exporting more autos to the United States than the United States exports to the rest of the world—68 percent more, according to trade consultant Charles W. McMillion of MBG Information Services.[3] After NAFTA, the North American Free Trade Agreement, went into effect in 1994, US auto companies relocated major assembly plants and parts production to Mexico to take advantage of cheaper labor. That was the basic idea behind NAFTA—creating a convenient offshore platform for US companies. Make it in Mexico, export it to the United States. The Peter G. Peterson Institute for International Economics, the think tank of US multinational corporations, predicted that NAFTA would bring the United States great gains in jobs and trade surpluses, but NAFTA, like other trade agreements, has produced the opposite results. The modest trade surpluses the United States used to enjoy with Mexico have turned into much larger trade deficits—more than $460 billion in the approximately fifteen years since NAFTA was adopted.

Nor did cheaper Mexican labor do anything to solve the deeper problems of the US auto industry. The nation's worldwide trade deficit in autos, trucks, and auto parts has tripled to $150 billion over the last fifteen years. The trade deficit in manufactured goods was $130 billion a decade ago. Now it's more than $500 billion. As it happens, the multinational corporations that sent US workers' jobs to Mexico have already moved many of Mexico's NAFTA jobs to China in search of still cheaper workers. Organized labor calls this global migration of jobs the "race to the bottom."

The biggest names in US banking and finance, led by Citigroup and Goldman Sachs, are forming partnerships with Chinese financial firms to establish beachheads for participating in China's booming capital markets. The next Wall Street, it is widely believed, will be located in Shanghai, and American bankers will be there. As China becomes a major player in the takeover of US companies, it will have expert advisors who hail from New York. The Chinese government's investment firm purchased 10 percent of the Blackstone Group, one of Wall Street's premier private-equity firms, in 2007. Economist Peter Morici of the University of Maryland observed that if China chose to redeploy its passive investments in Treasury bonds, it could own 5 percent of the US stock market.[4]

The US machine tool industry—once a premier sector in the country's manufacturing—has fallen from first to ninth in the world. American machine tool companies (many of them located in my hometown of Cincinnati, Ohio) were celebrated for their highly skilled workforce and efficient production systems. Now 70 percent of their American market has been captured by foreign manufacturers. When the good jobs migrate, something more precious than wages is also lost. It is the knowledge and experience people need to make things using the newest manufacturing technologies. Once these capabilities are lost, the workers and technicians as well as the managers no longer have the know-how needed for innovation and making continuous improvements. Though its impact and extent are impossible to measure, this loss of knowledge upsets people involved in American manufacturing far more than other aspects of globalization.

In general, American goods are in retreat. Imported aircraft engines, plastics-making machinery, and environmental controls products now claim more than 60 percent of the US market share. The list of American-made industrial products that have lost at least half of their domestic market to foreign competitors is long, with computers, broadcast and wireless communications hardware, navigation equipment, pharmaceutical preparations, telecommunications equipment, and heavy-duty trucks being just a few among them.

A study by the United States Business and Industrial Council, a lobbying organization of 1,500 small- and medium-sized companies, most in manufacturing, reported in 2006 that tires, switchboard apparatus, x-ray equipment, electricity measuring instruments, turbines, construction equipment, laboratory instruments, and others will be the next to go. These are not labor-intensive sectors with low-wage workers, the group pointed out. The "hollowing out" of American manufacturing, it said, "is [also] proceeding in capital- and technology-intensive industries."[5]

The principal agents in this great shift in production are US companies, not foreign firms. Even quite small firms are now offshoring jobs and production with the assistance of a consulting industry that finds small manufacturers abroad to take over product lines. But America's multinationals, the companies that were expected to lead US export growth, are still the major players. The overwhelming majority of their foreign sales actually flow from their foreign factories, not from their remaining factories in the United States.

In 2004, American multinationals exported $400 billion in goods from their US plants, but they sold $2.6 trillion produced in their overseas facilities. This geographical distribution illustrates why US exports will never catch up with US imports unless something fundamental is changed about the way US multinationals are allowed to operate. This is not hypothesizing about what might happen in the future. The deterioration is happening now.[6]

Whatever the dogma claims, using common sense helps clarify the meaning of these facts. With Americans buying more and more things made in other countries and producing less and less at home, the economic losses—jobs, wages, output, and wealth—are flowing one way. To be sure, some benefits, such as lower prices for goods, flow in our direction but, as I will explain, their relevance is destined to fade. In any case, being able to buy cheaper goods will not pay off the credit card when you're going broke.

The University of Maryland's Morici explained the losses with clarity. "Thanks to the record trade deficits accumulated over the last 10 years, the U.S.

economy is about $1.5 trillion smaller," he estimated. "This comes to about $10,000 per worker." In fact, trade deficits act like a dead-weight tax on the US economy. Because the goods are produced overseas, the value of excess imports does not add to the US GDP, but instead is subtracted, dollar for dollar. "Were the trade deficit cut in half, GDP would increase by nearly $250 billion, or about $1,500 for every working American," Morici explained. "Workers' wages would not be lagging inflation, and ordinary working Americans would more easily find jobs paying higher wages and offering decent benefits."[7]

Twenty years ago, US household debt was 70 percent of disposable income. Now it is 135 percent. Twenty years ago, families owned 70 percent of the equity in their homes—their nest egg for retirement. Now, their equity has fallen below 50 percent and they are borrowing from their savings to keep up with the bills. Earning less, borrowing more—that is what is keeping people up at night.

But the essential message behind these disturbing facts is not about the human losses. These facts tell us that the United States faces a more fundamental disorder that applies not just to the "losers," but to the overall economy. Working harder or going back to school or doing any of the other palliative measures the establishment recommends will not solve our economic problem. America's economic problem is rooted in how the United States engages with the globalizing economy and how our government has misunderstood and misstated what is in the national interest. The American predicament cannot be remedied by assailing the Chinese or anyone else.

Our problem was made in America, not in foreign nations. It will not be resolved unless and until the nation lets go of false pride, faces reality, and decides to change itself.

★　★　★　★　★

Perhaps I see the economic landscape differently because I have been around it for so long. As a reporter, I have been covering globalization's controversies and wrenching changes and trying to understand its dynamics for a generation or more. Staying with a story for a long, long time has advantages—you begin to see trends the economists will not acknowledge and you remember their predictions after they do not come true. In moments of crisis, you recognize official explanations for what they are—recycled platitudes of the last crisis. This experience has given me an abiding skepticism about the theory and theorists of free trade.

On the other hand, as a reporter, I have heard a very different story from practical-minded "realists" who are engaged directly in globalizing commerce and investment. These are businesspeople, mostly—the "in country" managers at overseas plants, for example, and the global strategists and economists for the largest multinational corporations—as well as sophisticated international financiers and investors. I have encountered them on three continents and in more than a dozen countries. I have also learned from talking to labor leaders and assembly-line workers (on safe ground, away from the factory) in rich and poor countries. The story they tell about globalization is a harrowing drama, one fraught with the uncertainty, real-world risks, and brutal realities that economists tend to leave out.

The multinational corporations' managers, both foreign and American, whom I've interviewed have not talked much about the "theory" except to say it has little to do with the messy combat they engage in. These are unsentimental business guys (and a very few women) who take the world as they find it. They describe the fierce competition among rival corporations and countries. They complain that other nations pursue strategies very different from those of the United States and, for better or worse, they do not expect this to change. They report seeing huge pressures and instabilities developing within the global economy, but have no grand solutions to offer. Their job is to make sure their companies do not wind up among the losers.

The book I wrote in 1997, *One World, Ready or Not: The Manic Logic of Global Capitalism*, drew mainly upon the real-world grasp these managers have of how the global system works. Their perspective, I would say, reflects the cheerful fatalism of realists as opposed to the more naive attitude of the theorists. Some of these businessmen are deeply concerned by what they see, others are indifferent. None assume it is inevitable that the United States will win this contest. Granted, they haven't gotten everything right over the years, but they certainly have been a lot closer to the realities of the unfolding industrial revolution than the economics textbooks.

My book made strong assertions and was not well received by academic economists. One Harvard professor explained, "From an economist's standpoint, Greider doesn't make any sense." Ouch. But he was right, of course:

My account did not make sense in terms of orthodox economics. On the other hand, I got the story right about the United States' growing economic vulnerability and the hole it was digging for itself. The storm I saw coming is upon us now.

★ ★ ★ ★ ★

Back in the 1980s, Ralph E. Gomory was senior vice president for science and technology at IBM and closely involved in negotiating with other nations as IBM began globalizing its production. Gomory watched in awe as Japan and other Asian economies began to capture advanced product lines from America's leading companies. He saw that Japanese capabilities in high-tech assembly were as good or better than IBM's. He marveled at the tiny city–state of Singapore that, with the assistance of US multinationals, swiftly became a world-class producer of semiconductors and disk drives. Although IBM had invented the disk drive, it dropped out of the business because it couldn't compete profitably with Asian companies.

"It was an unforgettable transformation," Gomory told me. "And it was pretty frightening."[8]

It also wasn't supposed to happen, according to orthodox trade theory. IBM and the other US giants held commanding advantages in technological expertise and scale of production, yet they were ceding market share to industrial beginners. Something had to be haywire in the two-hundred-year-old theory of free trade, because America was losing despite its overwhelming "comparative advantage."

The contradictions haunted Ralph Gomory and, in retirement, he pursued a scholarly investigation of why this was happening. An establishment insider, he has become a rare and important voice of dissent who explains why the establishment's conventional assumptions are both fallacious and destructive to the nation. When I wrote about him in *The Nation*, I playfully suggested that the "church of global free trade" may at last have met its Martin Luther. Gomory seeks not to overthrow the church, but to correct its fallacies. That will require thorough reform of the way the United States interacts with the global system— much like what was required of the Catholic Church after Luther launched his protestant reformation. One reason Gomory's critique is powerfully persuasive is that his thinking fuses the realism of the industry insider who has practical experience with the theory of the economist's abstract logic.

Gomory recognized that the "unforgettable transformation" he witnessed in Asia did not result from free-market forces, it was driven by deals—the business deals between US multinational corporations and developing countries that gave both sides what they wanted.

"The offer that many Asian countries will give to American companies," Gomory explained, "is essentially this: 'Come over here and enhance our GDP. If you are here, our people will be building disk drives, for example, instead of something less productive. In return, we'll help you with the investment, with taxes, maybe even with wages. We'll make sure you make a profit.' This works for both sides: the American company gets profits, the host country gets GDP. However, there is another effect beyond the benefits for those two parties—high-value-added jobs leave the U.S."

Singapore, for example, got economic growth and industrial development—new jobs and wealth, and rapidly advancing skills as a producer. The US multinationals got cheap labor, tax breaks, capital subsidies, and—above all—profits. Everybody was happy, everyone won. Except for the American economy.

The global deployment of capital and technology, Gomory concluded, is the core element in how some very poor countries are able to ratchet up their technological prowess, take over advanced industrial sectors, and rapidly expand their share of global trade—all with the help of US companies and investors roaming the globe in search of better returns.

China and India now are doing roughly the same as their predecessors, but more systematically and on a far larger scale. Over many years, the same basic transaction has played out thousands of times across companies, nations, and product lines. It is responsible for both China's extraordinary transformation *and* the deep hole of US trade deficits.

Ralph Gomory's systematic critique of the status quo involves three explosive assertions. First, US multinationals are fundamentally pursuing what he and coauthor William J. Baumol in *Global Trade and Conflicting National Interests* called the "divergence of interests" from those of their home country. By doing what comes naturally—maximizing profits—the companies can harm the broader US national interest, that is, its need to maintain the value-added production and high-wage jobs necessary for general prosperity. Self-interested success for the corporation "can constitute an actual loss of national income for the company's home country," Gomory and Baumol wrote.

Second, the US policy of putting corporate profit making ahead of the country's competing goals and interests is what makes the United States so different from other nations. US multinationals are free to make investment decisions that shift wealth-generating production, capital, and technology to other countries.

Most other nations, whether they are poor and developing or mature and advanced, pursue strategies designed to balance private profits with their other priorities. They may even suppress business profits in order to achieve longer-term goals such as an expanded industrial base or advanced technological prowess. How a society feels about profit is at the heart of the matter.

The United States is nearly the only major economy that focuses on encouraging short-term gain and private wealth. "The question is where do you put your technology and knowledge and investment?" Gomory explained. "These other countries understand that. . . . What countries want and what companies want are different."

Third, contrary to orthodox theory, the free-trade system does not necessarily lead to mutual gain among trading partners. The changing circumstances of competition between trading nations, Gomory told me, can produce losers as well as winners. The success of one nation may actively injure a trading partner. This is commonsensical to workers, but not to economists.

Even very rich nations may gradually lose their advantage as their poorer trading partners develop greater skills and assume the production of more advanced goods. In that event, Gomory and Baumol wrote, "the newly developing partner *becomes harmful* to the more industrialized country."

This is happening now in US–China trade and perhaps in US–India trade too, just it did twenty years ago in US trade with Japan, Gomory told me. The United States, he fears, is already "starting to go downhill," joining other loser nations on the wrong side of the trade equation. The injuries resulting from trade, in other words, are no longer localized to the people who have lost their jobs, but instead involve the overall national economy.

These assertions are considered pure heresy by the true believers. But

Gomory's critique fits remarkably well with what workers, labor leaders, and other uncredentialed critics (myself included) have been arguing for some years. A crucial distinction is that Gomory grounds his analysis in the formal logic of orthodox economics, which makes it much harder for authorities to dismiss him as a protectionist. In fact, having served as president of General Motors' philanthropic Alfred P. Sloan Foundation and as director of corporate boards, he is still a company guy, and largely apolitical. Gomory is making the rounds in Washington in an attempt to reeducate politicians about the realities of globalization.

"I want to stress it's a system problem," Gomory told me. "The directors are doing the job they're sworn to do. It's the system that says the companies have to have a sole focus on maximizing profit." I agree with his point, but I think he is being much too charitable toward corporate CEOs, many of whom seem absorbed in maximizing their own wealth rather than the company's or the shareholders'.

Baumol, Gomory's coauthor on *Global Trade and Conflicting National Interests,* is a well-regarded economist and former president of the American Economic Association. The two wrote a slender academic book that makes their case using clear prose suitable for the average reader, plus dense equations directed at professional economists.

Baumol has chided his fellow economists for overselling the free-trade doctrine, or perhaps misunderstanding it. "Many of our 'dismal science' colleagues speak unguardedly as though they believe free trade cannot fail, no matter what," he said at a Washington policy conference. "Our objective," Baumol said, "is to show how outsourcing can indeed reduce the share of benefits of trade, not only for those who lose their jobs and suffer a direct reduction in wages, but [also how it] can wind up making the average American worse off than he or she would have been."

Gomory is a lucid teacher. When I asked him to explain the changing US fortunes in terms people can understand, his response was a model of clarity and elementary economics. "What made America much wealthier than the Asian nations in the first place? We invested alongside our workers," he said. "Our workers dug ditches with backhoes. The workers in underdeveloped countries dug ditches with shovels. We had great big plants with a few people in them, which is the same thing. We knew how, through technology and investment, to make our workers highly productive. It wasn't that they went to better schools, then or now, and I don't know how much schooling it takes to run a backhoe.

"The situation today is that the companies have discovered that [by] using modern technology they can do all that overseas and pay less for labor and then import product and services back into the United States. So what we're doing now is competing shovel to shovel. The people in many countries are being equipped with as good a shovel or backhoe as our people have. Very often we are helping them make the transition.

"We're making it person-to-person competition, which it never was before and which we cannot win. Because their people will be paid a third, a quarter of what our people are paid. And it's unreasonable to think you can educate our people so well that they can produce four times as much in the United States."

The obvious implication is that Americans will be increasingly exposed to downward pressures on their wages and thus a falling standard of living. I asked Gomory if he agreed with that assessment. "Yes," he answered. "There are many ways to look at it, all of which reach the same conclusion."

But, I asked, could this produce greater equity in the world at large, where so many people are desperately poor? Could Americans be losing in order to make others less poor? Gomory agreed that reasonable people might choose to see it that way.

"But that isn't what people in this country are being told," he said. "No one has said to us: 'You're probably a little too rich and these other folks are a little too poor. Why don't we even it out?' Instead, what we usually hear is: 'It's going to be good for everyone. In the long run we're going to get richer with globalization.'"

Meanwhile, Americans are in for another ugly surprise. The cheap goods from Asia and elsewhere are gradually going to disappear. That is the most shocking assertion in the Gomory–Baumol analysis, and it will doubtless be rejected by the usual authorities. After all, the Wal-Mart stores that rely on lower-priced imports provide important comfort to citizens whose incomes are falling. Yet the United States will find itself paying more for all those imported goods from China and other fast-developing economies. Products whose manufacture were initially moved offshore to take advantage of low-wage labor will begin to cost more for both consumers and companies as these products claim a larger and larger share of US national income.

This striking reversal, which is already occurring in minor ways, is a response to the changing terms of trade between the United States and its poorer trading partners. As China and others gain higher levels of value-added production and have workforces possessing increased skills and sophistication, their exports will naturally cost more. China will gain a larger and larger share of global trade while US exports become a smaller share of the value of total trade—that, inevitably, will change the terms of trade between nations.

To put it more simply, the cost of one hour of US work used to buy many hours of Chinese or other low-wage countries' work. But as the foreign workers become more valuable—that is, more productive—the United States can no longer buy as many hours of labor in China, India, or elsewhere. Chinese productivity and wages are rising. Even if China suppresses domestic wages in order to sell more of its goods, the comparative prices will reflect the fundamental shift in productive strength. American incomes will buy less of the stuff Americans once got for cheap.

"That's why you start going downhill," Gomory explained. "Because you pay more for what you were previously getting."

Gomory and Baumol suggested that another fateful turn lies ahead for the global economy—one that could be very positive if poorer nations like China use their greater economic strength to distribute the gains broadly among their populations. That is how nations develop economies of middle-class consumers—enabling once-poor workers to buy the stuff they make. This potential opening could reverse the "race to the bottom" and instead foster a more balanced global system, one with nations that are less dependent on exporting goods to the US market.

On the other hand, the logic of business models tells companies they can always find cheaper labor somewhere else. The world has no shortage of desperate poor people looking for jobs, no matter what wages and working conditions they are offered. The pressures to keep moving production farther down the food chain in search of exploitable workers will not go away. That is how producers maintain their market share in the United States. But the positive outcome that can occur with globalization—global economic growth that is both more equitable and more balanced—is unlikely to occur so long as the United States—its government and companies—stick to the principles of trade that are failing the country.

★ ★ ★ ★ ★

If Americans swallowed their pride and looked around at other advanced economies, they would discover new ways to think about globalization and its impact.
Trouble is, Americans have been deeply misinformed by the major news media
outlets, which, when they examine other nations at all, generally adopt a conde-
scending tone of impatience. Why don't these countries become more like us,
they seem to ask. Can't Europeans or Japanese see that the American system is
obviously superior? This presumption is a stock element in news stories, which
regularly describe how political leaders in other nations—say, Germany or
France—are once again trying to "reform" their economies over the stubborn
resistance of the backward citizens. We are new and dynamic, the news stories
explain. They are old and tired.

This coverage has been repeating the stereotype for at least a generation,
and while it is flattering for Americans, it is ideologically biased and largely
untrue. The governments of Germany, Japan, and the others have not escaped
globalization's pressures and injuries, nor do they always get things to work out.
They have had to yield on important matters. But they are not converting to the
American system, despite predictions to the contrary by US foreign correspon-
dents. Japan's economy is presently a mess, yet it still doesn't abandon its basic
arrangement. Germany and the other European Union countries are arguably
among the most dynamic of the world's advanced economies, yet none has sur-
rendered its system, which permits government to impose national priorities on
business, to the American way. If Americans looked more closely, they would see
that EU policies are far ahead of the United States' on many emerging concerns,
from global warming to animal rights. Europe modifies but does not give up its
elaborate welfare state, which provides to citizens the social protections that
Americans are told are wasteful and injurious to the economy.

If you ask what makes these countries different, the essential answer is that
they value "society" more seriously. Though governing systems and techniques
vary from country to country, these older societies, by virtue of their longer histories, possess a deeper understanding of what can go wrong if the economic
system is allowed to overpower the concerns of the people. Each country is committed to defending society against threatening forces, including the potentially
destabilizing effects of economic life. The goal is not just making profits and getting richer. The goal is preserving what matters most.

Putting society first is frequently derided as nationalist or reactionary by critics in America, but the philosophy goes deeper than politics. The idea is anchored in a people's identity, in how a nation sees itself. But what exactly does "society" mean? The French discuss the question elegantly and endlessly. So do other nations, with perhaps less style and certitude.

Society is all that cannot be separated from the life of a country—the way people choose to live together, the things and values they feel they "own" as Germans or Japanese or French. Americans have their own definitions of what matters most, but by comparison, their idea of society is weakly represented in politics and economics. It is often ignored.

In Europe and Asia, defending society means, among other things, being reluctant to throw people over the side. Germans and Japanese learned this the hard way from the fascism of the twentieth century and do not wish to forget the lesson. Pushing people to extremes, marginalizing or destroying large groups, upending the lives and routines of ordinary citizens—destabilizing society in ways such as these leads to catastrophe, historic ruination. If a country has been through this once, it will not want to let it happen again.

Americans have been spared the fires that older societies have experienced, so we are perhaps less conscious of what's at stake. The business of "throwing people over the side" has become routine in American economic life, and it is generally accepted at least by the governing elites. No one can measure how deeply the insecurities and upheavals experienced by ordinary families have weakened American society, or predict what might follow from falling living standards.

Other nations pay more attention to the collateral consequences of policy. I recall my interviews fifteen years ago with Oscar Marx, a Ford Motor Company executive who was managing the dispersal of US auto-parts production to countries in eastern Europe and Asia, including China. "I do agree we have a fundamental problem," Marx told me. "We have been too incautious of the long-run impact of taking operations elsewhere. We are more prepared to move an operation than a Japanese businessman, who would be inclined to hold onto it."

The multinational managers and strategists I interviewed then talked a lot about the different strategies undertaken in other advanced economies. Sometimes they spoke with resentment, but often it was with resignation and respect. "We in the US are much more driven by rate of return," Marx explained. "The Chinese don't even know what that concept is." China was pursuing goals other than profit. Marx recognized China's great potential as an exporting nation, and he was assisting the process. But he was certain "the US will not permit another Asian country to do to it what Japan did to it. . . . Our people won't stand for it. Our policy makers won't let it happen." This was in 1994. As it turned out, he was overly optimistic.

★   ★   ★   ★   ★

Other nations defend their societies using many different approaches, some direct, some discreetly veiled. This has often amounted to forms of "soft" protectionism—implicit barriers or understandings. Although nothing's written in law, informal terms that limit how much will be allowed are communicated to exporting nations. Domestic stability is defended by labor laws that make it difficult and expensive for companies to shed workers. Strong labor unions and elected worker representatives are given direct access to corporate discussions of strategy. Labor federations participate in national bargaining on wages that sets industry-wide goals.

Japan's somewhat opaque governing system directs national savings to serve as capital for developing exporting industries, while it also redistributes the profits from those "winners" to subsidize unprofitable domestic sectors that are major employers.

In Europe, four nations came together in 1970 to create and finance Airbus. A generation later, Airbus is a private firm that is successfully competing head-to-head with US aerospace manufacturer Boeing. Boeing and McDonnell Douglas, another US competitor, did not file a formal complaint against subsidies given to Airbus because they were told by their customers—the European airlines—not to interfere. McDonnell Douglas subsequently went under, merging with Boeing in 1997.

US elites charge that these irregular methods not only violate the rules of the trading system, but also are stupid and wasteful. Government is not capable of picking winners and losers, they charge. Doesn't everyone know that? Evidently not. The European Union continues to launch public–private research and development consortiums with understandings of mutual obligations. In the United States, the government mostly hands private firms lots of money—in tax breaks and subsidies—and hopes they will do something useful with it. These are just a few examples of the many contrasts between the United States and countries that place a greater value on society.

The larger point is that, unlike the United States, nearly all of the other major industrialized nations develop and pursue national strategies that explicitly articulate the nation's collective economic goals and make sure that multinational corporations and investors honor them. This doesn't relieve these countries of enormous economic problems and fiercely contentious political disputes. In fact, it focuses the political debate on the larger and more meaningful questions.

National goals are advanced through law and government financial strategy, backed up by political pressures and popular persuasion. Ultimately, the strategy is enforced by broad public consent—the underlying cultural understandings that are often stronger than law. Citizens know in general terms what the social bargain promises them. When they think it is being violated, they take to the streets, marching in massive protests. The existing political system often folds. Many Americans might regard the theater of mass demonstration as somehow childish, but I suggest it is a more effective tool for democratic communication than is offered by the US media, with its top-down structure and bias.

The national strategies of the countries of Europe and Asia are essentially mechanisms for balancing inescapable economic conflicts—the tensions between short-term profit and long-term development, generalized prosperity and lopsided accumulation of personal wealth, market forces of efficiency and protecting the aspects of life that people need and cherish.

In France, the government subsidizes bread and every small village has its own baker who, seven days a week, turns out moderately priced, richly textured and flavored fresh loaves. The French evidently need this to exist. Good bread is part of their being. French people do not argue over whether this is inefficient, they argue over which village has the best bread.

In the US system, cultural graces deemed essential to life generally are not subsidized, but instead are sold at their true cost. They are thus rationed by price and available only to those who can afford them. Other nations regard this as backward. Some things in life, they say, must be available to everyone, regardless of their status or wealth.

In the late 1980s, Japan tried to explain its different economic system to American authorities. With prodding and financial support from Tokyo, the World Bank agreed to produce a study—*The East Asian Miracle*—that grudgingly conceded that Japan and the Asian tigers had broken all the rules of neoclassical economics, but had succeeded spectacularly. At the time, official Washington was trying to impose its "Washington Consensus" on developing nations in Latin America and Southeast Asia; it didn't want to hear about Asian heresies.

The "miracle" countries, the World Bank found, targeted infant industries and became major exporters by protecting and subsidizing them. Sources of foreign capital were invited to participate, but only on terms that fit the national plan. US partners were required to transfer technology and share production and jobs, as well as markets. Tokyo practiced what the World Bank called "financial repression." In addition to keeping its currency weak, interest rates on industrial loans were held down to foster development in what was in effect a discreet subsidy from savers to producers, from households to industrial sectors. Consumer credit was effectively rationed by high interest rates and stiff controls.

Orthodox economics holds that these measures should have collapsed the national savings rate, but the opposite occurred. As manufacturing exports grew, both private financial firms and the government built up enormous pools of investment capital, which were used as fuel to drive technological advancement still further. Asian consumers were essentially urged to buy products made in their own countries, though this was not exactly voluntary, given restrictions on their choices and compulsory savings programs.

The puzzle is how these governments persuaded people to accept such shared sacrifices. It was partly by force, which may have been easier for citizens to swallow because many of these nations were originally ruled by authoritarian regimes that sometimes brutally repressed individual rights. But it was also by social consent. As these nations rapidly built up their industrial capabilities, they demonstrated a substantive commitment to economic equity. The countries got a lot richer, and nobody got thrown over the side.

The urban dwellers enjoyed rising industrial incomes, but rural populations were not left behind. Land reform distributed basic assets among small landholders. Rice growers enjoyed higher prices because they were protected from importation of cheaper rice, notably from the United States. Various social welfare commitments—housing, full employment—created a basic floor for everyone's standard of living. In cultures like these, founded as they were on ethnic solidarity, extreme displays of wealth were socially taboo and discouraged.

Even the World Bank was impressed. "To establish their legitimacy and win the support of society at large, East Asian leaders established the principle of shared growth, promising that as the economy expanded, all groups would benefit," the organization's experts concluded.[9] The unorthodox economic strategy fostered unity, which persuaded people to forgo short-term rewards in the interest of promoting society's long-term progress. And it worked.

The point should be obvious, but I will make it anyway: US economic strategy in the age of globalization follows a nearly opposite path. Attention is paid to ensuring the success of the largest enterprises and enabling the extraordinary accumulation of wealth at the top, while ignoring the social losses down below. Not surprisingly, the American strategy does not lead to unity.

★　★　★　★　★

Germany illustrates a very different version of the same lesson in its recovery from World War II's devastation and national shame. The challenge was not simply to rebuild Germany's prewar industrial prowess, but also to create a new society inoculated against fascism. Stephen J. Silvia, PhD, professor of international economics at American University, put it succinctly: "The Nazis were seen as an excess of ideological extremism, and one of the ways to deal with that is to end this nasty class conflict and try to make a society where everyone can participate and everyone is given a share."[10]

The concept was elaborated in not only the political system, but also the industrial system. German politics involves an endless calendar of consultations and roundtable discussions that provide formal venues for declarations of purpose and bargaining. Virtually every sector gets to air its agenda and grievances. They may not be satisfied with the eventual decisions, but they are allowed to speak in serious, sometimes mind-numbing detail.

The contrast between the German model and US politics is instructive. America's democratic discourse goes for bright, provocative images—appealing story lines and slogans that are shallow substitutes for substantive discussions on the governing ideas. Germans talk—and talk and talk—with a thorough earnestness that can be exhausting. Many Americans would find it boring (as do many Germans). But political players understand that this is more than ritual. The inclusive process is necessary to create consent, or at least a general acceptance of governing authority.

Robert Dugger, an international investor with a major hedge fund, told me a decade ago that Germany's system probably would eventually be broken by global pressures. He has since decided he was mistaken. Germany has largely succeeded in preserving its basic welfare obligations and the most valuable core of jobs, those in value-added production and research and development.

"People look at the United States as the leader in national governance but that may no longer be accurate," Dugger said. "Countries like Germany have systems of governance that may be superior—more equitable, more decentralized with broader participation, and able to provide more open and informed discussions of the problems the country faces. German elites still have great power, but Germany involves labor in business and economic decisions more than the United States does."[11]

I don't want to romanticize the German system. German politicians are not lambs and the usual powerful interests (especially banking and finance) still act like lions. But one important benefit of maintaining this continuous national dialogue is that there are fewer surprises. One way or another, the German people are more likely to get fair warning about options their government intends to pursue. Because opposition sectors are all granted a formal voice, they are likely to identify the negative consequences of policy agendas, even when the governing party is trying to hide them.

The German economic system embeds the same principle in private enterprise—a system known as "stakeholder capitalism" because it formally recognizes all the important participants. A company does not have to listen just to shareholders, bankers, and capital investors. It must inform and regularly consult with workers, managers, labor unions, communities, and suppliers. The arrangement implicitly pushes companies toward more balanced corporate strategies. Profit is not their only goal. Return on capital must be weighed alongside competing objectives of employees or localities and the national economic strategy.

Labor union leaders sit on the supervisory boards of major corporations and are entitled to know in advance and to critique the company's strategic plans. Assembly-line workers and front-office professionals alike elect representatives to the works councils that continuously kibitz company managers. These and other, similar arrangements are required by law. US companies that operate factories in Germany have no choice but to accept democratic practices that at home they would denounce as socialist assaults on capitalism.

Conflicts between capital and labor are not eliminated by stakeholder capitalism. Labor federations still strike on occasion, sometimes in industry-wide protests over major issues. But the basic labor–management relationship in Germany is quite sophisticated and mature in comparison with the callous labor-dumping practices of the American system. And more to the point, German industry has followed a very different strategy in dealing with the global system. Multinational firms based in that country display far deeper loyalty to their home base than US firms do. And they succeed spectacularly, far more so than US multinationals, in boosting the nation's exports.

Twenty years ago, as globalization accelerated and financial capital was being internationalized, it was widely assumed that the so-called Rhineland capitalism could not survive. To compete on price and efficiency, it was thought, German companies would have to abandon their cooperative values, and the German state would have to whack away at its very generous welfare state. Many American media pundits and reporters still espouse this opinion of European economies. The old "social democracy," they assume, will give way to the force of the marketplace.

On the whole, it has not happened. Alexander Börsch of the European University Institute studied leading German corporations for *Global Pressure, National System.* He found that some had adopted limited practices of the US system—stock options for executives, listings on US stock exchanges—but they did not abandon their systems of corporate governance. Companies still complain about social welfare guarantees, but the political system has not enacted more than modest retrenchments.

"The prediction of convergence theory that stakeholder systems must converge toward shareholder systems in their entirety has not materialized," Börsch concluded. In fact, after the meltdown of the US stock markets in 2000, German companies backed away from offering stock options and began delisting their stocks on Wall Street exchanges. They also have resisted another familiar American feature—the market for capital control that makes a corporation's management vulnerable to takeover and ouster if the financial markets think its stock price is underperforming.

German firms prefer closely held ownership and executive management of very long tenure. Both are important elements for establishing the "patient capital" that can pursue long-term development instead of simply harvesting short-term profits. They are well familiar with the get-rich-quick scandals seen in US corporate governance. German investors have also been swindled in America's corporate frauds.

While German industry generally resists US-style capitalism, it has succeeded brilliantly on another front. German manufacturing more than doubled that nation's merchandise exports from 1994 to 2004. In the first half of the current decade, German exports grew by 65 percent, compared to only 5 percent export growth for the United States. In absolute terms, German export growth exceeded even China's. Those results may explain why public attitudes toward globalization are far less critical in Germany than in other industrialized nations.

Of course this does not prove that stakeholder capitalism is more efficient and effective in business terms than the American version. But Germany's outstanding performance dampens others' desire to mimic the US system. In his case studies, Börsch found that globalization does not erode the competitive advantages of stakeholder governance, if companies use the stakeholders' cooperation to adjust wisely to global competition. Celebrated firms like BMW and Porsche, he said, have demonstrated "that stakeholder governance can be associated with superior profits."

The adjustments German companies have made to globalization pressures have been quite different from what's been seen in the typical American story. Bosch, the German multinational electronics producer, initially cut domestic employment levels and clashed with its workforce in the early 1990s. But the corporation then embraced a cooperative strategy that has proved productive. It has globalized dramatically, doubling its foreign workforce over the last fifteen years, while its German employment numbers have remained more or less the same.

Yet the works councils representing Bosch's domestic employees endorsed this corporate strategy. "The main reason," Börsch explained in his book, "is that production was not withdrawn from Germany, but that additional work has been generated abroad." In consultations with works councils, Bosch management was able to explain the global challenge in depth and convince workers that the company's strategy was what was best for them and for the German economy.

The best jobs and value-added production stayed at home, while mostly less-skilled work was located offshore. Only 31 percent of Bosch sales are in Germany, but 80 percent of the research and development and 55 percent of the value-added production take place there. The company manages to balance its financial obligations with its support of its workers. American workers typically do not have this opportunity to participate. The company does not seek their consent, it simply notifies them when their labor is no longer needed.

★　★　★　★　★

China's story is so different from these others that it seems as strange as the far side of the moon. An ancient society is rising to greatness in modern circumstances, like a slumbering giant who has just now woken up. This drama is historically breathtaking and promising, yet it is also fraught with dangers. Chinese leaders are balanced atop a cauldron of popular unrest and they know it. We do not yet know if there will be an eruption from below. Communist Party leaders call their strategy "market socialism with Chinese characteristics."

The Chinese are doing what they promised they would do, including pegging their currency to the dollar to keep the price of exports low for the American market. Many US politicians complain about it, but they seem to have forgotten that US officials and economists applauded this arrangement when China announced it in 1994. Its effects were well understood even then. If China is breaking fair-trade rules, why didn't US officials object back in 2000 when Washington arranged for China to be admitted to the WTO? The political explanation is obvious: US business and financial interests were pushing hard for the deal. The Clinton administration pushed with them.

The biggest threat, if China doesn't alter its strategy, is that its enormous success might collapse not only the US economy, but also overwhelm the entire global trade system. Partly, this is simply a matter of scale. China has 1.3 billion people, compared to Japan's 127 million. If it follows the same development path Japan pursued, China has awesome potential for outproducing and underpricing the rest of the world.

The less obvious danger is that the Chinese people could be left without any underlying commitment to economic equity. No country in the world need be too self-righteous. Nearly every developing economy in industrial history— including the United States—has been built on the backs of exploited peasants, and sometimes slave labor. But China has no history or political precedent for pursuing equitable distribution of rewards among its citizens, much less for creating democratic governance. For more than one thousand years, China has been run by mandarins—a ruling class that exercises power brutally from the top down. The Communist Party Mandarins have not changed that.

China itself is threatened by civil dissolution. The spectacular industrialization is underway mainly in the booming coastal regions, where rising incomes and wealth have created a large, new middle-class—300 million people or more. But the rest of the population—the other billion—does not share in much of these gains, and China does not have a cultural tradition of ethnic solidarity, like Japan or South Korea did, to ensure that such reform will happen.

The Chinese economy has an endless supply of very poor people to draw cheap labor from as expanding production needs them. This is a fiendish advantage for a developing nation. It means China could continue to have it both ways for quite a long time—it could be a wealthy nation with high-end technological advancement and lots of rich people, as well as a very poor country that grossly exploits labor to reward the affluent.

The danger is that this tension between progress at the top and mass deprivation down below could blow the country apart. The nation is seething with thousands of localized rebellions that are put down forcibly, and the civic tensions do not abate. In Tokyo, a cynical Japanese economist assured me that Japan does not need to worry about a rising China because China will break up eventually into many bloody parts.

Some well-informed American experts are confident of a more optimistic turn of events. In consultations with Beijing, they are informed that China's leadership understands the imperative to create a more equitable society and intends to undertake a deep shift in strategy that will spread the new wealth more widely. This could relieve political conflict and create a broader consumer economy.

★ ★ ★ ★ ★

This discussion of alternative responses to globalization is not intended to judge which system is right or wrong, but to convey to American readers the vast range of possibilities that exist for nations that choose their own path. America is American; we are unlikely to copy the operating techniques of the social democracy of Europe, and we certainly won't adopt business relationships as seen in Japan or China. But other societies defend principles and follow effective strategies that official America ignores or dismisses as illegitimate. Americans ought to explore the possibilities on their own, even if the dominant political and media discourse implies there are none.

Up to now, I haven't discussed possible solutions for our predicament. The next chapter takes up that challenge and explains promising ideas and remedies. My main message is this: Despite what you may have heard from the authorities, Americans are not helpless.

CHAPTER SEVEN

SECOND THOUGHTS

Globalization is an awesome force of history, but the global trading system itself is more fragile than it appears. The trading system is essentially a political arrangement among national governments—the agreed-upon rules of the road—and it can be undone by unforeseen disturbances. Economic break-downs, willful ruptures by individual nations, popular rebellions of people resist-ing social turmoil and injustice—any one or combination of these might derail the system.

Roughly speaking, previous eras of industrial revolution have ended in one or more of these ways. Each time, global trade stalled out with it. An abrupt unwinding of economic relationships can impose massive suffering upon inno-cent bystanders and set nations against one another in self-defensive actions. No one should wish for such an unhappy ending.

For many reasons, the global system is at a fragile moment, and the hold that its political arrangements have on the world is weakening. Followers are no longer reflexively following. One reason is that Washington lost much of its com-manding luster as a leader once the cold war ended. The catastrophe in Iraq fur-ther undermined the US hold; so did America's fiscal crisis and weakening economic condition. What is not clear is whether the system will be reformed and rescued from its flaws or brought down by them.

The old order—the American political assumptions and economic princi-ples that have dominated the trading system for six decades—no longer prevails so easily. A small club of rich countries led by the United States used to get its way in devising new rules for international agreements, but its control has lessened. After six years of fruitless negotiations by the World Trade Organization, a new global trade agreement died on the drawing board. It was supposedly going to benefit the poor nations, but the gestures it included from the rich nations did not add up to much. Poorer countries, led by China, India, and Brazil, resisted and, for once, could not be muscled into line.

In Latin America, popular movements are in full rebellion against the financial orthodoxy imposed upon them—the so-called Washington Consensus that led many of their economies into ruinous dependence on foreign capital. One country after another has opted out, instead adopting either left-leaning populist agendas that offend international bankers or homegrown strategies for development.

China has reorganized East Asia with itself at the center. Around the world, this new powerhouse is making its own rich deals to secure oil from producing nations that are hostile to the United States. Meanwhile, China skillfully deflects US political pressure to ease up on exports and allow America to start digging itself out of its hole. In an earlier era, the United States might have acted forcefully—and unilaterally—to get its way. Under the current circumstances, Washington is afraid to press its case too aggressively.

In the United States, the hottest edge of political discontentment revolves around illegal immigration. The immigration issue is really about globalization, too. Angry citizens ask if the United States is still a sovereign nation. If it is, why does it not defend the national borders? In the global system, capital has wings and is free to land in any nation. Logically, labor is free to do the same. If companies can move jobs to Mexico for cheaper workers, why can't Mexican workers move to the United States for better jobs? This cosmopolitan view may be logical, but it is far too radical for politicians to sell to citizens.

The confusion spills over into George W. Bush's so-called Global War on Terrorism—the GWOT, in policy lingo. On the one hand, President Bush effectively demonized Muslims as a vague terrorist threat to the country. But in the name of globalization, he authorized a subsidiary of a United Arab Emirates government-controlled company to take over the management of five of America's largest ports. Muslims are going to operate our ports? Aren't they trying to kill us? You can see why many Americans got confused.

★　★　★　★　★

The most intriguing ferment about globalization, oddly enough, may be occurring within the American establishment itself. In some quarters of elite opinion, influential figures recognize that the system is in trouble. They can read the polls. With the Republican presidency in collapse and Democrats recapturing Congress in 2006, a fervent minority of the party campaigned against the free-trade orthodoxy. They demand "fair trade" instead.

In this political context, important authority figures began to disclose having second thoughts about globalization. Some of them acknowledged what for many, many years they had denied. Global trade, they announced, is not a win-win proposition after all. In fact, the losers include the American middle class. If nothing changes, they warned, the free-market trading system could be overwhelmed by a popular backlash. This represented a startling concession: Working people had been protesting for years about the inequitable results of globalization and were dismissed as wrong, but now their complaints were being deemed acceptable for discussion.

I thought it was a big deal when I first heard this message being expressed by prominent veterans of Bill Clinton's administration who had played an important role in shaping the global system. It looked to me like strategic repositioning. During my many years in Washington, I came to admire the establishment's adeptness at recognizing new political currents that threaten its position and moving smartly to defuse or co-opt the opposition. When elites change their minds about something fundamental, like whether globalization has a downside, then the political debate is sure to change, too.

In this instance, the door was opened by a most influential figure—Robert Rubin, Clinton's treasury secretary and the economic policy advisor who crafted the conservative fiscal policy and free-trade agenda that became known as Rubinomics (or Clintonomics, if you prefer). Rubin is especially influential within the Democratic Party, but also on Wall Street. After his tenure in Washington, he became cochair of the executive committee at Citigroup. Before joining the Clinton team, Rubin led Goldman Sachs, the important investment house that Republican Henry Paulson also ran before he became George W. Bush's treasury secretary.

In the spring of 2006, Rubin launched the Hamilton Project, housed at center-right think tank the Brookings Institution and cosponsored by a dozen investment bankers. Composed of business, academic, and public policy leaders, its members were committed to proposing new ideas for reforming government and the economy. Most of the Hamilton Project's ideas were not very new and were quickly labeled "born-again Rubinomics." But the central theme was quite different. Income inequality generated by globalization, the group announced, was "a deeply troubling fact of American life."

The Hamilton Project's strategy paper, cowritten by Rubin, explained, "Between 1973 and 2003, real GDP per capita in the United States increased 73 percent, while real median hourly compensation rose only 13 percent. Prosperity has neither trickled down nor rippled outward." In blunt terms, family incomes have stagnated or lost ground, while capital and corporate returns have soared. This disparity threatens the future of the trading system, Rubin warned, maybe even the stability of "capitalist, democratic society."[1]

This was not news. Critics of the global system (myself included) had been arguing the same case for many years, and typically were batted down by conventional economists and media cheerleaders who insisted it wasn't true. But Robert Rubin is a high-church figure. His saying these things was like an important prelate announcing doctrinal change in church theology.

The obvious intention of Rubin's Hamilton Project was to devise ways to take the harsh edge off globalization before popular resentments build into a major political backlash. In the United States, the system has generated a relatively small pool of fabulously wealthy winners alongside a broad tide of losing American families. This maldistribution of incomes has been growing for many years, both within the United States and in many developing countries. Until now, official America generally dismissed the evidence and blamed income inequality on other causes. New technology destroyed jobs and lowered incomes, not trade.

But Rubin's declaration about inequality made it okay for other influentials to talk about the once-taboo subject. The prestige media outlets began to examine questions they had largely ignored. Politicians were, likewise, tacitly authorized to talk about measures to reduce inequality or at least to provide modest aid to some of the losers.[2]

Rubin deserves credit for widening the terms of "respectable discussion," but his shift also demonstrates that our democratic dialogue is restricted to pronouncements made by a few powerful names. I asked myself, Where have these guys been? Why did Rubin and colleagues say nothing about the growing inequality and trade when they were in government and had the power to do something about it? Belated truth telling is better than never, but it fails my basic test for public officials—giving people "fair warning."

At about the same time, another high-ranking economic official from the Clinton administration came forward with a more alarming message. Princeton economist Alan Blinder, who served on Clinton's Council of Economic Advisers and later as vice chair of the Federal Reserve's Board of Governors, declared that American workers are going to face even worse consequences in the future.

"Tens of millions" more jobs, Blinder revealed, are vulnerable to offshoring. These are not only factory jobs, but also those in high-end occupations that are filled by well-educated people and members of the affluent middle class. In an essay in *Foreign Affairs,* Blinder estimated that as many as 30 million to 40 million jobs in professional and technological occupations can in theory be shifted abroad, thanks to long-distance digital communications. Accountants, lawyers, technical experts, software designers, and those in many other high-tech jobs are readily replaceable by capable people in other societies who earn much less for doing essentially the same work. He warned fellow experts: "If we economists stubbornly insist on chanting 'Free trade is good for you' to people who know that it is not, we will quickly become irrelevant to the public debate."[3] Blinder was hailed for telling the truth.

For many years, globalization's supporters (Blinder among them) assumed that the demise of US manufacturing jobs was inevitable, much as the collapse of agricultural employment in the late nineteenth century was when modern machinery and capital-intensive farming replaced labor. The loss of manufacturing jobs can be tolerated, the experts claimed, because factory jobs will be replaced by other, more highly skilled work that earns higher compensation. Instead of making things, the United States would sell services to the rest of the world—banking, insurance, design, lawyering, engineering, and other high-end professional functions.

Some cheerleaders claimed the modest US trade surplus in services would expand and someday eclipse the much larger trade deficit in goods. That comforting notion faded long ago; the trade surplus in services has been shrinking for many years. Blinder's insight essentially confirmed that counting on service jobs to rectify US trade problems was a hopeless proposition. Since he had been in government a few years before, I asked him why he had waited so long to sound the alarm on the offshoring of services. "I've been thinking about this for some years and I frankly got goaded into writing it down," he said. Robert Rubin did the goading, he said.

Another Clinton colleague, former treasury secretary Lawrence Summers, who is now Barack Obama's chief economic advisor, added his own second thoughts. "Let us be frank," he wrote in the *Financial Times* of London in 2006. "What the anxious global middle is told often feels like pretty thin gruel." The basic problem, Summers explained, "is the divergence between the fortunes of capital and the fortunes of labour." Summers had not been so frank when he held high public office. There would have been a scandal if he had talked that way as treasury secretary or chief economist at the World Bank.[4]

I do not question the sincerity of these new thinkers. They clearly hope to inject a little more realism into the policy discussions and head off the growing backlash against the status quo. As some of them assume their places in the new administration, I hope this informs the discussion. But the fact remains that they propose as solutions quite modest measures that have been around for years in conservative thinking. The most prominent is "wage insurance" to ease the pain for displaced workers—essentially, relief checks to tide them over while they look for new jobs. It doesn't do any harm. It also does not do anything to change the system that destroyed their jobs.

To put it bluntly, Rubin and like-minded "reformers" are not thinking deeply about what may have gone wrong. They are silent on the dissenting arguments Ralph Gomory and William Baumol have put on the table to challenge the orthodox fallacies. In essence, the establishment is offering a helping hand to the losers in order to defend the theory.

This became clear to me during a stimulating interview I had with Rubin. The ideal system, he agreed, would include rights for labor and for social values like environmental protection. But, no, he would not let those issues get in the way of achieving trade agreements with countries that refuse to reform labor rights or environmental laws. Was it fair, I asked, for capital and corporations to have protective rules when comparable rights for working people are denounced as protectionist? "Well, I guess it's true," Rubin said. "You can say, why distinguish between those [rules for capital] and labor conditions?"[5]

The interview reminded me of the old saw—you can lead a horse to water, but you can't make him drink. Rubin was willing to endorse elements of nonestablishment thinking in principle, but only in principle. He was not ready to grant that anything is wrong with the system itself.

Given the great trade imbalances that have built up with China, I asked if he had any second thoughts about the trading system he had engineered during the Clinton presidency. "Maybe I'm missing something," Rubin said, "but I don't think there's anything in the design of the system we would have done differently."

Global competition, I pointed out, is driving the gradual convergence of wages worldwide—the top is being pulled down toward the bottom—and this dynamic is what depresses American wages. Did Rubin think any of his proposals could have any positive impact on that?

"I don't know the answer to that," Rubin said. "I would guess the answer is no"—a startling admission, if you think about it. The authorities acknowledge economic inequality is squeezing the middle class and they endorse some ameliorative measures. But their solutions, Rubin guesses, will not impact the fundamental problem. We should help the losers in various ways. But we must not disturb the system that produces them.

Alan Blinder expressed the same fatalism and became a bit testy when I pressed him about the loss of US manufacturing jobs. "You can call it fatalism," Blinder said, "but, given the almost immutable laws of economics and history, I think this is the case. It's pretty inevitable. Now we have to be dealing with other kinds of jobs."

Manufacturing jobs, actually, are not disappearing from the global economy, only from America, where workers used to earn compensation that was in line with their output—wages that supported middle-class lives. Blinder became frustrated with my suggestion that something is wrong with the system. "What I'm resisting," he said, "is the argument that there's something wrong. It's like arguing, Is there something wrong with bad weather? Yes, but you can't do anything about it. It's like global warming. If there is severe global warming, you may have to change the preparations for bad weather."

Blinder's metaphor misstates the reality. Global warming is not an act of nature. It is caused by human activity—the burning of fossil fuels—and human actors can address the sources of the problem if they decide to do so. The negative forces of globalization are not an act of nature, either. They can be changed too, if political actors have the courage to do so.

Blinder's pessimism about American manufacturing is widely shared, though others usually aren't so candid. Few elected politicians are willing to tell their constituents, "Forget manufacturing jobs, find something else to do. Go back to school, become a software engineer." It sounds like a high-tech version of Marie Antoinette, who, when told that the French peasants had no bread to eat, supposedly suggested, "Let them eat cake."

What worries Blinder and like-minded thinkers is political backlash from the affluent and well-educated middle class. If those highly skilled people see globalization destroying their futures, they might also turn against the dogma. Politicians who were willing to hold off the working-class protests may yield more readily when the pressure comes from more influential citizens.

"I think the prospects for the liberal trade order are not great," Blinder told me. "There's a whole class of people who are smart, well-educated and articulate, and politically involved who will not just sit there and take it."

The not-so-subtle class bias in the elites' perspective is obvious to blue-collar workers. When working-class people lose their jobs, it is said to be an act of nature. When people with advanced college degrees start losing their jobs, it is a matter for national alarm. People in the upper reaches of government, academia, and media may see these "losers" as people like themselves. "Smart, . . . articulate, . . . politically involved," as Blinder said.

Blinder has no smart solutions for their predicament. He talks vaguely about reforming the educational system, though he cannot say how. Nor does he have much to say about how less-educated Americans are supposed to cope as wages continue to decline. These are the people who often do the less glamorous work of society, but their jobs are essential. We can't all become software engineers or doctors, lawyers, and professors. Someone has to drive the trucks and feed the livestock and take out the trash.

The free-trade orthodoxy is at an intellectual dead-end, though the true believers do not seem to recognize the depth of their dilemma. Acknowledging the economic pressures bearing down on ordinary citizens is helpful, but it does not resolve anything—not if official thinkers cannot think of a more substantive response. Admitting error is a nice first step, but it may further weaken the authority of those in charge. That leaves their doctrine more vulnerable than before.

Another Princeton economist, Paul Krugman, the liberal columnist for the *New York Times* and 2008 Nobel Prize winner in Economics, reflects the poignancy of the establishment's dilemma. Krugman, whose academic specialty is international trade, is a brilliant polemicist and fervent defender of the global system who has dismissed and debunked critics who claimed to see negative consequences. Lately, however, he has been compelled to concede that he was wrong about some things.

Ten years ago, Krugman explained in his *Times* column, he and other economists had "crunched the numbers" and determined that global wage competition was not to blame for the depression of US wages. The impact was, at most, trivial, he explained.

Unfortunately, the accumulating real-world evidence refuted this scientific conclusion. Like Rubin and the others, Krugman was having second thoughts. Things changed, he explained, and it turns out that American workers are right about the depressing impact on their wages. "So there is a dark side to globalization," he wrote. "The question, however, is what to do about it." Not much of anything, he decided. "Old-fashioned protectionism" would have ugly consequences for poor countries, he explained. Enacting worldwide labor rights policies might boost wages at the bottom of the global labor market, but could not have a positive effect on US wages for many years, he added. Therefore, Krugman concluded, it would be a mistake to tamper with the status quo.

"So what's the answer?" he wrote. "I don't think there is one, as long as the discussion is restricted to trade policy."[6] Like others, Krugman tried to come down on both sides of the question. Yes, he said, the workers are right after all about their injuries from globalization. But, no, they can't do anything about it.

Krugman suggested an alternative—enacting universal health care to help the "losers" and paying for it by taxing the "winners." That approach appeals to many politicians too. They could do something for the folks by improving the social safety net, but they wouldn't have to confront the hard power of the multinationals.

Reforming health care is an important goal, of course. It might help ease the pain for people whose incomes are falling. But it would not stop their incomes from falling.

"What's the answer? I don't think there is one." This passive avoidance defines the trade establishment's political dilemma. I suspect the church will lose respect and adherents as more politicians figure out the emptiness of the orthodox position. How does a senator or representative tell people back home that they are right about the trade problem, but government can't—or won't—do anything about it? Voters will soon enough recognize this as impotence. They may start looking for other politicians, other options.

An economic ideology loses coherence and influence when the advocates have no answer for the disorders their doctrine has helped create. The free-trade orthodoxy is now stuck at that crossroads, unable to change. The theorists acknowledge the "dark side" but seem trapped in their own convictions, unable to imagine plausible alternatives. The global system is approaching a turning point. It will either change or it will break up.

It is simply not true that Americans have no choice but to accept our fate. Experts who believe that "old-fashioned protectionism" is the only alternative to the status quo reveal the limitations in their own thinking. The United States could take many strategic actions that would confront its deteriorating condition. There are numerous possibilities for reengaging with the global economy using a very different national strategy that would produce very different consequences.

If these changes are pursued in US policy, it will of course be deeply disruptive to the status quo—after all, that is the idea—and Washington's merely announcing its intentions would rattle world capitals. Any fundamental departure from the past inevitably involves real risks. Big change has to be managed with patient, transparent diplomacy to avoid overreactions by trading partners that might unwind the system.

The United States can argue that the far graver risk to the system is doing nothing. Allowing the present dynamics to play out to a predictably bloody conclusion for the United States would very likely take down the global system, too. A wiser option is to change things now, gradually and equitably, before it is too late. Making reforms that create a more balanced trading system could avoid a bad ending for all by restoring equity at both ends of the system.

★　★　★　★　★

The greatest obstacle to action lies in America, not foreign capitals, and particularly in the official America of Washington and Wall Street. In order to act, the United States would have to give up its singular role as the global leader and acknowledge the enormity of its predicament. The United States would have to become more like other nations and take care of its own interests instead of trying to run the world. This would be embarrassing, for sure, and possibly humiliating for those who staked their careers on the notion that America would be "number one" forever.

The business and financial interests would naturally resist. The multinationals would flood the political system with dire warnings and mislabel any new idea as protectionist. But the measures I have in mind are all permitted under the existing rules of the global system. In the right circumstances, they can be taken unilaterally by a sovereign nation acting in defense of its own national well-being. Other nations enforce their national interest in distinctive ways of their own invention. The United States must learn how to do the same.

After the many years of cheerleading, Americans at large would no doubt be shocked to hear confessions of economic weakness from their political leaders. But once people digested what is happening, I expect most Americans would be thrilled to see their government finally taking aggressive action in defense of the country.

Suppose Washington did decide to act. What should it do? In crude outline, I can describe a plausible agenda in three broad strokes.

First, stop the bleeding. Cap the US trade deficits and force them to shrink gradually until the country reached a rough equivalent of balanced trade with the rest of the world. This can be achieved by a general emergency tariff authorized under the World Trade Organization's charter. It permits a nation to curb imports when threatened by financial crisis—an out-of-control deficit in its international capital flows. Such a crisis normally occurs in very poor developing nations, but the US vulnerability follows the same outline—a nation living beyond its means on borrowed money, sinking into unsustainable debt and dependency.

Second, impose national obligations on the actions of US multinational corporations and investment capital firms. These requirements can be enforced the old-fashioned way—with taxation. Ralph Gomory has proposed a straightforward approach. The corporate income tax could be reformed to tax companies in relation to how much of their value-added production remains at home versus how much has been moved abroad. A lower tax rate would reward corporations whose strategies are aligned with the national economic interest. A higher tax rate would penalize those whose strategies aren't.

Third, launch a broad, aggressive strategy to rebuild the national economy at home and restore economic equity and security in society. Among many imperatives, this change of priorities means reforming numerous laws, from the eviscerated regulatory system to the obscenely corrupted tax code.

More concretely, reconstruction requires vast federal spending devoted to public investments. Rebuild the common assets of society (ranging from worn-out bridges to social guarantees) and finance the development of new industrial sectors that will create millions of new jobs.

Together, these three strands of national action would send a powerful message. To trading partners, it would say that the United States is giving up its long-standing role as "buyer of last resort" because we can no longer afford it and to avert a ruinous ending that is in no one's best interest. Moderating adjustments in trade and production could be made gradually, over five years or more, without blindsiding anyone. But other nations must not doubt that the United States is prepared to take this step, with or without the world's approval.

Applying a general emergency tariff (or similar devices like import certificates) would put a temporary collar around the size of US trade deficits and then gradually shrink them. The virtue of this approach is that it applies to everyone and does not target individual nations or industrial sectors, as protectionist measures do. China would not be not singled out as the "bad guy." Tariff revenues could even be rebated to very poor nations.

This initiative would give every major trading nation a strong incentive to work something out with Washington and to readjust its own economic balance between exports and imports, between production and consumption. Developing nations would still be entitled to pursue "infant industry" strategies that subsidize and protect new industries. After all, the United States did so in its own rise to industrial power. But the global system cannot endure this race to the bottom that expands trade by exploiting workers at both ends of the system. The way the present system works, America's dilemma will ultimately be the world's.

If the United States does take more aggressive action, other nations might retaliate by refusing to import US goods, touching off a downward spiral of defensive actions that could shut down the trading system. In 1971, President Richard Nixon acted unilaterally—consulting no one—when he abruptly devalued the dollar, imposed tariffs, and dumped the Bretton Woods agreement, an international system regulating currencies. Today, the United States is in a much weaker position—dependent on creditors who can pull the plug tomorrow if they want to—and our leaders will have to act more respectfully.

One way to avoid crisis is to act with clear purpose to work out cooperative agreements among the major trading nations. Exporting economies, especially those with very large trade surpluses, have a strong interest in helping to sustain the economy of the debtor nation—their best customer—because US failure would darken their futures, too.

The United States now has a fortuitous opening to act boldly in ways that might not trigger a brawl with China or other major trading partners. The overall US trade deficit has subsided in the last few years as the national economy slowed and the value of the dollar was allowed to weaken. This was good news, but no solution. The same process had occurred in the 1980s, when Japan was the problem and the United States was borrowing about 4 percent of GDP to cover its trade deficits. For a few years, the nation got closer to balanced trade, but the trend reversed when China and others came into play as major exporters. The huge deficits returned and ultimately the borrowing went much higher, to about 6 percent of GDP. The challenge is to break this cycle and push events in a new direction.

To achieve this, Congress and the new president can impose a ceiling on future trade deficits, pegging it to move lower in step with the currently declining trade imbalance. The rule would follow the recession's improvements in the US trade imbalance, not force it down. This would give everyone, foreign nations as well as producers and importers, time to adjust to the new terms. But it would also state concretely that the United States will not allow another resurgence of unbalanced trade when it has returned to healthy growth. Finance firms and corporations have to make long-term decisions about deploying their capital investments, and they would begin to change their decisions, I predict, as soon as they were convinced that the government in Washington was serious.

Another risk in constraining US imports is higher prices. Inflation would be a real shock to American consumers who rely on cheap goods from abroad to sustain their comfortable lives. But, as Gomory and Baumol explain, the era of cheap goods based on cheap labor is already coming to a close. Because China and others are rapidly climbing the ladder of advanced production, the terms of trade are changing and the United States will find itself paying more for everything it buys from those nations.

Whether the effects of inflation are good or bad is controversial, but if the rate is moderately higher, it can actually provide therapy for what ails the world. It would be a blow to financial markets and wealth holders who insist that the Federal Reserve maintain an austere monetary policy to protect their wealth's value. But in moderation, rising prices can help heal the economic ills of working people by encouraging wages to rise and reducing the real burden of their debts.

For US multinational interests, the message would be blunt: Your free ride is over. A graduated tax rate on corporate profits would put a new price tag on the offshoring of US production and jobs, forcing companies to rethink their global strategies. The tax bill for moving US jobs and productive assets abroad would be modest at first, but it would be accompanied by an implicit hint that the price tag could be increased if multinationals continued to ignore their responsibilities to the home country.

These two measures—a cap on US trade deficits and a corporate tax on companies neglecting national obligations—would together introduce significant risk and uncertainty for multinational companies and their investors. The risk would be that they had located their production in the wrong economy—overseas—and their invested capital might become stranded on the wrong side of the US border. The uncertainty would be whether their foreign-made goods could get to US consumers.

Offshored production, you'll remember, was sent overseas to capture cheap labor and other benefits, always with the assumption that the products could be sold back into the wide-open American marketplace. But if the United States temporarily imposed limits on the volume of imports it would accept, market access would no longer be assured and might be a big problem for all overseas producers, US multinationals included. Corporate decision makers and investment bankers, the people who decide where to deploy the capital, would have to start hedging their bets. Just in case, they might have to establish new factories in their home country.

Uncertainty has powerful leverage on corporate behavior. At a minimum, a prudent strategy would make them be more cautious about offshoring. To compete on price, companies might ask themselves how the Germans do it, or the French or Swedes. The globalizing process would not be stopped, but the priorities of decision makers would be altered. Stripping the United States of value-added manufacturing would no longer be such an easy call. The footloose irresponsibility of US multinationals has always been illogical for the country. I wonder why it has been tolerated.

As Ralph Gomory points out, neither of these two fundamental reforms—capping US trade deficits and taxing US multinationals—is likely to succeed without the other. If the government taxes unresponsive US companies but does not also set a limit on imports, corporations could simply head out the door and become "Chinese" or "European" while still selling their foreign-made products to the US domestic market.

"That won't work," Gomory explained, "because you will say to the companies, 'This is how we're going to measure you.' And the corporations will say, 'Oh, no, you're not. I'm going overseas. I'm going to make my product over there and I'll send it back into the United States.' But if you insist on balanced trade, then the amount that's shipped in has to equal the amount that's shipped out by companies."

This is hardball. It is aimed primarily at American logos rather than foreign nations. The purpose is to divert companies from pursuing their narrow self-interest and persuade them to devote more capital and technology to redeveloping the home front—both the production and the workforce. Gomory believes that if these reforms are adopted, "you are going to develop internal companies that work the way you want."

Similar incentives and rules will be needed for any government programs designed to foster greater public investment at home. First, corporations whose globalizing strategies blatantly ignore the national interest must be told that they need not apply for federal contracts or assistance. They should be ineligible to participate in any ventures to rebuild the domestic economy with taxpayers' money unless they are willing to adhere to our national objectives. Otherwise, some corporate types will simply take the public's money to develop new technologies and new industries, then ship the new jobs overseas where the workers are cheaper. Government can enforce responsibility by retaining patents and licenses on technology developed with federal money and making them available to companies that want to help the country.

All this represents an American-style approach to imposing national obligations on multinational firms. It seems crude and legalistic compared to the more sophisticated and supple approaches employed by other advanced nations. It is less discreet than the cultural solidarity of Japan and the cooperative governance of Germany's industrial system. Americans could not copy those systems, even if we wanted to. Our politics and culture are too different, and so is our history.

Americans have to figure out American solutions. It is painful for me to say this, but in this regard the United States looks like an underdeveloped nation compared to some others. We still have a lot of economic and social relationships to work out in terms Americans will consider fair and effective. On the other hand, we are a young nation, strong and inventive, and I have encountered many positive-minded citizens who are working on solutions.

These ideas, I know, sound politically impossible. At the present, they are. This is why I have said from the outset that great changes in our condition are not going to happen unless citizens at large rise to the historic occasion and make them happen. I am not naive about the political obstacles, and I understand the intimidating barriers powerful interests have erected to prevent change. But I also sense that terrible events and foreboding about the future are creating an opening—the opportunity to think anew.

What is the alternative? Doing nothing? That is defeatist and very unAmerican. Rather than despairing, some citizens and even some politicians are trying to construct a plausible alternative path. The alternative ideas are all enormously difficult politically, and some are fraught with risk. We are trying to imagine a sea change in US history, not to make a utopia or implement temporary fixes, but rather to consider serious ideas that sound right and are tested with popular debate and examination. They deserve to be taken seriously by serious citizens. Do not turn away because the authorities say no. The authorities are lost.

In Washington politics, a small but promising foothold has been established for some of these ideas and others. A hearty minority of dissenters has introduced in the House and Senate a handful of bills that would cap trade deficits and create tax incentives for corporations to honor the national interest. In 2007, three senators and seven representatives, all Democrats, one of whom was Barack Obama, proposed the Patriot Corporations of America Act, which spells out the working principles of corporate obligations and proposes modest rewards for acting in the national interest. The measure does not discuss any penalties for acting otherwise, but it's a start.

The AFL-CIO and the US Business and Industrial Council—an odd-couple alliance of left and right politics—came together to endorse the proposition to invoke an emergency general tariff under Article 12 of the World Trade Organization charter and cap trade deficits. Others, prompted by thinkers like Ralph Gomory, are beginning to study the idea. Democratic senator Byron Dorgan of North Dakota, a stalwart critic of the global system, has introduced a series of measures advancing the idea of capping the trade deficits and suggesting other reforms.

None of these bills is going anywhere, not now anyway. But they provide a starting point for citizens to explore the situation and develop their own thoughts. Even if Washington were to act promptly, I cannot pretend that Americans would be spared all the hard knocks, including downward pressures on living standards. It is too late, I am afraid, to expect a painless resolution of our national dilemma. But the sooner people begin to dig through the facts and contradictions, the sooner we might have an agenda for redeeming the country.

Ralph Gomory, for instance, is an optimistic realist who thinks that way. He has a hopeful vision of reform that goes beyond the consequences possible with globalization. As an old hand from corporate management, Gomory wants to see corporations again take up an old understanding that has faded. The corporate institution is a trust not only for the shareholders, but also for the country, the employees, and the customers. Profit making is important, but it should not trump society.

"That attitude was the attitude I grew up on in IBM," Gomory explained. "That's the way we thought—good for the country, good for the people, good for the shareholders—and I hope we will get back to it. . . . We should measure corporations by their impact on all their constituencies. So in my utopian dream, we decide what we want from the corporations and that's how they make a profit— by doing those things. Failing that, I would settle for the general realization of this divergence of interests between corporations and the nation and let people argue it out."

If we had such a debate in America, I think I know how the people would resolve it.

★　★　★　★　★

Finally, we also have to address the moral question. Is right for us to worry about the losses Americans face when the rest of the world is so desperately poor? After all, even if the worst occurs, the United States will still be fabulously affluent in comparison. Maybe transferring wealth and opportunity from this very rich nation to very poor countries should be regarded as just. The people who feel that way typically are not themselves threatened by the losses. The viewpoint is superficially progressive, but it actually repeats a great fallacy preached by the "winners" in previous industrial revolutions.

Our contemporary industrial revolution, notwithstanding its wondrous inventions and modernization, is mimicking the brutal dynamics that played out in the technological revolutions one hundred and two hundred years ago. In pursuit of economic advancement, millions of lives are being sacrificed—mainly those of working people and the poor—while the fabulous new wealth flows to the fortunate ranks who are in charge.

The conventional reaction, then and now, has been indifference to the human exploitation. The world, we are assured, is on the high road to progress and prosperity, so it's best not to interfere. The uglier aspects can be tolerated because it will all work out in the end. The pattern of US indifference applies now on two levels. In the industrialized United States, able workers are stripped of their places in the country's economic life and often lose dependable livelihoods. Prevented from participating in the dynamic transformation, the workers naturally protest. They are dismissed as reactionary Luddites trying to hold back progress. But they are not against progress. They are against their exclusion from it.

Meanwhile, the new workers brought into the factories at the other end of the global system are exploited for their weakness. They represent a cheap and malleable workforce, one that is often composed of children and young women. They are doing industrial work that previously provided high status and incomes to workers in advanced economies. The new workers are utterly without status or protection and often are made to work in unspeakably harsh conditions, their protests brutally suppressed.

What's different about this industrial revolution is that the discarded industrial workers and those toiling in low-wage sweatshops are not located in the same country. They are literally on opposite sides of the world. This matters tremendously in political terms because it means the consumers in affluent societies who buy the cheaper imported goods do not have to see how the workers who make them are mistreated. Consumers benefit from the ugly injustices and are insulated from them, even as they are told that the new workers are grateful for the opportunity to earn wage income, however meager it is and however inhumane their working conditions.

Both the displaced workers and the new poor are victims who are being exploited by the system, albeit in different ways. Both are on the same side in opposing an economic system that extracts great profits from pitting the two groups against each other. This is a very old story in capitalism, of course. What's remarkable in our time is that sophisticated opinion leaders are preaching the same bromides and excuses that were used when American children toiled in coal mines or English girls labored in the factories that poet William Blake called "the dark satanic mills."

High returns on capital and great accumulations of personal wealth are literally built on the backs of workers because employers leverage the two groups against each other to suppress their demands for economic justice. The producers and investors further entrench this state of affairs by continuously moving production from one country to another—or threatening to do so—whenever workers begin to organize for improved wages or working conditions. This is why the old-fashioned term "exploitation" describes the modern system.

The present drama is essentially the same as that in the English Industrial Revolution of about 1800 (steam power, automated textile looms, steelmaking), when Blake wrote his memorable phrase. Our era also replicates the injustices and scandals of the industrial revolution in the United States circa 1900 (electricity, oil, cars, mass production). American children were in the sweatshops then. Adult workers repeatedly attempted to form unions and obtain a voice in determining wages and conditions, but many were suppressed or jailed, and occasionally some were killed.

Why are these ugly abuses repeated across the centuries? How can this be described as progress? I don't have an adequate answer. Perhaps it is because an industrial revolution always generates explosive disruptions in the existing order, and in response normal social restraints are pushed aside. Or perhaps cutthroat practices are encouraged by the fierce competition among companies to be the first to employ revolutionary technologies. Or perhaps it is simply the enduring power of human greed. The people in charge see that they are free to take advantage of other human beings—no one will stop them—and so they do.

The moral question for our time is different for Americans. Unlike in the distant past, we cannot pretend to be innocent about the potential consequences. We know the history, or have no excuse for not knowing it. Will our passivity allow these destructive forces to play out to their natural conclusions as we trust the establishment's assurances that everything will work out in the end? Or should we force governments to step up and confront the inhumanities before it is too late?

The history of industrial revolutions teaches that indifference to the deeper social injuries that are occurring leads eventually to explosive events, including economic breakdown. When government turns its back on immoral behavior, social movements form to struggle for justice and security. Both radical and reactionary political rebellions arise, promoting very different ideologies for replacing the system. History has demonstrated that the marketplace will not correct its own moral failures—it has no incentive to do so—and reforms are won only through popular political struggle. If politics fails, violent conflict may ensue.

The English Industrial Revolution of about 1800 led straight to Karl Marx and the communist alternative to capitalism, with its dreams of international revolution. The industrial revolution at the end of the nineteenth century spawned five decades of intense political and social struggle by workers, socialists, and reformers. That era of globalization crashed in 1929 and produced global depression. In Europe, the recurring upending of normal life—families being tossed about by continuous economic upheavals—created the seedbed for fascism. Hitler promised Germans he would restore order in exchange for their rights. To their own sorrow, Germans took the deal.

My point is this: Wrongful, inhumane behavior by powerful interests that is allowed to continue has consequences that are to be dreaded. Ultimately, it can derange and ruin societies that tolerate the excesses of greed and power. To put it simply, you can't teach civilized values to the next generation when they can see that the society no longer upholds those values. The moral imperative is to recognize this larger, long-term risk and act to defeat it.

To put it bluntly, American consumers are complicit in the injustices because we benefit directly and concretely from the brutal treatment of those young people making shirts and shoes and electronics. In my reporting, I talked with a lot of those young workers in numerous countries—Malaysia, Indonesia, Thailand, Mexico, and elsewhere.

Yes, they are grateful for the jobs and wage incomes. Most came to the factories from muddy poverty in the countryside, and they typically send home to their families money from pitifully thin pay envelopes. They are excited by their new status as industrial workers, and also bewildered. They are trying to understand their place in the world. They know something is wrong and have staged many wildcat strikes against employers across Asia and in other poor countries. The strikes are organized not by unions, but by the angry young workers themselves because authentic unions are illegal and callously suppressed. Brave young workers leave the workplace and stop production. They are herded back to work by the police or military.

Nobody has to tell the young people they are being exploited. They know it from the harsh working conditions and terribly low wages. When they try to protest, they learn how alone they are in their struggles against the multinational companies. At the international level, only organized labor groups, some churches, and social activists come to their aid. Governments, with rare exceptions, are on the other side, aligned with corporate power. This includes the US government.

I came home from my global travels haunted by these young workers, obsessed by the strange gulf that exists between the kids who make the stuff and the affluent American teenagers who buy it. Some young Americans do get the connection, and in the last decade they have organized political action groups like United Students Against Sweatshops to confront the famous brand names that make sports shoes or clothing in exploitative conditions. But where are the adults or, for that matter, the political parties?

Organized labor is the one important American institution that preaches and practices genuine solidarity with those distant young people and understands that the conditions for workers in advanced economies is deeply linked with those for workers at the bottom. If the conditions and wages at the bottom are not improved, if workers there cannot organize unions and gain political voice to air their grievances, then the workers at the top are doomed to lose more of what they have, too. This is why international labor rights are central to reforming the global system.

But organized labor is not enough; we need a shift in the public consciousness. In 1993, I was in Bangkok, where, ten months before, the worst industrial fire in the history of capitalism had occurred at a mammoth toy factory—188 dead, 469 injured. All but fourteen were women, some as young as thirteen years old. They made toys for American children—Muppets like Big Bird and other *Sesame Street* characters, Bart Simpson, Bugs Bunny. These were marketed by the best names in US toys—Fisher-Price, Hasbro, Tyco, Kenner, Toys"R"Us.

The human toll in the horrendous fire in Thailand surpassed that in the famous Triangle Waist Company fire of 1911 in New York City, in which 146 young garment workers died in similar circumstances. The Triangle fire became a galvanizing event for political reform in American history. The fire in Bangkok disappeared on the inside pages of leading US newspapers. The gruesome facts remained unknown to the American families who buy those toys. Scores of similar fires, albeit on a smaller scale, continue to occur across Asia, killing hundreds of young workers in textile and toy factories where the employers refuse to observe the most basic rules for safety in workplaces.

Cheaper prices can destroy innocent lives, quite literally. These injustices are entirely avoidable, but the competitive price pressures of the multinational system drive employers at every level to cut corners to win the contract. The steady erosion of US wages and good jobs represents the other end of the same process. Getting Americans to grasp the moral connection is not easy because people have to recognize that the suffering of young industrial workers in distant countries is linked to the displacement of American industrial workers. Lives are turned upside down in both places by the same system, which remains aloof from the social consequences.

America as we know it could eventually be destabilized if this destructive process is allowed to proceed without significant change. A decline in US living standards will be painful, but it may not be the worst consequence. The destruction of the social order—the curdling of optimism and human dignity, the swelling of bitter distrust—could be far more dangerous for us and for the world. The US imperative to defend its broader national interest is justified by this threat, but so are reforms to defend justice in the global system.

As we learned in the twentieth century, you cannot upend people's lives year after year without eventually driving some to extreme responses. They will try to defend themselves and their families, even if it involves irrational actions.

The global system's economic health is likewise threatened by the utopian notion that every poor country can become an industrial producer, more or less at the same time, without destabilizing the system. If wage incomes keep sloping downward, thanks to the race to the bottom, who in the world will have the wherewithal to buy all this stuff? Sooner or later, people will rebel. Some already have.

These contradictions can be resolved among trading nations, rich and poor, only if the system accepts new rules that assume a more patient version of progress. No country should be excluded, but the pace and scale of globalization has to be moderated and managed as a unified economic system rather than as an unregulated playing field for combat among multinational interests. That means instituting new global rules and social standards to establish equitable terms between capital and labor, between society's values and the profit interests of globalized companies and investors.

In other words, reforms must interfere with and gradually reverse the race to the bottom. We should begin by abandoning the World Trade Organization and starting over. WTO rules and similar trade agreements are designed for the benefit and convenience of multinational corporations and capital holders (whose lobbyists helped write them). A new regime might start with a social charter that sets basic behavioral ground rules for entry, makes commitments to poorer nations, and imposes accountability upon companies as well as advanced and underdeveloped nations.

Building a global floor for wage levels would effectively impede the companies from pitting the poorest nations against each other. Countries would be liberated to work out their own homegrown approaches to economic development. The system would likewise guarantee developing countries financing for development, currency stabilization, and other protections if these nations endorsed the goal of achieving higher social standards.

This is not a visionary scheme; it essentially follows the approach the European Union employed to promote the convergence of Europe's rich and poor economies. The wealthy EU countries provided financing and special concessions to assist in the rise of poorer nations like Spain, Portugal, and Greece. They, in turn, agreed to eventually meet the EU's unified standards. Scrapping the North American Free Trade Agreement and starting over could allow a similar model for North America, as Jeff Faux, president emeritus of the Economic Policy Institute, has proposed.[7]

Plausible reforms are difficult but possible, once leading nations agree that they must alter the world's direction. The United States could become a trustworthy broker in this new politics, urging others to face the system's contradictions and reviving the progressive spirit of cooperation the United States advanced after World War II. Now, however, if the United States is to be trusted, it first has to let go of the world.

CHAPTER EIGHT

THE NEXT WAR

The US military, despite its massive firepower and technological brilliance, has itself become the gravest threat to our peace and security. Americans may find this accusation disturbing, but I hope they will consider it seriously. Our risks and vulnerabilities around the world are magnified and multiplied because the American military has shifted from providing national defense to taking the offensive worldwide, from being a vigilant defender to being an adventurous aggressor in search of enemies.

The predicament this muscle-bound approach puts our country in is dangerous and new. Go looking for trouble around the world and you are likely to find it. The next war may be a fight that is provoked not by them, but by us. The next war may already have started somewhere in the world, perhaps in a small, obscure country we've never considered threatening.

Most Americans are used to seeing our country as the "good guy" in world affairs, so many naturally resist any assertion that the United States might be the source of future conflicts rather than the innocent peacekeeper. But a clear picture of this newly aggressive United States is outlined in the government's own plans.

The next war, the Pentagon's *Quadrennial Defense Review Report* proclaimed in 2006, will be against any or all "who seek to destroy our free way of life."[1] The struggle "may well be fought in dozens of countries [other than Iraq and Afghanistan] simultaneously and for many years to come." The Pentagon calls this "the Long War." The military has grandiose ambitions for how it intends to fight it.

One of its goals is "the creation of a global environment inhospitable to terrorism." To accomplish this, it is dispersing thousands of clandestine soldiers—special operations forces from all the service branches—to dozens of unnamed countries to root out agents of radical Islam and other hostile groups. The armed forces, meanwhile, aim to prevent any "near-peer competitors"— meaning Russia and China—from establishing even "regional hegemony" in their own parts of the world. The army and other uniformed branches expect to be equipped to wage two wars simultaneously—as they now are in Iraq and Afghanistan—"to remove a hostile regime, destroy its military capacity and set conditions for the transition to, or for the restoration of, civil society." Above all, the military intends to establish supremacy on land, air, and sea; in space and cyberspace; and also in nuclear arms.

To prevail, as the report, commonly called the *QDR*, explains, the United States and its allies must maintain the offensive. All these goals constitute a breathtaking challenge, even for a military as awesome as ours. The Pentagon's review describes the scope:

> *Long duration, complex operations involving the U.S. military, other government agencies and international partners will be waged simultaneously in multiple countries around the world, relying on a combination of direct (visible) and indirect (clandestine) approaches. Above all, they will require persistent surveillance and vastly better intelligence to locate enemy capabilities and personnel. They will also require global mobility, rapid strike, sustained unconventional warfare, foreign internal defense, counterterrorism and counterinsurgency capabilities. Maintaining a long-term, low-visibility presence in many areas of the world where U.S. forces do not traditionally operate will be required.*

The doctrine is not empty theory. Look around the world and you can see glimpses of the American offensive already underway. The United States is laying trip wires for war, betting that other nations will be too intimidated by our military power to respond. Sometimes, the gamble goes awry.

Iraq is an obvious example. The United States first announced its unilateral right to conduct preemptive war in September 2002. Then it invaded and conquered Iraq based on bogus premises. The unprovoked attack was arguably a war crime under international law—a "war of aggression" prohibited by the Geneva Conventions. After World War II, that treaty was sponsored and ratified by the United States as the historic answer to Hitler's unprovoked invasions of Poland and other neighboring European countries. The Bush administration dismissed international norms as irrelevant to its so-called Global War on Terrorism and proceeded to commit other egregious violations of international law, most notably the torture and inhumane treatment of captured combatants.

In central Asia and eastern Europe, the US quest for hegemony has taken shape differently. In Russia, we've been "taunting the bear," as a headline in the *New York Times* put it.[2] The United States has surrounded the old Soviet Union with new military bases and invited former Soviet republics to join western Europe's NATO alliance. Washington has supported Western-style political insurgencies against pro-Russian leaders in former Soviet satellites. The republic of Georgia was encouraged to challenge Moscow provocatively by the US buildup of Georgia's army with advanced US weaponry and military trainers.

The bear pushed back. In August 2008, when Georgia sent troops to subdue two breakaway provinces allied with Moscow, Russia responded by invading and easily decimating the American-sponsored Georgian military. The Bush administration's aggressive diplomacy had triggered the conflict, but it did not come to the rescue of its beleaguered new ally. The United States already had two wars going, and its armed forces were in a depleted condition.

Vladimir V. Putin, the Russian prime minister, was widely denounced for thuggish behavior, but he was hailed at home for defending the nation against American meddling. Some Russians noted that Putin was merely doing what the United States has done many times before in Central and South America—using military force to protect its sphere of influence from outside intruders. Washington has for many decades used invading armies or CIA intrigues to topple governments and eliminate unfriendly leaders in the Western Hemisphere—in Nicaragua, Haiti, Panama, Chile, and Cuba, to name a few.

In Asia, Washington pursues a similar strategy of military encirclement of China, though less provocatively. The United States is trying to establish "alliances" among China's smaller neighbors while it simultaneously acquires advanced weapons systems designed to fight a large-scale war against "potential hostile powers." China, the *QDR* says, "has the greatest potential to compete militarily with the United States and field disruptive military technologies that could over time offset traditional U.S. military advantages."

If that is so, then why has the US government permitted US companies to share advanced technologies with China? Strange as it sounds, China lends the US capital to pay for the American military, while the United States helps equip China to become a major military rival.

It is hard to imagine that China will be intimidated by an alliance of smaller neighbors like Singapore, Taiwan, Japan, the Philippines, and even India. Some of those nations hesitate to join in the US military strategy, given China's overwhelming influence in their region. But the relevant risk for Americans is whether the US government has already implicitly (and secretly) promised to defend those countries if China should threaten to push back.

In Africa, the American military has opened another front for potential conflicts. The Pentagon announced in February 2007 that a new regional command center, AFRICOM—the United States Africa Command—will oversee its military forays on that continent, including the dispersal of Green Berets and Navy SEALS to some places without the approval of local governments. The United States is already engaged sporadically in a little-noticed, undeclared war against Somalia, a pitifully poor and chaotic nation believed to harbor Muslim terrorists. The Pentagon arranged for Ethiopia, Somalia's Christian neighbor, to invade Somalia and the United States engaged in high-tech bombing attacks to kill selected Somalis it had identified as jihad leaders. Using military weaponry to assassinate individuals is prohibited by US law and may also represent another war crime.

Terrorists are the ostensible targets, but all of these localized conflicts tie into the fierce competition for access to the future oil supply. That motivation is never candidly acknowledged by the US government. "War for oil" contradicts our supposed purpose of liberating other nations and spreading democracy. Besides, using military force to acquire the resources of a foreign nation is defined as a war crime under the Geneva Conventions.

The most fundamental provocation by the United States may be its aggressive stance on nuclear arms. The United States is seeking what it was never able to achieve during the long-running cold war—"first strike" nuclear supremacy. By deploying its missile-defense system, the United States could in theory have the ability to strike first without fear of nuclear retaliation. Though still untested, the US system is designed to shield the country from incoming missiles. With that protection, America could launch a first-strike attack against an adversary and block any return fire.

The United States denies having this intention, but other nations understand what the missile shield would accomplish. Even if the system doesn't work, its introduction effectively destabilizes the prevailing balance among nations. It helps explain why so many countries are anxious to acquire their own nuclear bombs or are seeking the protection of larger nations that already have them.

In these and other ways, Washington is acting on a dangerous presumption: If the US provokes, nobody will dare push back or be able to circumvent the superior high-tech weaponry in the American arsenal. The United States assumes that merely deploying its overwhelming advantage in military power will persuade other nations to defer to Washington's wishes. As the *QDR* puts it, "projecting power"—pre-positioning troops and arms in far-flung locations—is a way of "shaping the choices of countries at strategic crossroads."

But what happens if a rival nation decides to ignore US power and goes ahead with its ambitions? The answer, presumably, is war. The *QDR* puts it more delicately: "Should deterrence fail, the United States would deny a hostile power its strategic and operational objectives."

But there are ways to strike back despite the overwhelming power of the United States. That is why relatively small bands of insurgent agitators turn to irregular methods of violence, better known as terrorism. The question is whether deploying thousands of US special operations forces to seek out, capture, and kill local Muslim radicals will reduce the threat or make it worse. The *QDR* extravagantly compares the jihad threat to nazism and communism. But, as we have learned from Iraq and Afghanistan, people tend to resent foreign armies occupying their country, whatever good intentions are claimed. They find irregular ways to resist, and they regard them as acts of patriotism.

The great contradiction in these war plans is that US efforts to impose influence over far-flung nations through military power may very likely produce the opposite results. Instead of controlling potentially threatening forces, we will become hostage to them, randomly expanding our vulnerability to ugly surprises. More intrusions create more recruiting arguments for the radicals. The US war in Iraq revived fading jihad insurgencies in Algeria and other countries.

Nations do push back—when they can. If that occurs and the situation escalates beyond what the United States intended, then American national honor will suddenly be at stake. And then comes the intractable question: Should the United States back away from the fight, or should it step up to maintain its credibility? Wars waged in the name of credibility can prove to be bloody disappointments, long and unfulfilling.

The worldwide deployment of US military forces has always been described as being part of national defense, and it has proceeded under the idealistic banner of freedom and democracy, with the generous goal of liberating other peoples. When American intrusions provoke a blowup in some unexpected place, it is too late for public debate. When the shooting starts and Americans are under attack, no one in government is likely to admit that the war was an unfortunate mistake.

The tragedy of America's military dilemma is that it reflects a missed opportunity of historic proportions—the lost chance to reorganize global relationships in more sensible ways after the cold war ended. There was a brief interlude of perhaps ten or fifteen years after the fall of the Berlin Wall and the breakup of the Soviet Union when the United States could have designed a different future. Other nations were ready to follow our lead, just as they had after World War II. When a half century of conflict between two ideological realms ended, conditions were ripe for more normal interplay among nations—a reunified world no longer organized by rival empires with massive arsenals poised to destroy one another.

The possibility was not addressed. Washington was instead enthralled with its own triumphant power and fell under the spell of the "winner's complex" described by Mikhail Gorbachev. The United States decided to reshape the world in its own image and use its military and economic powers to promote itself as the model for everyone else. George W. Bush and Republican neoconservatives became the most ferocious (and lawless) advocates of this new doctrine, and they rightly get the most blame for putting forward extreme assertions of US power. But the idea of Pax Americana was broadly embraced by policy thinkers and politicians of both parties. The premises for Bush's war making and aggressive diplomacy were established in the years before he came to power. Democrats and Republicans both assumed that other nations wanted to become more like us and, given America's dominance, could be made to do so.

Bush's father, President George H. W. Bush, expressed the spirit of the new American posture by declaring his "new world order" following the quick military success that liberated Kuwait from Iraq in 1991. The Clinton administration continued US military action against Iraq by bombing it occasionally. Bill Clinton was the first to declare formally that Saddam Hussein was a menace who must be removed from power, the goal fulfilled by Bush II's invasion.

The Democrats were more hesitant warriors than the Republicans, but they, too, intervened with military power, in the Balkans. Without a United Nations sanction, Clinton conducted an intensive bombing campaign against Serbia to liberate the rebellious province of Kosovo—a precedent Russia recently cited to justify its invasion of Georgia to liberate two pro-Russian provinces.

The Clinton administration might have been even more aggressive were it not for the objections US military leaders expressed to some proposed interventions. Madeleine Albright, Clinton's secretary of state, once tartly expressed her frustration with the reluctant generals: "'What's the point of having this superb military that you're always talking about, if we can't use it?'"[3]

Unlike its actions in the aftermath of World War II, the United States committed a grave and shortsighted error following the end of the cold war. This time Washington decided to punish and humiliate the loser—Soviet Russia. US strategy determined that it must shrink Russia's domain of influence and swiftly dismantle the state-owned Soviet economy, replacing it with Western-style "free market" capitalism.

The expansion of NATO membership located new Western bases on or near Russian borders and planted the flag in at least half of the fourteen former Soviet republics, from the Baltic Sea to central Asia. This helped newly independent nations get out from under Moscow's dominance, but also provided new customers for US arms manufacturers, whose lobbyists had pushed hard for the enlarged NATO. With financial aid from Washington, Poland dumped MiGs and bought F-16s, made in the United States of America by Lockheed Martin.

Meanwhile, Boris Yeltsin's government in Moscow was manipulated into accepting American-inspired "shock therapy" economics—the abrupt privatization of Russia's state-owned enterprises, which stripped away social protections and created the new Russian billionaires known as oligarchs. The sudden transformation induced probably the most severe depression that any modern industrial society has ever endured. The Russian people suffered through a decade of rising poverty, falling living standards, and shortened life expectancy. The United States agitated for our favored candidates inside Russian politics and in surrounding nations, further weakening its old adversary.

At one point, Secretary of State Condoleezza Rice encouraged the Russian people "if necessary, to change their government."[4] Stephen F. Cohen, a scholar in Russian studies at New York University, called this strategy "the new American Cold War." His conclusion that Washington had provoked this new confrontation was at first widely disputed, then powerfully confirmed by the US–Russian collision over Georgia.[5]

During the 1990s, while the Washington Consensus was imposing US economic doctrine on poor, developing nations, the US military was expanding its reach and influence around the world. The unified armed forces were supervised in various regions by a new system of joint-service commanders-in-chief, or CinCs, who became powerful figures in the Middle East, the Asian littoral, northeast Asia, Europe, and Latin America (and Africa, beginning in 2007).

The CinCs, as Dana Priest described in *The Mission,* have developed greater influence in foreign affairs than the State Department. Unlike diplomats, admirals and generals can hand out vast amounts of money and armaments to foreign governments.[6] The United States, as critics have observed, has more people playing in military bands than officers in the Foreign Service.[7]

When the cold war ended, the military institution suddenly lacked a convincing enemy to focus defense thinking and justify Pentagon budgets. The armed forces were pulled this way and that. "Humanitarian wars" came into vogue, but neither the public nor the armed services had much enthusiasm for them. Senior military leaders and defense intellectuals argued against the emerging notion of a "constabulary army" that would act like the world's police force. Armies are for fighting wars, they insisted, not settling domestic disputes.

The Pentagon's procurement budget declined for several years in the 1990s, but always with the understanding that it would start rising again when the new and very expensive high-tech weapons systems came into production. Development of these advanced tanks, ships, and planes, including three different fighter planes, had begun during the cold war—they were designed to fight World War III against the Soviets—but no one in government found the nerve to cancel them. Now the United States was selling or giving away some of its finest weapons to its new allies. If the United States wanted to maintain superiority, military planners claimed, they would need a new generation of even better weapons for their own forces.

The confusion of purposes was resolved by the shocking events of 9/11. The new enemy was identified—Muslim terrorists—and swiftly hyped into a universal threat. Anywhere and everywhere, networks of murderous agents are said to be plotting to destroy the US way of life. Public anxieties about terrorism have subsided, but the hyped-up defense plans remain in force.

Now there was no need to choose among competing strategies. The US military would pursue all of them: clandestine special operations forces working in "denied areas" to root out terrorists, large-scale readiness for worldwide war against rival powers, selective invasions to destroy hostile governments preemptively, high-tech counterinsurgencies to convert the backward natives to our modern way of thinking, and a strategic military vision for manipulating the "global environment." The United States now has 761 active military bases in 151 countries around the world, according to scholarly critic and author Chalmers Johnson.[8]

The grandiose expectations have encouraged a preposterously inflated militarism to flourish. It chases after unlimited objectives that defy practical reality yet is largely unchallenged in domestic politics. Neither political party has the courage to reject the blueprint for endless war and adventure or to reconsider the open-ended risks and costs. Politicians are fearful, but not so much about foreign enemies. What they fear is looking like weaklings in their next campaign.

Former president Bill Clinton slyly warned fellow Democrats about the danger of criticizing Bush's war against Iraq. People, Clinton explained, "would rather have someone who is strong and wrong than somebody who is weak and right." His cynicism neatly expresses the general absence of courage in politics.

The Pentagon is a machine running out of control without a reliable brake—no one will say no to its expansive plans. This is dangerous for the country for reasons I have suggested. Ultimately, it is also dangerous for the American military. Uniformed leaders welcome the enlarged funding and influence they have secured for their services, but they also set themselves up for failure by making promises that cannot be kept and claiming capabilities for which their fighting armies have little or no competence.

Each time the US military falls short in its efforts to control and subdue the world at large, its natural response is to ask for more—more troops, more high-tech marvels, more clandestine agents, more money to sustain a permanent global struggle that is anywhere and everywhere. Given the nation's weakened financial condition, the Pentagon is headed for an ugly collision with citizens over its relentless calls for larger military budgets. Government may have to sacrifice broadly popular social protections, like Social Security and Medicare, in order to keep paying for the continuing military buildup. If people are compelled to choose, which form of security will matter most to them?

Each time a new war disappoints the Pentagon's expectations of victory, the military forces will feel trapped by an absence of realism on the part of politicians and the public. People in uniform are sworn to do their duty, however recklessly it has been defined for them. They are committed to following orders (or else resigning), even when the orders make no sense. Yet fighting wars that do not lead to victory because they are misconceived leaves its own poisonous residue— bitter losses and lingering arguments over what went wrong.

Many military people, from among the ranks and at the highest levels, recognize the trouble their institution is in. Some are demoralized by it. Others have spoken out bravely, telling the truth even though that effectively ended their careers. Soldiers are can-do people who find it very difficult to say, No, the mission cannot be accomplished. It requires a special brand of courage, a willingness to dissent from accepted wisdom that does not make any sense.

This is what the country needs, I believe, to discard our overblown version of militarism: brave voices, both within and outside of the military, active and retired, to speak honestly about the dilemma threatening the country and our armed services. I will return to this subject later because I am convinced that military people can be a crucial element in the rescue of the country. They are credible witnesses to the dangers of war because they have been there. They have to find ways to speak up without violating their code and to inspire a forthright discussion about where "the Long War" is leading us. People in uniform take an oath to defend our country, whatever price they might pay. They do not sign up to waste their lives for mindless militarism.

★   ★   ★   ★   ★

Since I have written critically about the US military's condition, I will say for myself that I have one small advantage over many of the armchair warriors who are so eager for military adventures: I actually served in uniform. This was long ago in my youth, when the US Army was between the wars in Korea and Vietnam. I cannot say I enjoyed the experience, but it must have been deeply educational because I still remember military life in vivid detail. My old Army Reserve serial number was BR 15 585 780, and I had to recite it endlessly in response to the officers' and drill sergeants' commands.

I came away with an abiding admiration for how the military functions and an understanding of its core competencies (and also with a lowly private's loathing for the repetition and tedium). The armed forces is a very different institution from the rest of society, and in those days, when the universal draft was still in effect, it was a rare experience for those of us who served our time. Back then, the army was one of very few places in American life where people came together across the dividing lines of race, class, income, geography, and educational status. This was especially true for those who joined as enlisted men. We raw recruits shared the same lowly standing—our heads shaved and our personal identities stripped away, we were "sad sacks" reduced to crude equality in the barracks.

The truth is, we were a sorry bunch of soldiers whom the career regulars constantly belittled as worthless cannon fodder—a bad joke at the expense of the armed forces who had fought and died to win World War II. The lingering draft was a big problem in peacetime because it netted far more bodies— millions more—than the army could possibly use. So the draft was deliberately porous and easy to avoid. Get a doctor's excuse or marry early and have a child and you were let go. Many of us selected another popular evasion of the draft by joining recruits in the Army Reserve or National Guard—six months on active duty, then six years of Reserve meetings and two-week summer camps at military posts.

The reservists and draftees were mostly farm boys and urban working class kids, with a sprinkling of "college punks" like myself. We got along because we were not given a choice. Racial tensions, though present in the barracks, were mostly suppressed. It was new for most of us—white and black, northerners and southerners—this living and working together in close proximity, adhering to the official policy of racial equality. The military had been racially integrated a decade earlier, but American society was still overwhelmingly segregated, often by law.

The drill sergeants, many of whom were white southerners themselves, enforced the new program. I remember an obnoxious white boy named Goss from rural Arkansas who started bullying an undersized black kid from Dayton,

Ohio. The platoon sergeant did not ask Goss to back off. He took him out behind the barracks one evening and beat the crap out of him. This discreet method of instruction taught the lesson well enough.

What was also new to most of us, whether from the North or the South, was encountering black men in positions of authority and taking orders from them. In basic training, drill sergeants rule every hour of your life and you learn rather quickly to avoid displeasing them. In fact, the recruits found themselves competing to please. Our favorite was Sergeant Dorsey, a barrel-chested, bow-legged black man from Mississippi who still carried shrapnel in his body from the Korean War and World War II.

He was a natural-born leader—stern, clever, melodramatic, and entertaining, even when he chewed you out. Sergeant Dorsey spoke in the unfamiliar vernacular of the Delta Deep South when he lightly mocked our lame performance. We listened reverently to his stories. He whipped us into shape. An impertinent college punk once asked him why such a talented man would devote his career to the army. Sergeant Dorsey snickered. "You never did plow behind a mule in Mississippi, did you," he said.

I also remember Private Friday, a frail little white boy also from the rural South. He was too small to carry the heavy pack and M1 rifle. We discovered he was illiterate when he asked us to read him the letters he got from home (in which he was usually asked to send money). Friday was thrilled to be in the army—you got terrific boots and shoes, well-made clothing, and wholesome food, plus $72 a month in pay. It was more cash than Friday had ever seen, and he'd send some dollars to his folks but then splurge on stuff at the PX and have to bum cigarettes for the rest of the month.

Private Friday couldn't keep up. We took turns carrying his pack or rifle on the long marches. When the sergeant wasn't looking, we filled out written exams for him. But the sergeants knew all this. When basic training ended, they sent him home to Arkansas.

Join the army and see the real America, the country you didn't know existed: That valuable experience was part of what I got from my military service. It was a short course on the lucky and the unlucky who live together in our affluent society. I definitely am not in favor of reinstating the universal draft, but it would be good if more Americans got to experience our diversity in this way.

I learned something else important about military life: Soldiers know how to teach people, even when the students are untalented or uninterested in learning. After basic training at Fort Knox, Kentucky, I was sent to Fort Sill, Oklahoma, for advanced training in artillery. My "military occupation" was fire-direction controller for 105 mm howitzers. We were taught to use terrain maps and slide rules to calculate precisely how to aim an artillery battery so its shells would hit distant targets scattered across the prairie (on Fort Sill's vast firing range, the targets were junked cars).

The classroom training was tedious, involving mind-numbing repetition and lame jokes told by the instructors. They assured us that 105 mm howitzers were obsolete and would never again be used in warfare, so it hardly mattered if we were incompetent. But they were wrong about the howitzers; a few years later, the 105s were firing again in Vietnam.

Nevertheless, after eight boring weeks, everyone in the classroom had learned exactly what the army set out to teach us. We were trained and ready, even feeling a little proud of ourselves. When the battery went out to the field to practice, we fire-direction controllers were directing live fire for the first time. And our howitzer rounds (some of them, anyway) actually hit the old cars.

The military may seem lumbering and rigidly by the book, but it is a highly capable institution. It knows how to accomplish what it sets out to do. It produces soldiers from whatever raw material society provides, and they march off with a high degree of competency. The military teacher operates on a scale of mass production, taking young people to higher levels of performance than they or their families had imagined possible. The modern army has raised this training process to an extraordinary level of technological complexity. What the military does not do so well is fulfill overwrought national ambitions that are mismatched with reality.

Before Iraq, there was Vietnam. I did not fight in that war because I was honorably discharged, with the rank of sergeant E-5, from the Army Reserve just as it got underway. As a reporter, I did cover the fallout at home, the monster antiwar mobilizations and other political conflicts of the 1960s. What I mainly learned from that tragic conflict was a simple truth: The government sometimes lies to the people. Naive as it sounds, I was shocked to know this.

Big lies, along with other, smaller lies, kept that war going. In my reporting, I was told by street-level activists—antiwar agitators and "black power" radicals—that the government was spying on them. They said the FBI and CIA, even army intelligence units, tapped their phones, infiltrated political groups, and subverted political dissent with provocateurs. I thought their radical talk was paranoid. But it turned out to be true. Thereafter, I learned to listen to the people in the streets. Sometimes, they know the truth when official America is lying.

During that long war, I also spent a fair amount of time among returning veterans, hearing their version of truth telling. Some of them suffered the harmful health effects of Agent Orange or the strange disorder that is now known as post-traumatic stress disorder. Lyndon Johnson's administration denied the complaints and shortchanged veterans on GI benefits and health care, essentially to hold down federal spending. I was struck by the veterans' sense of aloneness. They shared gruesome war stories among themselves and tried to help each other get well. Many had turned against the war. Their patriotic sacrifices, they felt, had been betrayed.

The closest I got to the combat was in an army courtroom at Fort Benning, Georgia, where I covered the trial of Lieutenant Rusty Calley for actions committed in the My Lai massacre. Calley had led his company through the village, where they systematically killed hundreds of unarmed civilians— women, children, the elderly, even an occasional water buffalo. The grotesque trial testimony from GIs in Calley's unit revealed the dark side of war and what happens to warriors in a fraying army. My Lai was the worst massacre, but it was only one among many barbarisms. The jury was composed of six career army officers, from captains to colonels, who sat expressionless through the months of witnesses and legal arguments. The damning evidence against Calley was overwhelming, but the cynical expectation was that these army officers would never convict one of their own. Lieutenant Calley was widely portrayed as a scapegoat victimized by antiwar politics, an all-American soldier who had done his duty and been abandoned by the army brass. The sentiment was strongest in the military ranks and among veterans, who felt that they themselves were on trial.

When the jury delivered its guilty verdict, the country exploded in angry protest. Both liberals and conservatives denounced it for different reasons. People everywhere demanded Calley's immediate release on appeal, and the Nixon White House quickly complied. I felt sympathy instead for the six jurors. They had done the right thing, despite knowing they would be reviled for convicting the young man. But if they had acquitted Calley, they would have been denying the truth and discarding principle, which would have had devastating long-term consequences for military conduct and order, for law and justice. I admired the jurors' bravery. It had been a lonely act of honor that would not be rewarded.

"Honor" in the military institution involves a selfless commitment to duty and principle. The understanding applies up and down in the military ranks, a two-way commitment of mutual responsibility between the institution and its members. The troops commit to the good of the service—the mission comes first—and in return they can count on the institution's loyalty to them. That concept has been tarnished in the war in Iraq, just as it was in Vietnam, but honor still demands principled action. A sense of honor is what has led many old soldiers and younger ones to stand up and tell the truth about the war in Iraq. These actions are not rebellions, but rather expressions of a deeper loyalty.

The military is an intriguing contradiction in the American setting—a spartan society that exists within the larger prosperity and operates according to very different values. The military requires top-down discipline and closely regulated behavior, but these are mediated by the troops' communal obligations to one another, an interior system that somewhat resembles socialism. Promises are made, the commitments are shared. Take responsibility for the mission. The service will take care of you and yours. The system's success depends on those promises being kept by both individuals and organization.

All this is vaguely alien to what the larger society preaches and practices, though it claims to admire the military's values. Civilian life is freewheeling and opportunistic in contrast, aggressively individualistic and often indifferent to what happens to the unlucky people of lower social ranks. I am not recommending a militarized society, but Americans at large could learn a lot about their own social dislocations by exploring how the military sustains discipline and cohesion alongside equity and opportunity.

As Vietnam was winding down in the 1970s, the army was disintegrating. Some enlisted men were refusing orders on the battlefield, even fragging—killing—their officers with grenades. Back home on some military posts, the chaos found expression in the form of racial violence—vicious nighttime clashes between roving bands of white and black soldiers. I covered the story for the

Washington Post, and it was genuinely scary. When I asked commanding officers at several bases what had gone wrong to prompt this behavior, they did not invoke complicated social factors. The explanation, they said, was "a failure of command." I thought at the time that this was an evasion. Later, I came to realize they had been right. It was the officers' way of saying, Don't blame the troops, blame us because we failed them. This, too, was an expression of honor.

In the late 1990s, I returned to military bases and toured air force, army, and navy installations. The cold war had ended and I was focused on the obvious dilemma presented by the United States being the sole superpower. The nation had not demobilized. Yet, without a convincing enemy, what would it do with all this massive military power? Did Americans still need a war-fighting army or a global police force?[9]

At Fort Hood, Texas, I drove for six and a half miles alongside the army's gigantic motor pool for armor. It was stupefying to behold—an exhausting lineup of M1 Abrams tanks, Bradley fighting vehicles, trucks, tankers, Humvees, and assorted other heavy equipment. At the end of the line, the escort sergeant told me I had observed 14,000 idle vehicles of war. Little did I know that George W. Bush would find a place to use them.

At Nellis Air Force Base outside Las Vegas, I saw personnel in F-16s still training to shoot down Soviet MiGs in the Red Flag exercises that were still being conducted ten years after the Soviet empire disappeared. And why not? No other major adversary yet existed. Many of the contradictions that arose in those early post–cold war years are still not resolved.

But what really grabbed my attention were the young people. Very young men and women in uniform were running the complex machines and repairing them, servicing all the computerized systems that are now standard in weaponry, fiddling with the innards of high-speed, high-precision aircraft. As a veteran of the old draftee army, I was taken aback, impressed in entirely new ways.

It is not just the advanced technology of the modern military institution, though the complexity is awesome, but also the texture of the organizations. The all-volunteer services have transformed the capabilities of the people and increased their skill levels. More to the point, the new military distributes authority among the ranks, encouraging and requiring enlisted personnel to take the initiative to solve complex problems on their own. It seemed a long way from the by-the-book tedium I had known.

Again and again, I encountered in all three services young people of humble origins who were performing extraordinarily complex tasks, who were in charge of vital processes and teaching others who were even younger. They were performing tasks like overhauling the jet engines that power a navy destroyer, monitoring the dogfights of combat aircraft on large-screen computer maps, and repairing engines upon which lives depended.

I dropped in on the USS *Arleigh Burke* by helicopter as the destroyer steamed off the Virginia coast. Deep in the belly of the ship, six stories down in the engine room, I found Eddie Ramirez, a petty officer from Los Angeles. He was teaching two younger sailors how to clean and refit the plumbing inside a huge jet engine equivalent in size to those in DC-10 aircraft. This is a not a task you assign to beginners. Ramirez was twenty-two years old.

"I'm mechanically minded," he told me, "but I really learned this hands-on, mostly. The navy's taught me just about everything I know since I was a kid, since I came in at seventeen. I got five guys working for me now. I'm responsible for three of the six engines."

As it happened, Ramirez had just signed up for an officer-training program called Seaman to Admiral. He did not really intend to become an admiral, he said, but he liked the idea that this was possible in the modern navy. "Number one, I want an education," he explained. "Number two, it's like payback time. The navy did for me. I'm going to do for the navy."

My point is, the mutual responsibility ingrained in military organizations is a powerful glue that can enable remarkable accomplishments. The armed services, in my experience, is possibly the American institution that most effectively advances equal opportunity. Whether people know this or not, service in the uniformed forces is a ladder for upward mobility that really does work.

The military is, likewise, more advanced than most other institutions in creating real racial integration and overcoming discrimination against women. True, it has not yet let go of its bias against gays and lesbians. But I am confident that, when the order comes down, the institution will comply promptly rather than risk the disorders that result from "command failure."

A couple of years back, I met with a group of black women in Baltimore who were low-wage workers trying to organize themselves for political action. As we gathered around the conference table, one of the women announced that, after several failed attempts, her son had just passed his GED test, the high school equivalency exam.

The other women immediately recognized the meaning of this and congratulated her profusely. It meant that her son was now eligible to join the navy. The recruiter, she said, had already signed the papers and told him where to report for his basic training. Getting into the armed services was a life-altering event for him. It meant he had gained a foothold on the ladder. Now he had a shot—an opportunity, with hard work and a bit of luck, to escape the predictable trap of urban poverty. The navy would do it for him and he would do it for himself. Americans need to understand this about the military institution. Whatever else has gone wrong with its war making or plans for the next war, the people in uniform have a lot to teach the rest of society.

★   ★   ★   ★   ★

Generals, it is said, have a tendency to fight the last war because that is the war they know. That propensity is certainly evident in the Pentagon's plans for the Long War. The counterinsurgencies being waged against radical Muslims in various countries replay what was tried to no avail in the Vietnam War, as well as the dirty business and secret wars the CIA undertook during the cold war. The United States' plan for "projecting power" by encircling Russia and China is modeled on cold war containment strategies. The unannounced war for oil resembles the gunboat diplomacy of the nineteenth-century wars for resources fought by colonialist powers. The clandestine use of special operations forces has the flavor of America's own Indian wars that set out to conquer the native populations.

These various strands are intertwined in US strategy in complicated ways, but no matter how hard Pentagon leaders try to sell their tactics, the logic remains strained. US leaders cannot bring themselves to acknowledge that military power is the wrong tool for dealing with the nation's adversities. Instead, the *Quadrennial Defense Review Report* offers a medley of strategies culled from old wars that may evoke nostalgia for America's past triumphs. However, the real result is confusion and multiple contradictions.

Confusion over China is a breathtaking example. The United States evidently wants to see China both ways—as a market-friendly partner and as a future military adversary. This straddle serves many US interests at once. Google,

Microsoft, and other high-tech companies and banks gain entry to China's burgeoning market economy, while Lockheed Martin, Boeing, and Northrop Grumman get to supply the costly, large-scale weapons to defend us against China.

"Preparing for war with China is to be the future cash cow for the giant U.S. weapons-making corporations in the military-industrial complex," explained Michael T. Klare, professor of peace and world security studies at Hampshire College. If China should someday play its hand as our leading lender and withdraw its capital to punish the United States, the militarists may claim this is a hostile act of war, though of course the United States has done the same thing to scores of lesser nations.

The logic of targeting China also has an entirely different rationale—oil and the intensifying global competition for sources of it. As China's fast-growing industrial base creates a burgeoning demand for energy, China has been brilliantly adaptive and assertive. Instead of waging wars to secure oil supply, as the United States seems to be doing in the Middle East, China buys its oil with cash, drawing upon on its enormous surplus wealth from trade. China wins friends and supply contracts by sponsoring infrastructure projects in oil-rich but very poor countries with underdeveloped resources. As Klare put it, China employs "charm and the conspicuous blandishment of economic benefits" to win new friends, including US allies.[10]

In the last few years, China has developed new oil supply relationships with some traditional US suppliers—Canada, Venezuela, Saudi Arabia, Indonesia, and Nigeria. But it also has signed major contracts with nations the United States regards as hostile or unreliable—Iran, Angola, Sudan, Kazakhstan, and Myanmar. It is unclear how a larger US naval fleet, not to mention war, can be expected to enhance the United States' position in this competition for scarce resources.

Another official contradiction involves the so-called Global War on Terrorism. As it happens, the nations in which the United States most earnestly pursues nation building are countries with oil resources or countries in close proximity to those countries. For that matter, if the strategy is to promote democracy as a way to counter terrorist threats, why does the United States sell more of its weapons to countries ruled by dictatorial regimes that abuse their citizens?

"In the last six years," the Center for Defense Information in Washington reported in 2007, "the Bush administration has demonstrated a willingness to provide weapons and military training to weak and failing states and countries that have been repeatedly criticized by the U.S. State Department for human rights violations, lack of democracy, and even support of terrorism."[11] Indeed, the American-made weapons may be used to subdue the very people who are struggling to win democratic freedoms.

People in other countries know this, even if many Americans do not. This is one reason why US military technological advances sometimes lead to ugly surprises. Are we fighting the jihadists, or is antiterrorism just a sideshow to larger worries—the potential for a great-power rivalry and for a "long war" for oil supply? It is very difficult for most Americans to see the outlines of this new struggle because they are so poorly informed about how other nations understand the play of events. US media outlets generally tell only one side of the story—the US establishment's version. We know some people don't like us, but so what? When other nations react and push back, their behavior is interpreted as proof of their hostile intentions. American popular opinion is misled by a closed loop that nearly always blames the other guy and almost never concludes that the United States transgressed against peaceful relations.

Americans might understand the situation better if they were able, now and then, to hear how other peoples see us. Dilip Hiro is a playwright and journalist born in India and living in Britain who specializes in Islamic nations and regularly challenges establishment wisdom in the United States. One of his provocative essays was entitled "The Sole Superpower in Decline."

> With the collapse of the Soviet Union in 1991, the United States stood tall—militarily invincible, economically unrivalled, diplomatically uncontestable, and the dominating force on information channels worldwide. The next century was to be the true "American century," with the rest of the world molding itself in the image of the sole superpower.
>
> Yet, with not even a decade of this century behind us, we are already witnessing the rise of a multipolar world in which new powers are challenging different aspects of American supremacy—Russia and China in the forefront, with regional powers Venezuela and Iran forming the second rank. These emergent powers are primed to erode American hegemony, not confront it, singly or jointly.[12]

After describing some of the conflicts, Hiro observed, "No superpower in modern times has maintained its supremacy for more than several generations.

And, however exceptional its leaders may have thought themselves, the United States, already clearly past its zenith, has no chance of becoming an exception to this age-old pattern of history."

Is Hiro right? He is describing a worldview widely shared by other nations. Many, including some true friends, earnestly desire a less powerful America. By itself, that is not an expression of hostility. At its deepest level, it is not even anti-American. It is an age-old yearning to be free—free of domination by others, free to pursue self-determination in one's own way. Many Americans ask themselves, Why should our country stand in their way? That is a question worthy of national debate. Belligerence increasingly looks like a losing hand.

★ ★ ★ ★ ★

Nuclear proliferation is arguably the gravest result of US aggressiveness. It is also a striking example of the new push-back dynamics in global affairs. For nearly forty years, the practical reality was a nuclear stalemate between the United States and the Soviet Union, the implicit truce known as mutual assured destruction. Both powers accepted that either could destroy the other, but it would be suicidal to try.

Now the genie is out of the bottle again. Elsewhere in the world, reasonable people conclude that aggressive US behavior is encouraging nuclear proliferation, stimulating lesser nations' sense of urgency to get the bomb themselves. The old stalemate was destabilized not by rogue nations, but by the United States.

During the 1990s, as the United States became the only superpower, Saddam Hussein had reason to seek protection. He was warned again and again by the Clinton administration and Washington policy hawks that the United States intended to remove him. After 9/11, George W. Bush broadened the message by identifying an "axis of evil"—Iraq, Iran, and North Korea—that must be stopped and their rulers removed. Bush policy makers subsequently added Syria, Libya, and Cuba to the list of proscribed "rogue nations."

If you are on that list, it makes sense that you'd want to develop a nuclear bomb or other so-called weapons of mass destruction. Developing a nuclear bomb provides insurance of a sort against a threatening big power or hostile neighbors. Plus, joining the "nuclear club" confers status upon otherwise weak countries. Washington's bellicose language gave lots of nations motivation to acquire the bomb. The US invasion of Iraq seemed to confirm the urgency.

Of course it would be crazy to attack the United States and suffer national obliteration in retaliation, but what if the alternative is abject submission to American power? The essential objective of wannabe nuclear powers is to defend themselves; it is protection against US attacks rather than first-strike aggression. Yet US war planners usually portray their adversaries as irrational and suicidal— mad dictators who will do anything for their cause, even destroy their own countries. Some adversaries depict the United States in similar terms.

The United States undermined nuclear stability with the missile defense system first proposed by Ronald Reagan in 1983; officially called the Strategic Defense Initiative, the complex system for missile combat in space was soon dubbed Star Wars. In 2002, George W. Bush withdrew the United States from the 1972 Anti-Ballistic Missile Treaty that prohibited such systems, and then he ordered the Pentagon to go ahead and build the missile defense system, the technological feasibility of which even now has not been confirmed.

The idea—a shield that could protect America from incoming nuclear warheads by shooting them down in space before they reach their targets—is politically appealing. Trouble is, this innovation is provocative because it destroys assurances of a nuclear stalemate. If one country has a fail-proof defensive system, unprotected countries see themselves as being at greater risk of unilateral attack and will take countermeasures.

Bush launched this massive public works project, which ultimately will cost far more than $100 billion, with very little debate. The system in Alaska is supposed to block incoming warheads from Asia—think China—while another deployment in Europe will defend NATO nations against Russia or other nuclear powers. Even if doesn't work, it undercuts everyone's calculations because no one can be certain it doesn't work. Stephen Cohen explained, "The United States is attempting, by exploiting Russia's weakness, to acquire the nuclear superiority it could not achieve during the Soviet era . . . the capacity to launch a nuclear first strike without fear of retaliation."[13]

The nuclear advantage works as well against China, which is also a nuclear power possessing long-range ballistic missiles. This may explain why China did its own successful demonstration in January 2007, when it shot down an orbiting satellite in space with a ground-launched missile just to show that it could. It might further explain why China is modernizing its defense forces—whose equipment has mostly consisted of obsolete Soviet weaponry from the 1950s and 1960s—and buying fighter planes, diesel-electric submarines, and destroyers from Russia. According to Klare, China has expanded its arsenal of short-range missiles that can reach Taiwan and Japan.

None of China's new weapons compares to American weaponry, but the acquisitions have prompted fresh warnings from Washington about the need to counter China's military expansion. Russia, likewise, has undertaken its own arms buildup and now is less cooperative with US programs to keep the old Soviet arsenals of nuclear, chemical, and biological weapons from passing into terrorists' hands. The Bush administration was adamant that Iran not be allowed to develop a nuclear bomb, but it did not suggest the Middle East become a nuclear-free zone. Iran, if it told the truth about its intentions, might perhaps say that it is trying to establish a more level playing field against both the United States and Israel, which has had its own nuclear arsenal for decades. In South Asia, Bush breached the terms of US antiproliferation law by making an exception and agreeing to share our nuclear technologies with India. India already has its own bomb and has always shunned UN supervision of its nuclear weapons production—no differently than Iraq and Iran. Washington may be eager to ignore India's violations because it wants to recruit the country as a major partner in its alliance to encircle China (India so far seems ambivalent). The contradictions invite suspicion. Does the United States truly want to stop the spread of nuclear weapons, or does it simply want to stop those countries it considers potential rivals from having them?

If the United States continues along its present path, insecure nations may very well opt to join clusters of countries that are sheltered by the nuclear umbrellas of larger powers like Russia, China, India, and Pakistan. None are likely to announce this arrangement, but it will become clear that certain nuclear powers are providing security to assorted client states. The system might be chaotic, even unstable, but its purpose is to protect the vulnerable against bullying.

★　★　★　★　★

US counterinsurgency forays into smaller nations evoke an older memory in the military imagination—the "Indian wars" fought against America's own indigenous peoples during the nineteenth century. As it was in those conflicts, the US military is said once again to be fighting "stateless" tribes in order to "civilize" backward peoples, the righteous cause of conquering missionaries. The cowboys-and-Indians metaphor is evidently in common usage among the special operations forces that are fighting insurgents in dozens of countries.

Robert D. Kaplan, a correspondent for the *Atlantic Monthly,* toured their remote outposts in seven countries and wrote a highly romanticized book about the clandestine American warriors who carry civilization to primitives. "'Welcome to Injun Country' was the refrain I heard from troops from Colombia to the Philippines, including Iraq and Afghanistan," Kaplan wrote. "The War on Terrorism was really about taming the frontier. But the fascination with Indian Country was never meant as a slight against Native North Americans."[14]

Kaplan interviewed Marine Brigadier General Mastin Robeson, commander of a joint task force in Ethiopia and surrounding nations, who explained the subtlety of their approach. "'The new Economy of Force model we're working on is to whack people quietly, while running a lot of aid projects that generate good publicity in the areas affected,'" the general said.

Kaplan's book, *Imperial Grunts,* employed Rudyard Kipling's racist line "the white man's burden" from the age of British colonialism. Kipling, Kaplan insisted, "meant only the righteous responsibility to advance the boundaries of free society and good government into zones of sheer chaos."

If this is the ethos guiding US expeditionary efforts, "winning hearts and minds" is going to make big problems for the military and for the American people. As we might have learned from the experiences of Iraq and Vietnam—and, for that matter, from the original "Indian wars"—people, even in the bleakest circumstances, do not welcome occupying armies and tenaciously resist "civilizing" forces.

Teams of special operations forces are far too small to subdue any country, but they are lethal enough to provoke the rise of opposing insurgencies, Muslim and otherwise. If the rebels gain strength, the call goes out for more special forces. If that fails, the "grunts" call in air strikes. This road leads to larger conflicts while also stimulating recruitment for indigenous opponents.

One such "little war" is underway in East Africa. Ethiopia, Africa's second-most-populous country and a Christian nation surrounded by Muslim neighbors, was recruited by the United States to invade Somalia in 2006 to attack "Islamist militants." The much larger Ethiopian army's lightning strike on Somalia's eastern border had the objective of wiping out an Islamist movement that controlled much of the country and the United States claimed had a connection to al Qaeda.

US Army Special Forces guided the Ethiopians and made their own forays into that troubled country. A month or so later, the US Air Force launched two ferocious air strikes against Somalis with AC-130 gunships. *Washington Post* op-ed columnist David Ignatius described this as "an Ethiopian-American pincer strategy."[15]

The facts were clouded. The Pentagon said it was shooting at "al Qaeda targets" and that several were among the eight people who had died. But Oxfam, the British humanitarian group, reported that local sources said at least seventy people had been killed. US "bombs have hit vital water sources as well as large groups of nomads and their animals who had gathered around large fires at night to ward off mosquitoes," Oxfam said.[16] On the other hand, *Post* columnist Ignatius reported from intelligence sources that eight thousand "Muslim fighters" had died in this "brief war."

Ignatius had doubts about the value of these actions. "A successful proxy war, from the American standpoint. But then what?" he asked. Ignatius compared the defeat of Somalia to the US conquests of Iraq and Afghanistan. "A decisive military strike has destroyed one threat," he explained. "But what's left behind, when the dust clears, is a shattered tribal society that won't have real stability without a complex process of political reconciliation and economic development." Winning meant the United States would now have to rebuild Somalia, too.

Ethiopia is an unlikely partner for "winning hearts and minds" since its army is notorious for abusing people, including its own countrymen. The government has been cited numerous times by international authorities for thousands of cases of torture, arbitrary arrest, and extrajudicial killing. Jeffrey Gettleman of the *New York Times* managed to get into Ogaden, a remote corner of Ethiopia where the army has been putting down a separatist movement of impoverished nomads.

"In village after village," Gettleman reported, "people said they had been brutalized by government troops. They described a widespread and longstanding reign of terror, with Ethiopian soldiers gang-raping women, burning down huts and killing civilians at will."[17] Ethiopia, the *Times* reported, is holding forty-one terrorist suspects from seventeen other countries who were captured in clashes with Somalia's Islamist movement. US intelligence agents acknowledged that they have interrogated some of these captives, but denied that Ethiopia has revived the "rendition" system for torture by surrogates that previously disgraced the CIA.[18]

None of this made big news in America, but East Africa was shattered by the violence and controversy. "U.S. policymakers seem determined to replicate the Iraq experience in Somalia," said AfricaFocus, a US-based advocacy bulletin. "They are building up long-term problems even while chalking up military 'victories.'"[19]

"This is a very, very ominous turn of events," wrote Issa Shivja, a Tanzanian scholar and retired law professor. "If we keep quiet about American military planes flying over African skies, they will paint our lands red with blood. . . . This air-strike is a curtain raiser to expand the Middle East War theatre to Africa."[20]

Salim Lone, a former UN official and columnist for Kenya's *Daily Nation*, lamented the United States' tilt toward war. "The best antidote to terrorism in Somalia is stability," he explained. "Instead of engaging with the Islamists to secure peace, the United States has plunged a poor country into greater misery."[21]

AFRICOM, the new US command center, intends to locate permanent military bases in sub-Saharan Africa, according to actor Danny Glover, who is chairman of the board of directors of TransAfrica Forum, the US-based advocacy group.[22] Like other skeptical observers, TransAfrica suspects that US militarization of Africa is not about terrorism.

Instead, AFRICOM is about blocking China over Africa's oil. Among China's ventures in the region are long-term oil deals and development investments made with the government of Sudan, which the United States has accused of committing genocide in its Darfur region. Even celebrated humanitarian causes become entangled with the contest for oil. China has protected Sudan by blocking UN peacekeeping interventions in Darfur.[23]

Somalia, meanwhile, is a dysfunctional society rampant with bloodshed and starvation. Nearly a year after the US attacks, Gettleman reported that in Somalia there was crisis and chaos far worse than anything experienced in Darfur. Somalis told him the government of warlords installed with US help was more brutal than the Islamist movement they displaced. "'We want the Islamists back,'" an elderly retired taxi driver told him. "'At least we had food.'"[24]

Why exactly has the Pentagon opened a new front in Africa? Not for humanitarian reasons. Not even to combat terrorism. Robert Kaplan, the enthusiastic advocate of clandestine forces, wrote in the *New York Times*, "It's no secret that a major reason for the Pentagon's decision to establish its new Africa Command is to contain and keep an eye on China's growing web of development projects across the sub-Saharan regions."[25]

China sends capital to Africa. The United States sends Green Berets.

★ ★ ★ ★ ★

The Pentagon's containment strategy sounds vaguely like "national defense," the long and generally successful strategy employed in the cold war—impede a foreign power and influence its behavior by surrounding its borders with US power. But Andrew J. Bacevich, professor of international relations at Boston University, a retired army colonel and a Vietnam veteran, has described how the military strategy evolved into something quite different and more dangerous.

"For the Department of Defense and all of its constituent parts, defense per se figures as little more than an afterthought," Bacevich explained in *The New American Militarism: How Americans Are Seduced by War.* "The primary mission of America's far-flung military establishment is global power projection." In military circles, "supremacy" is now seen as an end in itself, Bacevich wrote. He cites Pentagon strategy papers that invoke muscular claims like "'sea supremacy beginning at our shore lines and extending outward to distant theaters is a necessary condition for the defense of the U.S.,'" "'overwhelming precision firepower,'" "'pervasive surveillance,'" and "'dominant control of a maneuvering area, whether sea, undersea, land, air, space or cyberspace.'"[26]

A West Point graduate, Bacevich emerged as a leading military critic of the Iraq War, and in his book, he argued for a major downsizing of our far-flung military forces. By 2009, Bacevich calculated, US military spending will exceed the cold war average by 23 percent. Defense strategy, he explained, has gradually been taken over by academic theorists, who have displaced the career officers with real experience fighting wars. In May 2007, First Lieutenant Andrew

Bacevich, a platoon leader in Iraq and the colonel's twenty-seven-year-old son, was killed by a suicide bomber. "As my son was doing his utmost to be a good soldier, I strove to be a good citizen," Bacevich wrote. Father and son shared a melancholy kinship "in picking the wrong war at the wrong time."[27]

As Stephen Cohen has written, the United States' containment of Russia by aggressively expanding NATO and deploying new bases around the defunct Soviet Union provoked heightened nationalism and paranoia among Russians. A "'hostile ring tightens around the Motherland,'" former prime minister Evgeny Primakoff warned. Novelist and former Soviet dissident Aleksandr Solzhenitsyn saw the "'complete encirclement of Russia and then the loss of its sovereignty.'"[28] The United States, it was widely suspected, was ultimately after Russia's oil.

This version of events is very different, of course, from what Americans read and hear in the US media. Cohen described US actions as an effort to humiliate Russia and its people in historic terms. The new cold war, he wrote, is founded on "a US-built reverse iron curtain and the remilitarization of American-Russian relations."

China has encountered similar attempts at containment by the United States, but without the dramatic economic suffering inflicted upon Russia. While the United States develops sophisticated new weaponry to maintain its superiority over China, Washington simultaneously pushes "what can only be described as the encirclement of China through the further acquisition of military bases and the establishment of American-led, anti-Chinese alliances," Michael Klare wrote. "None of these efforts are being described as part of an explicit, coherent strategy of containment, but there is no doubt from the testimony of US officials that such a strategy is being implemented."[29]

Klare felt the true intentions were expressed by Admiral William Fallon, then head of the US Pacific Command, in congressional testimony. Fallon worried about matching Chinese military improvements and called for a "tiered system" of missile defense that would be aimed at blocking China's short-range missiles, as well the long-range missiles that presumably target the United States.

"Note that Fallon is not talking about a conflict that might occur in the central or eastern Pacific, within reach of America's shores," Klare explained. "Rather, he is talking about defeating Chinese forces in their home waters, on the western rim of the Pacific." This forward deployment of US firepower was meant to reassure "potential coalition partners"—Japan, Singapore, the Philippines, Australia, and South Korea—who were wary of the US resolve to stand and fight another war in Asia.

China is expanding its defense budget, but it remains quite small in comparison with that of the United States. The estimates range widely, but its declared military spending of about $45 billion to $60 billion is one-tenth of the US defense budget, though China's population is four times larger. In a speech given at an Asian-Pacific military strategy conference in Singapore in 2005, then–defense secretary Donald Rumsfeld coyly asked, "'Since no nation threatens China, one must wonder: Why this growing investment? Why these continuing large and expanding arms purchases? Why these continuing robust deployments?'"[30]

Given the aggressive US approach toward both China and Russia, no one should be surprised that those two nations have found mutual self-interest in their new situation. "Moscow is forming a political, economic and military 'strategic partnership' with China," Cohen wrote, "lending support to Iran and other anti-American governments in the Middle East and already putting surface-to-air missiles back in Belarus, in effect Russia's western border with NATO."[31] Both Russia and China are pursuing what is in their self-interest by supporting some ugly, authoritarian regimes that are hostile to democracy and human rights (the United States, of course, does the same whenever it seems to serve our strategic purposes).

The China–Russia convergence may seem familiar to defense hawks in Washington. Our two great ideological adversaries from the cold war are united again, and we are told that we must thwart them. But what unites them is our own bellicose behavior. US containment strategy assumes that both Russia and China have ambitions for territorial expansion and must be physically blocked by the deployment of US forces. But there is no evidence (or obvious incentive) for territorial expansion by either country.

China is so large it hardly needs more people or real estate. Its influence has spread to other nations mainly through the Chinese diaspora— the many millions of Chinese who migrated to neighboring Asian countries and established a strong presence in commerce, politics, culture, and education.

Both Russia and China do expect, however, to exert influence in their own regions and hemispheres, as they have historically, and to see their power respected by other nations. It is folly—dangerous folly—to imagine that more US gunboats or nuclear missiles will somehow dissuade Moscow and Beijing from asserting their historic spheres of influence as great powers.

China and Russia are rising, in different ways, as economic powers. Even if the United States were reckless enough to engage in a real war, it is not clear how that would alter the basic realities. China is gaining economic power through its spectacular industrialization. Russia is a major source and supplier of energy— oil and natural gas—and that is the foundation for its remarkable economic recovery.

Russia is flourishing and accumulating new wealth because Putin renationalized the energy industry, but also mainly because of the sky-high oil prices. You might say Putin got lucky, but the truth is that he should thank George W. Bush, whose invasion of Iraq triggered the soaring prices. Short of war, US military force cannot reverse or even impede this shift of power to Russia and China. The United States can police the sea-lanes to ensure the free movement of oil, but it cannot alter the market force of scarce supply and surging demand.

Western Europe now gets 25 percent of its natural gas from Russia. Hungary, Germany, Poland, and even Britain are dependent on Russian oil. According to Dilip Hiro, Bulgaria, Estonia, Finland, and Slovakia get 100 percent of their gas from Russia; Turkey, 66 percent; Poland, 58 percent; Germany, 41 percent; and France, 25 percent. The Kremlin is now flush with more than $400 billion in foreign reserves, up from $12 billion in 1999.[32]

In other words, Russia has a degree of energy leverage that is similar to the financial leverage China has with its great lending to the dependent US economy. It is not in Russia's interest to cause the collapse of the European economy, but in theory it could. It can also exercise devastating influence on some of its closer neighbors and former Soviet republics simply by withholding energy supplies, charging the full market price, or shifting sales to eastern customers like China. Russia has not played the oil card, China has not played the financial card. But they can if the United States gives them a good reason.

Envisioning China as our new military rival seems especially detached from reality. America is China's best customer; China is America's best banker. The unbalanced relationship is very unhealthy for reasons I have already explained. But if Pentagon planners are serious about making China the new threat, they may find themselves targeting some of the best names in American business and finance.

During the cold war, the United States developed a shrewd though cynical strategy to bring down the Soviet empire—the ongoing nuclear arms race. We could afford it, the Russians couldn't. Over thirty years, the United States repeatedly raised the ante on the Soviets by developing succeeding generations of increasingly sophisticated strategic weapons systems, while always claiming the Soviets were dangerously ahead of us in nuclear capabilities.

In fact, as the Soviet Union's state-owned economy declined, the relentless arms competition was steadily bleeding its scarce resources. In the end, the Soviet leaders had to give up the chase. The cold war ended peaceably. At that point, some US policy makers frankly credited the US arms buildup as an important element in producing the final triumph.

If that's what the US military and hawkish policy elites have in mind—provoking an arms race with China—the strategy is especially wrongheaded. What the Pentagon and its industrial allies do not seem to understand is that the strategic advantage has been reversed since the cold war days. China is now the ascendant economy amassing production and great financial surpluses. The United States is the debtor country losing factories and wealth. Spending many more billions on weaponry will not bankrupt Beijing, but it will definitely bleed Washington.

The most intriguing and potentially ominous collaboration between China and Russia concerns oil. China is a major consumer; Russia is a major producer. Together, they are participating in an innocuous-sounding organization China started called the Shanghai Cooperation Organization. The SCO is a diplomatic club that occasionally brings together selected oil-producing and -consuming nations for talks on "international security."

No one can say exactly where this group is headed. It might emerge as an alternative alliance to NATO. Or it could become a club for friendly deal making outside the global oil market dominated by Western capitalism. Think of "'OPEC with nuclear weapons,'" as one worried analyst suggested to Cohen.

China started the Shanghai club in 1996 with four adjoining nations, Russia and the former Soviet republics of Kazakhstan, Kyrgyzstan, and Tajikistan. Uzbekistan was later added to the fold. The original subjects were drug smuggling and terrorism, according to Hiro. In 2003, regional economic development became the formal focus of discussions, and observer status was granted to Pakistan, India, Mongolia, and Iran. That put more oil, and more nukes, at the table.

When the United States asked to be included as an observer, it was turned down. More recently, according to Hiro, the SCO nations conducted their first joint military exercises in the Ural Mountains of Russia. The maneuvers were code-named Peace Mission 2007.

All of these underappreciated facts could be used to tell Americans a very scary story about potential adversaries in a world of scarce oil. But that would raise some embarrassing complications for US policy elites. They might have to acknowledge the truth of what they had dismissed as a left-wing fantasy: an undeclared war for oil. Many Americans who opposed the Iraq invasion insisted from the start that oil was the real purpose. They raised a raw antiwar slogan, No Blood for Oil. In their reporting on the invasion, the media and politicians ignored oil as if it were a taboo subject. It fell to retired Federal Reserve chairman Alan Greenspan, never known for his public candor, to state the matter clearly.

"I am saddened," Greenspan wrote in his memoir, "that it is politically inconvenient to acknowledge what everyone knows: the Iraq war is largely about oil."[33]

Bush himself obliquely confirmed the oil subtext in September 2007 when he declared that US troops should maintain an "enduring" presence in Iraq, as they have in South Korea for nearly sixty years. This would explain why the United States is building vast permanent bases and the largest US embassy in the world in Iraq.

Did "everyone" know oil was the real cause for war? Or maybe Greenspan meant "everyone" who is a Washington insider like himself. Americans at large were not told that "blood for oil" was on the government's agenda. If they had been, popular consent might have required a more honest discussion before the public backed the march to war. People could have discussed whether military action is a rational response to the oil problem, whether young people should be asked to risk their lives to maintain the excesses and waste of consumer tastes in the hydrocarbon economy. Michael Klare's disturbing book—*Blood and Oil: The Dangers and Consequences of America's Growing Dependency on Imported Petroleum*—makes that case, as others have for the alternative vision. To escape the oil dilemma, the United States must undertake a profound industrial transformation that will shift it to alternative fuels and reduce the great wastefulness of US consumption. That is the only lasting way to reduce US dependence on foreign sources of energy. Bullying other nations with military force, Klare explained, makes the already adverse circumstances worse:

> *The question of truth telling may not bother civilian policy makers, but it is an important point of honor for the uniformed military. It is one thing to lead young men and women into battle, but another to mislead them about why they are fighting. Their families will want to know—need to be reassured—that their sacrifices were not for nothing. Imagine the commanding officer who has to tell a soldier's parents, "Your son died to keep the oil flowing" or "Your daughter was maimed so we will have cheap gasoline."*

CHAPTER NINE

WHY NOT VICTORY?

Why does the United States keep losing wars? The US military is extraordinarily powerful and capable, yet in the last half century it has experienced three embittering failures—Korea, Vietnam, and Iraq—plus a smattering of minor embarrassments. Reforming the US military for the good of the country needs to begin with finding an answer to that question.

Ignorance is an important element in the explanation. Ignorance has been a hallmark of modern American war making for decades. Most recently in the Iraq War, leaders of the armed services did agree to send troops into battle under false pretenses, but we cannot lay the blame primarily on the military. US wars have been launched based on gross misunderstandings or active deceptions not once, but three times in the last sixty years. Each one ended badly—that is, with bloody humiliation for the country and its armed forces.

The United States was already four years into the Iraq War when Jeff Stein, national security editor of *Congressional Quarterly*, began a mischievous experiment. He regularly interviews high-ranking intelligence officials, FBI executives, and congressional members who serve on intelligence committees. Stein decided to ask them, in passing, if they knew the difference between Sunni and Shiite Muslims, the two sects killing one another in Iraq's civil war.

"Most American officials I've interviewed don't have a clue," he reported.[1]

Willie Hulon, chief of the FBI's national security branch, was flummoxed, but attempted an answer. "'The basics goes back to their beliefs and who they were following,'" Hulon said. When Stein asked whether Iran and Hezbollah are Sunni or Shiite, the FBI expert guessed, "'Sunni.'" Wrong.

Stein asked Representative Jo Ann Davis, a Virginia Republican who chaired the House intelligence subcommittee on the CIA at the time, if she knew the difference. "'Do I? You know, I should,'" she said. "'The Sunni are more radical than the Shia. Or vice versa.'"

Stein had to explain the difference to Representative Terry Everett, an Alabama Republican who was then vice-chair of the intelligence subcommittee on technical and tactical issues. "'Now that you've explained it to me,'" Everett said, "'what occurs to me is that it makes what we're doing over there extremely difficult, not only in Iraq but that whole area.'"

Ignorance makes it easier to go to war. If the congressman had paused to learn something about the people of the country the United States was about to invade, the complexities might have tempered his enthusiasm for the war. Like most of his congressional colleagues, Everett did not bother.

The military is implicated, too. Recall the Pentagon's confident assurances that "shock and awe" bombardment would stun Iraqis into submission. And the defense secretary's hearty prediction that the defeated Iraqis would welcome Americans as liberators.

The blame, however, belongs mainly to the political establishment—people from both political parties and the deep ranks of foreign policy experts, academic advisors, and media opinion leaders. With noble exceptions, they were oblivious to the complexity of what they blithely supported. They embraced the pro-war arguments once it became clear that the president wanted to go to war. Ultimately, the culpability resides with the man who was at the pinnacle of power, the poorly informed politician who was president.

Did anyone explain the differences between Sunni and Shiite Muslims to George W. Bush before he went to war? Four years later, the president righteously complained that Iran was meddling in Iraq and would gain dominance there if the United States withdrew. Did Bush understand when he began the push for war that Iran is next door to Iraq? Did he not know that the Shiite ayatollahs who rule Iran are close brethren of the Shiite leaders in Iraq? Didn't he recognize that deposing Saddam Hussein, for better or worse, was sure to empower the long-suppressed Shiite majority and thus their patrons in Iran? Surely Bush remembered that when Iran fought an extremely bloody war against Saddam in the 1980s, the United States aligned itself with the murderous Iraqi leader. Bush's father was vice president at the time.

Bush Jr. may be an extreme example of ignorance in high places, but this pervasive ignorance did not start with his presidency. When things go wrong, commentators like to identify the "mistakes" the commander in chief is making and recommend that the next guy who is elected correct them. But bloody and baffling blindness has been a recurring stain on US war making from Korea to Vietnam to Iraq, and it's been shared by Democrats and Republicans, liberals and conservatives, hawks and even a few doves.

The war in Korea was a hideous mistake. The conflict between North and South Korea was essentially a postcolonial civil war over how to reunify a nation divided by the cold war. Korea had been occupied by Japan from 1910 through the end of World War II and then arbitrarily divided into two nations in response to the cold war rivalry between the United States and the Soviet Union. The war was triggered inadvertently in 1950 by a colossal US foreign policy blunder—South Korea wasn't listed among the nations the United States explicitly pledged to defend in the event of a Soviet attack. That omission invited North Korea's Soviet-backed invasion. Then that ignorance was compounded on the battlefield when US miscalculations led it to charge northward, only to find itself face-to-face with the vast ground army of Red China.

The United States couldn't win and it couldn't get out. Some thirty-three thousand Americans were killed and one hundred and nine thousand wounded, not to mention the nearly 2 million Korean and Chinese troops who were killed. Washington was grateful in the end to settle for a stalemate (the final truce was arranged by an old general, President Dwight Eisenhower).

Lessons were not learned. Less than fifteen years later, the United States was fighting another land war in Asia, this one also based on erroneous presumptions. The United States went to war in Indochina based on Washington's belief that North Vietnam was merely a stand-in for Red China and therefore had to be opposed. Washington's great obsession in those days was the so-called domino theory. If Vietnam was lost to the communists, experts argued, US resolve would be discredited and the "balance of power" would tip toward the communists throughout Southeast Asia. One by one, nations would go "red" like falling dominoes.

Only the premise was utterly mistaken. The truth was (and still is) that all Vietnamese, regardless of their internal political differences, shared an ancient enmity toward China, and vice versa. Scholars and journalists who knew Indochina and its history kept trying to correct the ignorance of policy makers at the Pentagon, State Department, and White House, but to no avail. The United States, they explained, had waded into another postcolonial civil war thinking they were fighting "commies," but actually confronting deeply rooted nationalism. North Vietnam was authentically nationalist and very likely to prevail, given its determination and popular support. The US client state, South Vietnam, was just that—a client state propped up by Washington.

Very late in the war, the US government obliquely admitted its error. President Richard Nixon went to China and "normalized" relations with its communist government. "Red China" swiftly disappeared from US political rhetoric. By then, fifty-eight thousand Americans had been killed, one hundred and fifty-three thousand wounded. North Vietnam lost 1.1 million soldiers, South Vietnam another two hundred and fifty thousand. Four million Indochinese civilians died in the war.

The casualty accounting for Iraq is as yet incomplete, of course, and won't be known for some years. The loss of Americans in this war seems trivial compared with those previous wars. But the horrendous losses incurred by Iraqi civilians, and the utter destruction of Iraqi culture and social structure, suggests on the part of the United States a callous indifference to life that borders on the criminal.

US ignorance is perhaps inspired by arrogance—the "winner's complex." After all, we are not an uninformed people. There is no shortage of US experts who know quite a lot about the rest of the world. The government can draw from a vast variety of sophisticated scholars and astute diplomats who understand the underlying complexities. For that matter, many experienced military officers are equally well informed. Yet every lost war produces the same melancholy tales about knowledgeable people's insights that were ignored until it was too late. Or is it that US leaders are arrogant because they are ignorant? Either way, the result is a military apparatus that has gruesome killing power and is accident prone, to put it generously. No one is held accountable afterward. Nothing fundamental is changed that might prevent the repetition of essentially the same "mistakes." That seems both arrogant and ignorant.

★　★　★　★　★

Many critics explain America's aggressive war making with a more forceful charge—the United States has become an empire. They contend that US military power is being employed to act out the wishes of a presumptuous imperial power that aspires to rule the world. This interpretation of events has gained wider support in light of the aggressive actions of the Bush administration. The implication is that the United States' use of force has been more purposeful than it may have appeared, and therefore more effective. Despite the errors and losses, the objective is global dominion.

In this analysis, the United States is the modern equivalent of Rome or Great Britain when Britannia ruled the waves. US military power spans the globe with awesome reach, consisting of hundreds of bases and deployments that situate US military power far, far away from our national borders. The military presence accompanies American capitalism in its global expansion, serving as protector and policeman for US multinational corporations and investors who, in turn, exert a colonizing influence on the economic lives of other nations.

In this reading of events, occasional wars can be explained as useful tools in the thrust for empire—teaching deference and fear to less powerful nations. Even if the wars go badly, the United States' willingness to use its thunderous power encourages obedience and thus advances the logic of US domination. Scholarly arguments aside, this idea of America as empire is widely believed—and widely resented—elsewhere in the world. One of the most impressive arguments for the reality of US empire building is the grim trilogy produced by Chalmers Johnson, a legendary scholar of international relations. In three books—*Blowback*, *The Sorrows of Empire*, and *Nemesis*—he lays out a comprehensive case that the American republic has been undermined by aggressive militarism, the US Constitution effectively rendered moot by the imperial quest. It is a chilling portrait that demands respect.[2]

Still, I don't buy it. There is no doubt that imperial impulses are present and active among governing elites. Many foreign policy thinkers are comfortable with the concept of a Pax Americana that exercises global control. Nevertheless, I am not convinced that "empire" accurately describes our condition.

The radical depiction of the United States as the new imperium flourished on the left during the cold war, but, strangely enough, the concept has gained greater mainstream respectability since that era ended. Foreign policy elites and influential media commentators began extolling the United States as a benign empire and endorsed the supposed virtues of having an indispensable Goliath in charge of world affairs. A single superpower, some opinion leaders argued, was required to avert catastrophe and war. Who better to fill the role than well-intentioned Americans?

In fact, the thirst for empire is a deeply embedded impulse in our history, and it has been present from the start. New York is called the Empire State because empire building was a widely shared understanding of our national purpose during the nineteenth century. When the nation expanded westward in North America, it did so by conquest and absorption, subjugating the native inhabitants and developing a highly productive economy in their lands. This was described as our Manifest Destiny. Many Americans (maybe most of them) believed our territorial acquisitions fulfilled God's will.

Historian William Appleman Williams described that path in *The Tragedy of American Diplomacy*, *Empire as a Way of Life*, and other books. The thirst for continental expansion was carried into US foreign policy, he wrote, and shaped US ambitions to acquire power and territory in the rest of the world. Empire drove the foreign policy of the so-called imperialist era at the close of the nineteenth century, when the United States defeated Spain in war and took over Cuba, Puerto Rico, and the Philippines as US colonies. Religious missionaries accompanied the troops abroad to convert "our little brown brothers" to Christianity, as one US president proclaimed. This imperial impulse, Williams explained, was active and visible again in the cold war deployments and other military intrusions abroad.

Williams's interpretation of American history radically upends the popular faith in American innocence. The American story, he contends, is not just about the search for freedom and justice. It is also a saga of conquest—new lands, new vistas—and the expansion of US territory nourishes the nation's prosperity and opportunity. Those who get in the way—starting with the indigenous peoples we call Native Americans—are dealt with harshly.

The Williams critique is compelling, and it is pointless to argue with the facts of our history. But American history and culture produced a countervailing story as well—the continuing struggles of Americans who opposed and resisted the imperial impulses and military adventurism of those in the higher echelons of power. These people were usually in the minority, but they were not always trampled. Again and again, they rallied in opposition by focusing on two issues—the practical consequences of wrongful wars and the nation's founding principles.

Abraham Lincoln was in Congress in the 1840s when he was among those denouncing the war against Mexico. The United States annexed the Philippines in 1898 in the face of fierce political opposition. An Anti-Imperialist League was founded by celebrated figures like Mark Twain, Andrew Carnegie, and Samuel Gompers, the American Federation of Labor leader. The cold war years, likewise, produced intense political opposition to US behavior abroad, including to the surrogate wars and CIA plots to kill or unseat foreign leaders. Popular resistance was expressed forcefully again on the war in Iraq, and rather swiftly it became the majority opinion, eventually dragging hesitant political leaders to reconsider their war making.

Williams, notwithstanding his harsh critique of the American past, was committed to optimism. We understand the past so that we may change the future, he wrote. The question for our time is whether, as a country, we have learned from the past. Or are we doomed to repeat the same bloody patterns until eventually the rest of the world forces us to stop?

We have changed as a people, though not yet as a nation. That is my conviction, and the confirming evidence is everywhere around us. This is why I reject the notion that the United States has evolved into an imperial state, that it is no longer a democracy. People in other nations have changed as well, and the commitment to humanitarian principles and a world without empires is now widely shared.

To be sure, most governing elites in the United States have not yet converted to the broad popular perspective of the American people and this remains another crucial breakdown in our weakened democracy. But this story is unfinished and still unfolding. It represents a central challenge in the restoration of representative democracy. War and peace can be resolved in sensible, progressive terms, once people learn to assert themselves with force and reason.

Americans today did not sign up to build an empire, any more than our soldiers enlisted to fight an endless war for oil. If government officials privately consider themselves in charge of an empire, they had better not tell the people. Authorities well understand how deeply the people oppose the idea of empire. Imperialistic impulses are disguised with virtuous rationales like liberation, not subjugation, or spreading democracy. If the United States is now an empire, then why is this empire afraid to speak its name?

The values of contemporary Americans are not derived from the country's nineteenth-century brutal conquest of the Native Americans or the frequent Marine Corps invasions of small Central American countries or the CIA's illegal overthrowing of foreign governments. In fact, in conventional views of history, those events have been papered over as though they never happened.

The noble conception of our country's purpose endures in popular belief because it was inspired by the broad-shouldered, progressive America that saved the world from fascism in World War II. Americans were then strongly anticolonialist, and they still are today. Check the opinion polls if you doubt this. Americans overwhelmingly express the desire not to get into foreign wars, but rather to let international organizations like the United Nations act as mediators and peacekeeping forces. The American soldiers who fought and won World War II are now enshrined in the culture as the Greatest Generation. Some Americans observe the results in Iraq and ask where the greatness has gone.

If the United States is an empire, why does it keep losing wars? If the country is an imperial power intent upon gaining economic surplus from the rest of the world, then why has the global economy turned into a losing proposition for us? Above all, why doesn't the United States apply the full enormity of its military power with the fierce thoroughness expected of a real empire?

If the United States is supposed to be the new Rome, it is an incompetent version. I suggest that popular opinion's resistance to empire provides an answer to these questions. We have the equipment for empire, but the people lack the bloodthirsty enthusiasm. They are squeamish about inhumanities like torture. They do not want to be bullies and brutal conquerors. Some frustrated policy thinkers say we have "gone soft" or that we have lost our thirst for "national greatness."

Perhaps so. But I believe instead that we are maturing. Americans are gradually developing a more confident regard for the rest of the world, a more grown-up sense of what matters to us as a nation. The process of maturity is far from complete, but it is promising. The wrongful war in Iraq, launched after official propaganda promoted fear and hysteria, led to ordinary Americans learning, with sorrow and embarrassment, that other peoples in the world were shocked and disappointed by our nation's thuggish behavior. That is not who we are, we told ourselves, and not who we want to be. Americans are pragmatic people; we learn from experience, from the past. Now, we would like official America to do the same.

★ ★ ★ ★ ★

The United States can display the fullness of its awesome power, but it cannot use it. Our modern military machine certainly has the capacity to enforce imperial rule—the United States could bomb people back to the Stone Age if it chose—but that is not a real option, for either military or political leaders. As a nation, the United States wants to be both noble and tough, to use military force with some regard for human sensibilities. The war in Iraq instead has degraded our sense of American rectitude in numerous ways. These degradations turned the public against the war and explain why so many brave military people—officers and enlisted personnel—have raised their voices to expose inhumane practices or to condemn the ill-conceived strategy. Military people see themselves as honorable inheritors of the greatness and glory of World War II, which exemplified the generosity of US power. They too feel degraded by how this war was fought and lost its legitimacy.

The world's greatest military power keeps losing wars for a fairly straightforward reason: The United States does not go to war to win in the classic sense. Political leaders talk a lot about victory and offer changing definitions of what that will mean. But there is no "victory" in store for US forces that satisfies the traditional meaning—one side conquers, the other side loses.

When empires go to war, the purpose is neither vague nor complicated. They fight to win in old-fashioned terms—conquer, crush, destroy—and the objective normally is to secure two things—real estate and resources. Throughout history, this has always been case, though religious fervor and ethnic hatred often are mixed up as added motivations with the acquisition of real assets. The Romans (and Greeks before them) did not conquer other Mediterranean peoples to bring literature and law to backward tribes. They wanted land and colonies and, when they were victorious, they routinely slaughtered their male captives.

Instead, the United States goes to war on the cheap after calculating what it intends to accomplish, how much it is willing to expend. This is uncharacteristic of a self-confident empire. Imperial powers do not plan wars of limited purpose. They do not shy away from using their overwhelming firepower against poorer nations. Nor did the early United States push the Native Americans westward to "civilize" them. The commonly held belief in the nineteenth century was that those indigenous tribes were doomed and would vanish, as defeated cultures often have in the path of a conquering empire. Today, the Indian wars are understood more accurately as genocide—the attempted destruction of an entire people.

World War II changed the meaning of war profoundly, altering historic sensibilities and the basic standards by which nation-states relate to one another. We Americans changed, as well. Because the United States and its allies success-fully opposed the last great imperial wars of conquest, our victory led to new understandings. These new values have not taken over entirely, of course, but they are generally accepted. The victors did not slaughter the captive losers. They helped rebuild their societies and economies. The defeated empires were pun-ished for their crimes against humanity.

Hitler's aggression against Europe, both eastern and western, and Japan's colonization of East Asia were so unspeakably horrible that no one needed to question whether the United States and its allies had any subsidiary motives. The aggressors were war criminals who were tried and convicted, and many of them were executed. Nor did the US victors pillage the losers' assets and annex their real estate. Instead, new values arose from that great war. Those enlightened val-ues were strengthened considerably by the new threat of nuclear devastation. Total war was now unthinkable, and nations had to collaborate to ensure that it did not happen.

My point is that the United States' reluctance to fight a full-out war for real estate and resources is not simply a function of heightened American moral-ity, but rather because no great power can do this any longer. It will be broadly opposed if one of them tries. The United States brushed up against such objec-tions with its single-minded preemptive invasion of Iraq. Likewise, if the US invasion was really intended to acquire control of Iraq's oil, the United States had to deny that this was so. The allowable reasons for going to war have been circumscribed, even as the technologies for war have become far more lethal. The United States is not exempt from these new understandings, though it sometimes pretends it is.

When the United States goes to war now, it has to define goals that are more limited and more abstract. The purpose, of course, is always broadly described as "national defense." But the actual conduct of the war itself is usually distant from the logic of defense and involves the chess game of great powers contesting for influence. When the adversary has not directly attacked the United States, the United States has to find other reasons to confront it.

Why does the United States fight wars? To show others that it can; to send political messages, or to uphold diplomatic threats and promises; to spread democracy and "improve" foreign governments; to "shape the behavior" of other nations; to retain its credibility as a powerful nation that keeps its commitments; to intimidate troublesome nations before they become aggressive; to show the world it is willing and able to shed blood.

If the true objective is acquiring oil or real estate, the United States must conceal this from the world community and lie to its own citizens and soldiers. The United States draws a line on the map and goes to war if the wrong people cross it. The United States projects its own bellicose intentions onto rivals and then depicts them as evil or irrational. It says they want to "destroy American civilization" by blowing up our cities.

Once at war, the United States fights to defend its sacred honor, even when honor already has been lost. In Vietnam, the United States sought a negotiated peace that would allow it to exit. "Peace with honor," President Nixon called it. When the enemy would not agree to these terms, the United States bombed it again as a final gesture of diplomacy.

If we look back again at the failures—Korea, Vietnam, and Iraq—each of those wars had a mixture of these qualities. They were wars about statecraft and geopolitical abstractions, not territorial conquest, and therefore they lacked the concreteness necessary for traditional victory or defeat. The United States was not threatened in any direct way, but it saw the need to insert itself into civil wars or conflicts between other nations.

In every case, the US rationale for war was dependent upon complicated geopolitical premises and policy abstractions about what might happen to the "balance of power" if the United States failed to fight, what a malevolent dictator might attempt if the United States did not take him out first, how the lives of foreign peoples might be improved if we changed their government for them, and how changing a government through armed violence would enhance world peace.

Desert Storm, the first Iraq war, might seem like an exception because the United States achieved its limited objectives and brought the troops home. But that was not really the end, because the US war against Saddam continued on a less obvious plane. The Clinton administration continued vowing to remove Saddam from power. It imposed severe restrictions—US overflights of "no-fly zones" in northern and southern Iraq and periodic bombing, plus economic sanctions that inflicted harsh conditions upon Iraqi civilians. The strategy was designed to squeeze Iraq and bring about Saddam's fall. Though that didn't occur, Bill Clinton continued to portray Iraq as a monstrous threat to Americans. George W. Bush agreed and ordered his preemptive invasion.

In wars with limited objectives, the United States can't fully exert its superior firepower because it would be seen as disproportionate. In Vietnam, the United States bombed the North in an extraordinary blitzkrieg that exceeded the explosive tonnage expended in World War II. Yet the other side did not give up. The Vietnamese were fighting for the precious real estate of their own country, while the United States was fighting to prevent the consequences of the abstract domino theory, which held that Asian nations would fall to communism if North Vietnam was not defeated. Hanoi had a very tangible understanding of "victory." But what was Washington fighting for? The "balance of power."

The American goals in war are too complex for straightforward explanation. Evidence of this is the frequently changing rationales Bush offered for his war as he redefined "victory" again and again. But changing the terms of war creates impossible dilemmas for soldiers, especially if they are supposed to be enforcing order in the world.

Fighting "limited" wars sets up the US military to look incompetent. It can go only so far in the conflict, not all the way. It wins battles, but those victories swiftly lose their meaning because the troops are fighting to win a political point, not to capture the real estate and hold it.

If the objective is to change public opinion in enemy territory, aerial bombing becomes the preferred substitute for troops on the ground. Employing airpower against civilian populations is another form of terrorism, though American war planners describe it as pristine and mostly free of US casualties. High officials in Washington, and even some at the White House, get to pick the bombing targets they think promise maximum persuasion. War making is reimagined as a sophisticated form of pain management, wiping out discrete hot spots of disorder in the hope of making the whole function normally. Combat veterans know war is otherwise.

The confusion of purpose is why many Americans look back at the lost wars and question what might have been. All those thousands of dead bodies, but to what end? How exactly did those sacrifices make Americans or the world safer? The answers, like the reasons, are abstractions, but lost lives are not.

I am reminded of an angry complaint voiced by hard-right conservative politicians and bitterly frustrated retired generals during the war in Vietnam. They demanded to know "Why not victory?"

I remember thinking as a young reporter that their complaint seemed like a reasonable question. The right-wingers accused the Johnson administration of conducting the war with one hand tied behind our back. They were right, of course, and they never got much of an answer.

Some of those discontented conservatives wanted the United States to use nuclear bombs to resolve the matter, to decimate the Vietnamese and then send US troops northward to occupy Hanoi. That was what the United States had mistakenly attempted to do in North Korea. "Total victory" sounded good compared to incremental war fighting, but waging total war opens the door to nuclear exchanges in which everyone can be destroyed.

That way lies madness. This is the essential dilemma with fighting limited wars: When a great power goes to war to make a political point, victory in the authentic sense is not in the cards. Victory in real terms was never an option in Vietnam, nor is it one now in Iraq. The United States could flood Iraq with half a million troops and bomb every town and village to rubble. If that failed, it could double the devastation. That still would not achieve an outcome Americans might recognize as a victory. More likely, it would amount to national disgrace.

Here is the real question: When should this nation go to war, and for what purpose? What do Americans regard as justifiable reasons for war? What objectives do they think are unworthy and unreasonable?

For obvious reasons, neither political parties nor the military institution can preside over this discussion. It has to be organized by the people themselves, including those in the military. For the good of the country, we need an interlude of honest conversation, a great debate before the momentum generated by military plans and posturing pulls us into the next war.

I have become something of a "fundamentalist" on the question. Wars should not be fought at all unless they absolutely must be, and if they are fought, they must be won. Do not go to war, in other words, unless genuine victory is the only acceptable option and policy makers are committed to allocating the resources necessary to achieve it. Anything less is political gamesmanship that uses citizens and soldiers as expendable pawns to make a point. I am not a pacifist. Some wars in history have been necessary and righteous. If the United States is attacked, of course it must respond with whatever force is needed to prevail. But Americans should be vigilant and deeply skeptical about attacking enemies concocted by ignorant politicians or manipulative intelligence agencies.

Wars are not chess games. I want the establishment of a standard that puts an end to the careless bluffing, secret war making, and false claims of "national honor" that have drawn us into wrongful and stupid wars. The standard must severely limit the acceptable conditions for war and bring a complete halt to the half-baked conflicts that end in dishonorable failure.

When armies are needed to enforce peace among previously warring nations, the task properly belongs to the United Nations or regional alliances (the same view a majority of Americans have repeatedly expressed). The United States can contribute to such efforts, but not unilaterally. In the past, the United States has not been particularly effective or selfless in its motives when it has chosen sides in civil wars. Because of Iraq, it will be quite some time before the United States will again be trusted when it unilaterally declares the need for preemptive invasion.

Even the so-called humanitarian wars are suspect in my mind, first because there is nothing humanitarian about war making, and second because these interventions are inevitably highly selective and politicized. Amid all the world's suffering and cruelties, where do missionaries want to send the troops? If you look around the world, there are dozens of examples of people caught in brutal tribal conflicts or being abused by tyrannical governments. Shall we make a list of the worst ten or twenty and intervene in each one?

I am not insensitive to the killings and violence in Darfur, for instance, but I am skeptical of applying the genocide label to justify intervening in Sudan. Is genocide also present in neighboring Somalia, where the conditions of oppression and starvation are at least as severe? The United States has even contributed to that nation's misery by bombing it and installing a brutal, unstable government. At the risk of offending people of conscience, I wonder if some Americans charging genocide in one African country may be displacing our own guilt over having slaughtered innocents elsewhere. Killing is killing. The United States has done quite a lot of it over the years, whatever the motives and methods.

My goal is to see established a standard that makes it far more difficult for the United States to go to war, but accepts that if a war must be fought, genuine victory will be pursued. This proposition might provide a starting point from which warriors and antiwar citizens can look for common ground. Unless Americans engage each other with these questions and develop commonsense answers, the nation may not be able to rid itself of the bloated militarism and the poisonous cycle that follows failed wars. The military has a special stake in breaking out of that cycle. When generals send soldiers off to fight in wrongful wars, their honor is also lost.

★ ★ ★ ★ ★

The most promising development in military matters is the rebellion among generals (and colonels and sergeants) that became an important factor in the political contest over Iraq. An astonishing insurgency unfolded inside the government, one that was slyly managed by career military officers and senior civil servants who were desperate to introduce some truth amid the White House propaganda. They bravely countered and contradicted what the commander in chief and some of their own military leaders were telling the public. Some of the rebels remained anonymous, generating embarrassing news by passing along to reporters government documents that exposed the duplicity and incompetence of the Bush administration. Others retired early from the armed services and went public with what they knew, sacrificing their careers to warn the country of grave misdeeds and wrongheaded policies.

I call them "embedded patriots" because they stepped forward to tell the truth when major media outlets and opposition politicians were meekly going along with Bush's confused war making. "It's a wonderful country in a way," veteran *Washington Post* investigative reporter Walter Pincus told me. "People in the government community are really concerned about what can happen. They get upset with themselves when they see things going wrong. So they are willing to raise questions. But I also think for some the failure to stand up before the war started is emboldening them now."[3]

Richard J. Whalen, a conservative Republican and high-level insider during the Nixon years, wrote an illuminating article for the *Nation* called "Revolt of the Generals." Whalen is close to a number of retired generals, former intelligence officers, and Pentagon officials and aides. He explained that senior military leaders who were junior officers during Vietnam were determined not to remain silent, as their superior officers had three decades ago. "'For our generation,'" a retired major general told him, "'Iraq will be Vietnam with the volume turned way up.'"[4]

Active-duty officers, Whalen reported, "are working behind the scenes to end the war and are preparing for the inevitable US withdrawal." Retired officers of higher rank, meanwhile, hope to become a "potentially powerful factor" in future political debate by "publically opposing reckless civilian warmaking in advance."

This development—old generals getting active in politics—may disturb some, but I find it hopeful and promising. It suggests that the narrowly confined national security debate can be refocused to address the broader realities and practical questions. When so many speak up, it means that although the military's sense of honor may have been damaged, it will not be silenced. Their dissenting voices could start discussions that open the way for fundamental reform of how and why this nation goes to war.

Those who worry that this might mean there is a politicized military are a bit late with that concern. The military institution is already politicized, not in electioneering, but in the broader sphere of determining foreign policy by coaching Congress and presidents, who defer to the military's open-ended appetites. US politics has always been enamored of military heroes. Twelve generals have been elected president, starting with George Washington. Most were undistinguished as political leaders, but not any more bellicose than other commanders in chief.

Dwight Eisenhower was a distinctive exception. Perhaps because he had been the allied commander who won World War II, Ike as president was a well-informed (and well-loved) skeptic of military ambitions. He was wary of the generals' more extravagant ideas and rejected, for instance, the use of nuclear weapons or US entry into the war in Indochina. Eisenhower tamped down defense spending during his tenure and famously warned the country of the danger lurking in the "military-industrial complex." Other presidents who followed him—notably John F. Kennedy and Richard Nixon—served as junior officers during World War II. In the White House, they were far more deferential to the general officers who had outranked them in uniform.

If Americans are to rescue themselves from militarism, we will need experienced warriors among the active agitators for reform—authoritative critics who can spell out the danger of bloated military commitments and show the people plausible ways out of the predicament. Enlisted personnel have a story to tell, as well. Perhaps somewhere among the critics are political voices who will argue, like Eisenhower, for realism and restraint.

What I envision is a "popular formation" of citizens dedicated to confronting US militarism. It would not be an "issues" movement in the familiar sense or a political party as such, but rather a loose assembly of citizens committed to the same broad goal or goals, regardless of whatever else divides them. It is perhaps too much to hope that military types and peaceniks could meet in the same hall to air their views, but they could at least learn to respect each other and coordinate their political actions when they seek a common solution. If such a formation could acquire the scale and skills to act collectively, it could be a political force that might change the agenda for elected politicians. The members could also find ways to punish unresponsive politicians of all parties, or even present their own reform candidates for office.

My discussion of formations is stimulated in part by novelist Walter Mosley's slender book on democratic revival, *Life Out of Context*. Mosley's primary vision involves restoring black Americans to active citizenship and collective political power, but the concept has nearly universal application. A formation organized to counter militarism would be one among many. I return to the possibilities of this device and others later in the book.[5]

Confronting militarism is without question the most difficult challenge in reviving our decayed democracy. Governing elites are incapacitated by either fear or conformity and obedient to the primacy of militarization regardless of their partisan or ideological differences. They are elected representatives, but they are unable to speak candidly about their doubts. Therefore, people must learn to speak for themselves.

An antimilitarism formation would both teach the public about the military reality and confront the political order with tough demands and nagging intrusions. Think of it as a guerilla force organizing to take on a much larger army. Nonviolence is the operating principle for this kind of politics, but the objective is to disrupt and discomfit the status quo to compel it to change.

To develop real leverage (that is, power), people must learn again how to act like citizens, not supplicants. A formation has to be freestanding and independent of established political institutions, aloof from both parties and willing to threaten them with reprisals. But first, its adherents have to develop their own rough consensus—what they will fight for—with no central command handing down instructions.

To move politics and incumbent politicians, citizens have to invent ways to induce fear and insecurity within the comfortable and complacent regular order. That is, they need to demonstrate that people associated with the formation have a real ability to cut short political careers. The initial challenge is not so much to acquire a majority in Congress or to capture the White House, but to instill a general dread of the formation's power in established political circles.

The best way to alter the views of the incumbent members of Congress, in my experience, is to defeat a handful of their colleagues—blindsiding them when they have not taken citizen demands seriously. Other incumbents will get the message and want to avoid the same fate.

Despite having dissenters among their members, both political parties are, in practice, united in a "war party" that supports and finances militarism. Most voters are unaware of this complicity in aggressive war making because they have bought into the distorted rhetoric of national security politics. This is one of the things that freestanding citizens have to change by targeting and picking off the most vulnerable politicians first, then advancing on the leaders who are militarism's enablers. This kind of politics requires both patience and stubbornness, as well as a refusal to settle for phony gains.

In his book *The New American Militarism*, Andrew Bacevich, the former Army colonel, provides a valuable text for thinking about reform. Although not all military dissenters agree with his proposals and principles, his moderate blueprint is a good starting place for the discussion. Militarism, he observes, flourishes with the passive consent of both politicians and people.

Reforming the military means reducing its size and reach, but above all, it means restoring it to its original purpose—defending the nation, not searching for new enemies and the next war. "View force as a last resort," Bacevich wrote. "Organize US forces explicitly for national defense.[6]

"Focusing on defense rather than power projection," Bacevich explained, "implies jettisoning the concept of 'national security,' an artifact of the Cold War and employed as a device to justify everything from overthrowing foreign governments to armed intervention in places most Americans could not locate on a map."

Among other things, this will allow maintenance of a considerably smaller military force—"shedding unnecessary obligations . . . bringing US troops home from stations abroad where an immediate need for their presence no longer exists, withdrawing from the vast 'empire of bases.'" As Bacevich wrote, it also means repealing the Bush doctrine of preemptive war and dumping the open-ended ambitions for sustaining a global war on terrorism.

"Drawing down US overseas garrisons may or may not save money, but [it will] reduce the prospects of the United States getting dragged into a conflict in which its own interests are marginal or altogether non-existent," he explained.

This shift in US commitments would compel allied nations to share the costs of self-defense instead of letting American taxpayers pick up the tab. But it will also require US leaders to treat allies "as partners rather than vassals," in Bacevich's words.

Much of Bacevich's agenda requires political reforms that are beyond the Pentagon's reach. He proposes restoring the separation of powers and the decision-making role of Congress, enhancing the alternative instruments of state-craft and foreign policy, and "[reviving] the moribund concept of the citizen-soldier," not by restoring the draft, but by returning Reserve and National Guard troops to their traditional focus on domestic concerns and community self-defense. As I explained earlier, this is fertile ground for national reconciliation. The armed forces have much to learn, but they also have much to teach the country.

Provoked by Bush's go-it-alone war, many hopeful dissenters have presented initiatives for reforming the political system that call for moving away from a unipolar world with a single superpower and toward a multipolar world in which decision making is shared among many nations. Both policy scholars and leading Democrats are calling for diplomacy that at least reestablishes contact and con-versation with our presumed adversaries. They promote using US aid and diplo-macy in a manner that is more like China's supple approach to winning friends.

This would be real progress. Yet the rhetoric will not be convincing if the advocates are unwilling to take on the military's outsize role in shaping foreign policy. With few exceptions, the advocates for revived diplomacy either talk around that issue or fall silent altogether. Many politicians try to have it both ways by endorsing the military's open-ended designs while also urging the use of softer, more sensitive diplomacy.

This is an elementary evasion. As a practical matter, military action trumps "soft power." So long as the Pentagon gets all the money it wants or needs for its ill-defined Long War, the Pentagon will dominate US foreign policy. If the military continues to pursue an undeclared war for oil and demands to have permanent bases in Iraq, or to make little wars in Africa, foreign governments are unlikely to be convinced that much has changed. They ask, For what purpose does the United States wish to keep troops in Iraq for the indefinite future? The answer is either to control Iraq's oil spigot or to keep it out of other hands.[7]

The oil problem will not be solved by military power or adventures in foreign lands. It will only be solved at home. The debate has at least begun in higher political circles about the industrial reforms that will be needed to shift the economy to alternative fuels and less wasteful methods of production and consumption. But the efforts will not get serious until the United States realizes that the military institution is the wrong agent for solving this historic challenge.

Bacevich does not try to estimate how much his ideas for downsizing the armed forces might reduce military spending, but he proposes a new way of calculating how much is enough. War advocates say the answer is simple—more money next year than last, more or less in perpetuity. Bacevich's is a modest alternative: In the absence of any great-power adversary, the US defense budget could simply match the combined military spending of the ten next-biggest military powers.

That is hardly a radical proposition. The US defense budget has constituted 46 to 48 percent of the world's total military spending in recent years. The closest rivals spend no more than 4 or 5 percent of the world's total. By my rough calculation, Bacevich's approach would mean cutting the Pentagon budget by something like 20 to 30 percent, which is about $180 billion. In 2006, the Pentagon spent $529 billion, compared to the $382 billion spent by the next ten nations. Over the last ten years, worldwide spending on military forces grew by one-third. The United States accounted for 80 percent of that increase.[8]

The United States is conducting an arms race with itself, and there is no end in sight. Actually, the United States is losing the arms race with itself: The sole superpower is compelled to spend more and more each year, not because of its imagined opponents, but thanks to its own plans and projects.

More than two dozen new and very expensive weapons systems, armaments that prepare us to fight another world war, are in development or early production. The plan is to expand US ground forces in case another regional war or two begins somewhere. China and Russia are rearming modestly, as is Japan. But no one can possibly catch up with the Pentagon, which, as Bacevich observed, is surpassing its old cold war budgets. Yet even so, the military does not have enough money to do what it says must be done.

In fact, Defense Department leaders are warning Congress that its budget—pumped up to fight two wars simultaneously—will have to remain at that elevated level after the war in Iraq is over. Admiral Mike Mullen, chairman of the Joint Chiefs of Staff, called a press conference with defense secretary Robert Gates in October 2007 to deliver the bad news. Mullen is the former chief of naval operations who expressed such enthusiasm for the Long War strategies outlined in the *Quadrennial Defense Review Report*.

"'I think as a country we're just going to have to devote more resources to national security in the world that we're living in right now,'" the admiral warned. "'And I don't do that lightly.'" Mullen added, "'I recognize that the budget is higher now than it's ever been.'" But, he said, more money is needed to repair and replace the weapons worn out or destroyed in combat zones, to refocus on risks in Africa and the Pacific Rim, and to take care of military personnel and their families.[9]

Given the competing claims, even inflated defense budgets will not be able to cover all the costs. George C. Wilson, defense columnist for *National Journal* and for many years a legendary Pentagon correspondent for the *Washington Post*, explained why. The rising price tags on new weapons systems are combining with the rising costs of people—providing for the health care, pensions, and other benefits for the men and women in uniform.

More and bigger weapons, or fewer people in the armed forces? The fiscal implication, Wilson wrote, is that the Pentagon will be forced to choose, roughly speaking, between the people and the war machines. Wilson predicts that, despite the congressional decision to add 90,000 troops to the rolls, "a bigger budget means . . . a smaller force."[10]

The war machine may likewise preempt domestic priorities. The cost of war making has never become a potent issue in US politics. During the cold war, liberal critics tried again and again to explain the wastefulness and contrasted the military's wish list for new spending with the country's other needs. How many new schools, hospitals, or roads could be built, they asked, if the United States did not spend hundreds of billions of dollars on new weapons it did not need? These comparisons never had much traction with voters. If forced to choose between domestic priorities and protecting the country, people typically opt for national defense, whatever it costs.

However, this familiar preference will be challenged in new ways by approaching events. The United States' indebtedness to foreign governments will be grossly enlarged if the nation tries to finance record defense budgets and significant domestic improvements at the same time. The old debate about "guns versus butter" will be renewed on fiercer terms. If they cannot have both, people and politicians may have to decide which they really want.

Given the public's disenchantment with the war in Iraq, voters are likely to be hostile to new military expeditions, at least for a time. Governing elites, on the other hand, are targeting the most important entitlement programs for budget cuts as their solution to the fiscal problems. "Reform" to them means whacking the benefits people have been promised by the government. Would Americans prefer to cut Medicare, Medicaid, and Social Security, or would they rather cut the defense budget? If people understand the choice in those terms, the Pentagon will be squaring off against much stronger adversaries in domestic politics.

Putting the choice that starkly, however, assumes that ordinary Americans have something to say about the matter. Normally, they do not. The media and policy thinkers typically obscure the meaning and declare the "responsible" choice to be shrinking social guarantees in order to replenish the machinery of war. Political leaders may try to work out a bipartisan agreement—both parties acting together—to cut people's benefits so neither party can be held solely responsible.

This could turn into one of those situations when an independent formation of well-prepared citizens could make a real difference by explaining the trade-off in plain English. Voters could then rally in opposition and put the members of the "war party" on notice that they would not escape retribution.

Anxiety and anger are agents of reform. Both are widespread in the general population at present. People's distrust of as-usual politics is very high. People are eager for change—big change—if they can see a way to achieve it. Many citizens doubt it is possible.

In the next chapter, I turn to the domain that is the core anxiety for ordinary Americans—the deteriorating conditions of their lives and prospects, the encroaching doubts about what lies ahead for their children and grandchildren. I cannot describe easy, overnight solutions to these problems, which they are deeply grounded in the deformed economic system, and in society and politics. But I can describe great possibilities for deep reform. For better or worse, the country is in the beginning stages of making difficult adjustments and a profound transformation.

In crisis lies opportunity, but there is no guarantee that this political opening to remake America in more promising terms will be realized. Standing in the way is the dysfunctional democracy and a political system severely distorted by the influence of concentrated power. The Republican Party has been punished dramatically for its failures. But that is not the end of our challenge. The confusion of democracy is a bipartisan failure.

CHAPTER TEN

THE END OF THE
CONSERVATIVE ERA

merica has arrived at a critical political juncture that seems confusing
and threatening, but also hints of promising changes to come. The conservative economic doctrine that has governed the country for a generation and
reshaped society in many harsh ways is collapsing, though not yet fully dis-
lodged. We are witnessing the dying groans of a political ideology. The market-
first theory failed as a governing regime essentially for practical reasons. It did
not deliver what it promised—reliable and widely shared prosperity.

Government was pushed to the side, disabled, and purposefully starved for
revenue, and essential functions were privatized. Private enterprise and financial
markets were empowered to decide large, public questions free of the constraints
of rules and supervision. Yet this did not lead to Morning Again in America, as
Ronald Reagan's warm-hearted campaign slogan promised.

Some people have prospered fantastically, but most Americans do not feel
liberated by the free market. Their lives are instead ensnared in the stresses and
strains of encroaching losses, of economic insecurity, stagnating incomes, and
the fear of falling. The national economy has not achieved the high plateau of
prosperity. Instead, it is sinking deeper and deeper into debt. These and other
practical contradictions explain the deep ideological shift that is underway.
Long-reigning convictions are in free fall.

This is a momentous turn of events for the nation. It amounts to good news
for those of us who believe the conservative order has gravely damaged the country. We, the people, have an opportunity to think anew. It gives Americans the

chance to reimagine what our society can look like if an era of progressive reform confronts the accumulating disorders and develops new governing principles.

The bad news, of course, is that no coherent alternative presently exists. The old order is falling, but there is no governing agenda ready to replace it. On the contrary, most politicians, even those in opposition, seem shy and intimidated by the uncertain political circumstances, reluctant to think in terms of big ideas. Neither party appears to grasp the full, awesome dimensions of what the nation now faces. The vacuum of ideas is unlikely be filled by risk-averse Washington insiders. That is why citizens must rally to force change upon the status quo. With their distance from power, outsiders see the big picture more clearly.

A governing ideology collapses when it no longer addresses the disorders disturbing the country, when it provides no answers for the questions people are asking; it is a rare event, one that comes along in American politics only every thirty or forty years. No one announces it in the *New York Times*. The shift will not be recognized as newsworthy until the accumulated facts have already made it obvious to most people.

The last time something like this occurred was in the 1970s, when economic liberalism lost its way and eventually broke down. The liberal ranks— somewhat like today's right-wing true believers—reflexively adhered to governing principles they had inherited from the New Deal, but those assumptions no longer matched the nation's changed economic circumstances or addressed its new disorders—price inflation, stagnant growth, and lifeless stock prices. The dynamic postwar prosperity fostered by the New Deal came to an end. The liberal order ended with it.

Unwilling to question orthodoxy, too cozy and complacent from their long stay in power, liberals could not figure out how to respond to the new economic realities and make timely adjustments in the governing agenda. Democrats fumbled in confusion for several years while conditions worsened, and then liberals began to retreat grudgingly on one major issue after another. Liberalism's collapse was announced with a thunderclap—the 1980 landslide election of Ronald Reagan. Unlike in today's implosion of the Republican Party, a concrete alternative was waiting to replace liberalism. For two decades, the conservative movement had been developing its ferocious critique of liberalism and a set of governing principles that would fundamentally dismantle forty years of liberal politics: a smaller, less powerful federal government, and a private sector free of Washington's meddling regulation and taxation. Conservatives described their agenda as a restoration of freedom, of "getting government off our backs," and the theme resonated persuasively with popular anger and disappointments on many fronts. Government had failed. People were ready for something different.

Thirty years later, Republicans have been rattled by the loss of power, but are still clinging to old bromides. Like generals stuck in an intractable war, conservatives cannot win unless they change strategies, and they cannot change without betraying the faith. That does not mean they will fade away gracefully, any more than liberals did in similar circumstances.

The market-first doctrine is dysfunctional, but it remains in place and powerful because so many influentials in high places still believe in it. The presumptions that favor the marketplace over government are deeply embedded in law, politics, the media, the judiciary, and the economic system. Besides, powerful interests in industry and finance have a huge stake in keeping the dogma alive. They are among its principal beneficiaries.

Politics is muddled for the moment. One major party looks backward with nostalgia for its faded glory, and the other party lacks a confident vision for the future. A normal transition between eras, one that unfolds gradually as both parties adapt, is what you might expect to happen. But we are not in normal times. The nation is at a historic turning point that is not quite like anything that has come before. Those in the political system tend not to talk about this, though I am sure some politicians understand it. Who among them would want to announce the eclipse of American power and the loss of American innocence?

While America is in this vulnerable condition, forces have converged to deepen the national predicament, threatening to overwhelm the political system's weakened capacities. Neither party wants to deal head-on with the consequences of globalization. Neither is willing to oppose the dangers presented by the nation's overreaching military commitments. Meanwhile, the financial crisis and the ever-growing income inequalities demand dramatic interventions from Washington. And an even larger reckoning may be at hand with the twin threats of global warming and the approaching scarcity of oil added to the mix. Washington is not ready for all of this.

The federal government has deliberately been weakened by the right-wing ideologues in power, many of whom detest government and were pleased to see it fail. They routinely ignored established laws and federal obligations, like protecting the environment and policing corporate malfeasance. The party of business proved to be incompetent managers of the country, whether they were fighting a war or rescuing New Orleans from catastrophe.

Democrats should by nature be more conscientious governing stewards since they are the party of big government and do believe in it. On the other hand, contemporary Democrats see themselves mainly as responsible managers rather than reformers. Many have internalized the market-first ideology and support its basic tenets. Most leading Democrats do not seem convinced that deep reform is what the country needs or people want. Their hesitation could change if conditions get a lot worse, but the undertow of conventional wisdom and the influence of entrenched private interests work against major political change.

★　★　★　★　★

The conservative order basically produced more of two things—billionaires and borrowing. The United States accumulated record amounts of debt along with spectacular heaps of personal wealth. In 1982, when *Forbes* magazine first published its annual list of the four hundred richest Americans, there were only thirteen billionaires among them. Twenty-five years later, the Forbes 400 consisted entirely of billionaires. Eighty-two billionaires were left off the 2007 list because they were not rich enough to make the cut.

Meanwhile, earnings for working people have changed hardly at all. In 1982, as author Holly Sklar explained, the average wage for full-time workers was $34,199 in 2006 dollars. Twenty-five years later, it was $34,861.[1]

This great divergence in fortunes explains why families have had to take on extraordinary levels of debt as they try to stay afloat and keep up with mortgage payments when their incomes are no longer rising. They borrow to hold on to their standard of living. In 2005, US household savings went negative—people spent more than they earned—for the first time since 1933. In 2007, households took on another $1 trillion in borrowing. During the first seven years of George W. Bush's presidency, family debt expanded by $7 trillion—a virtual doubling.[2]

One place from which people borrow heavily is their own savings—the equity they have built up in their homes by paying down their mortgages. At the dawn of the Reagan era, American home owners owned 70 percent of the value of their homes (with the remainder still owed to the mortgages' issuers). Toward the end of Bush II's second term, home owner equity fell below 50 percent and was heading lower.

This snapshot of weakened debtors and wealthy winners conveys the human drama of the widening income inequalities stimulated by a generation of conservative doctrine. The top 1 percent of earners—primarily from the financial sector—has doubled its share of the national income since 1985. It now gets 21 percent—more than one-fifth of all income. That is to say that 1 million or so people get more than the 68 million people on the bottom half of the income ladder. Basically, those at the top lend their surplus to the debtors down below.[3]

The federal government is in roughly the same fix, thanks to the conservative order's distinctive approach to fiscal policy. Drastically cutting taxes for businesses and those in the upper income brackets while pumping up federal spending has led to huge budget deficits. Cutting taxes further while fighting costly wars has compelled Washington to borrow trillions more.

George W. Bush added $3 trillion to the federal debt, but it was Ronald Reagan who invented the politics. In Reagan's first year as president, the federal debt passed $1 trillion for the first time in US history. The federal debt has since reached $9 trillion, despite the intervening years of fiscal restraint Bill Clinton and the Democrats imposed in the 1990s.

All this borrowing caused the financial sector to expand spectacularly, since it is the intermediary between lenders and borrowers. An economist friend sourly refers to Wall Street as the debt industry. He has a point. As nuts-and-bolts manufacturing receded in US economic life, finance capital claimed the space. Financial deregulation took the brakes off banking and finance by doing away with limits on interest rates and laws against usury, for example, so profits soared and financiers invented esoteric new ways to lend and borrow.

Between the debtor government and the debtor consumers, the US economic engine is essentially running on fumes—the borrowed money we get from foreign creditors—and no easy vehicle for correction is in sight. Republicans could have raised taxes along the way to better balance the economy, but that ideological heresy would have enraged the monied interests that finance the GOP.

Despite scolding from economists, most consumers cannot boost the level of their savings without forfeiting their standard of living. If families stop borrowing to spend, they will essentially have to accept the diminished circumstances they have struggled so hard to avoid. And more to the point, if consumers are compelled to pull back, some experts fear the US economy is likely to tank. Consumption now accounts for a record 72 percent of GDP. Reducing that to a normal figure of about 65 percent will leave a huge hole in aggregate demand. Who's around to fill it?

Most Americans, I feel sure, see our predicament as an economic failure, and so do I. Any governing regime that cannot produce a stable prosperity that is generally attainable by the broad middle class is not likely to last. Sooner or later, the majority will lose patience with the false promises and look for something else. That shift began with the 2006 elections, when Democrats won slim congressional majorities, and was dramatically confirmed in 2008, but it still awaits definition.

Some distraught Republicans, alarmed by the implications, are urging their party to return to its core values of fiscal responsibility and smaller government to win back majority control of the legislature. Their nostalgia betrays a complete misunderstanding of the nature of the modern conservative movement. The New Right that came to power with Ronald Reagan never sought balanced budgets or smaller government, except as rhetorical flourishes. Fiscal responsibility was never their guiding principle. Ignoring unbalanced budgets, indeed, may have been one of their secrets to winning elections.

Once in power, the modern Republican Party pursued a far more radical objective—remaking American society by returning the federal government to an earlier era when it was much smaller and weaker. The Right literally set out to roll back the twentieth century. They wanted to return Washington to the time before Franklin Roosevelt and the New Deal Democrats constructed a big government endowed with powers to intervene and manage the national economy. The GOP agenda was reactionary by definition, as some principled right-wingers frankly acknowledged. Conservatives felt sincerely that they were liberating America from the error known as the New Deal.

Governing power, the Right explained, should be returned to private hands, to business enterprises and the holders of capital who had been cut down to size by liberals. Regulatory controls on businesses and markets should be repealed or eviscerated. Liberal social programs, including the vastly popular Social Security system, should be dismantled. As much of government as possible should be privatized, with essential functions handed off to profit-seeking firms. Corporate management should rescind its part of the "social contract" and cancel its obligations to employees and communities. Labor unions, the fiercest opposers of these ideas, should be hammered.

All of these initiatives were more or less successful, and in different ways, they caused economic rewards to move upward on the ladder. Basically, power and income shifted from labor to capital, from workers' paychecks to the employers' bottom lines, from consumers' needs to corporate profits, and from serving the broad public interest to enhancing the personal benefits for corporate shareholders.

The Right's core complaint, however, was taxation. Its central goal was to dismantle the progressive income tax that had efficiently financed big government. It had done so essentially by redistributing incomes in a way that served the collective general welfare—taxing the relative few at the top of the income pyramid at a much higher rate than the broad population with moderate incomes. Conservatives insisted that the graduated income tax was unjust, and they set out to flatten the rate structure for both the wage income of the wealthy and the income derived from capital assets like stocks and bonds (once known as unearned income because it is not derived from work).

Reagan himself seldom put it so bluntly, but movement conservatives candidly discussed their long-term goal of eliminating the income tax. They want to replace it with a single flat tax rate on consumption, a kind of national sales tax that would naturally hit those among the lower income ranks the hardest. The Right's first objectives were to bring down the highest rates for the wealthy and provide generous tax relief to businesses.

But the Reaganites faced a monumental political problem. How could they persuade ordinary Americans that cutting taxes for the rich would be good for them or for the country? The idea sounded a lot like the "trickle down" economics Republicans had preached in the 1920s—reward the wealthy and their gains will eventually trickle down to others. At the same time, economists were warning that massive tax cuts would generate huge federal deficits since Reagan also planned to double the defense budget.

The Republican old guard was alarmed by the prospect—huge budget deficits signaled fiscal irresponsibility to them—but the aggressive new generation of Reagan conservatives fractiously challenged their elders. Republicans would forever be the minority party, the Right argued, so long as they adhered to what the Right called the "root canal" economics of demanding balanced budgets. Why should big-spending Democrats have all the fun, they wondered. The Democrats' tax-and-spend politics had won elections and created loyal constituencies. But the right-wing upstarts had their own strategy for winning elections—cut taxes *and* spend more.

A new and somewhat magical theory dubbed supply-side economics emerged to solve the political problem. It said, Don't worry about budget deficits, they will only be temporary. Cutting income tax rates across all income levels, the supply-siders explained, would actually increase federal revenue. The tax reduction for working stiffs would be trivial compared to that for the wealthy, but that would give them an incentive to work harder and make more money. The well-to-do and wealthy would invest their tax windfalls in stocks and other financial assets, thereby financing expanded industrial production for the "supply side" of the economy. That would lead to greater output and profit, more jobs and work, and larger personal incomes. Bingo! People in prosperity would pay more taxes and the government would collect more revenue than it lost from cutting taxes.

Do you believe in miracles? Politicians in Congress evidently did. Nearly all of them, all but a handful of dissenting Democrats, voted to implement this dubious logic. Most Democrats were intimidated by Reagan's popularity, but they were also eager to cut taxes. When it was finally passed, the tax bill was overstuffed with budget-busting corporate goodies and bizarre new loopholes proposed by both parties. Republican Senate majority leader Howard Baker called it a "riverboat gamble."

The supply-side illusion was squelched abruptly. Two months after passage, Reagan's budget director, David Stockman, announced that the government was facing huge budget deficits "as far as the eye can see." Stockman also debunked the supply-side theory as convenient sleight-of-hand. The massive tax cut "was always a Trojan horse to bring down the top rate," Stockman confessed in my *Atlantic Monthly* article "The Education of David Stockman." The supply-side theory simply provided cover for the hoary Republicanism of trickle-down economics. "It's kind of hard to sell 'trickle down,'" Stockman told me, "so the supply-side formula was the only way to get a tax policy that was really 'trickle down.'"[4]

Reagan Republicans won their political gamble, notwithstanding the failed theory. The conservatives were marketing a new version of "feel good" politics, and it worked for them. They were not punished at election time for regressively cutting taxes by rewarding capital, corporations, and the wealthy instead of the broad population. Working people were told the tax cuts were for them, so ordinary folks could keep more of their money instead of letting the government spend it. George W. Bush added new tax cuts to the pile every year.

But the country lost the "riverboat gamble" in economic terms. Under Republican rule, federal revenues never caught up with federal spending. The principal source of the current $9 trillion in federal debt was the gap between taxes and spending. Aside from new weapons systems, very little of the accumulated debt built anything new and productive. It mostly wound up in bank accounts as private profits.

Running large budget deficits and accumulating debt is not itself necessarily harmful to the country. It depends on how the government spends the money. World War II, for instance, was an era of epic federal deficits and debt, but it also fueled the most dramatic economic advance in our history. Washington used the borrowed money to invest in the national economy by financing new technologies and production that spawned six or eight new industrial sectors. This provided the platform for the long-running postwar prosperity.

Now, Washington looks a lot like those indebted families who are living beyond their means. Both essentially borrow to live month to month, using the money to consume rather than invest. Like debt-soaked households, government can do this for quite a long time—at least until the creditors decide the United States is no longer a good risk. The difference is that the government has a way out, at least in theory. It can raise taxes, restore revenues, and bring back the progressive income tax. It could also wipe out the multitude of tax gimmicks and loopholes that now litter the corrupted US tax code.

★　★　★　★　★

Among the many remarkable things about this era is that both political parties have drifted away from their ideological moorings. While the GOP was running up unprecedented debt, the Democratic Party switched roles with Republicans and became the party of fiscal discipline. That required Democrats, the inheritors of New Deal liberalism, to adopt the root-canal economics Reagan Republicans had just discarded. Railing about the deficits, the Democrats in power imposed tight limits on domestic spending and even briefly achieved a balanced budget under Bill Clinton.

To embrace this shift in values, however, Democrats had to abandon a core legacy of liberal governance—the importance of public investment. Liberals had invested public money not only in public infrastructure works like roads, bridges, schools, and hospitals, but also in the kinds of forward-looking government initiatives that had famously fostered technological breakthroughs and launched new industries ranging from the Internet to nuclear power. Government's role in the liberal view was as a financier of ideas and projects that private capital wouldn't touch because they looked too risky or insufficiently profitable. The abandonment of that government role over the last generation has crippled the country's infrastructure and its technological advancement. Collapsing bridges are one symptom of the neglect. But Washington also denied funding for long-range industrial research and development that might help us address major problems like global warming. The one exception is military hardware; public capital still flows freely for its development.

Democrats pursuing a policy of "fiscal responsibility" experienced what Republicans had learned before them: Rigid budget discipline sounds righteous, but it is the enemy of an activist government. It forecloses the creative initiatives that can reshape the future. Wearing the hair shirt of reduced spending is not much fun for politicians, and it's also not especially popular with voters. When asked, people say they want balanced budgets, but what they really expect is that government will take action to solve problems. Years and years of antigovernment propaganda have not changed that.

Those who determine the Democratic Party platform did not execute the rightward turn at the behest of their constituents. They did it on the advice of Wall Street and, indeed, had to quash the resistance of many liberal rank-and-file Democrats. The shift began in the early 1980s with coaching from Robert Rubin, later Clinton's treasury secretary, who came to government from Goldman Sachs and returned to private life as chairman of Citigroup. Not coincidentally, the party was at the same time allying itself much more closely with the financial sector, cultivating these new friends as major donors of campaign money and as conservative counselors on how to best govern the economy.

The point is that both major parties changed on the fundamentals. Despite their substantial differences, both moved toward the same broad objective—serving the elite sources of power, the people and firms that in earlier political eras were called the monied interests. Democrats became "responsible" managers who adhered to the conservative economic perspective of the bond market, as Rubin and others counseled them to do. Republicans became the borrow-and-spend fun guys who delivered the boodle to more or less the same clientele. In different ways, both parties turned their backs on these policies' economic consequences for the broader ranks of Americans.

The political system, media influentials tell us endlessly, has become dangerously polarized and is unable to work out reasonable compromises in a civil manner. I suppose this is true if they are referring to the head banging that takes place in Congress or the increasingly vicious smears used to caricature and demonize opponents. Governing elites, such as media influentials, want politicians to be "rational," like them.

I have a completely different view. In looking back over the politics of the last thirty years, I see bipartisan collusion and complicity on the biggest issues. Maybe that is why partisan friction is so intense on secondary issues that matter much less. Smart pols understand that they are ducking the truly hard questions that divide the country. There are crucial differences between the two parties. If you push me into a corner and make me choose, I'll take the Democrats. But, like a vast number of voters, my confidence in the two-party system has been severely eroded by watching how the two parties actually behave cooperatively.

In one sense, the Democrats' ideological shift may have done greater damage than the Republicans' because the Democrats were always the party of the working people, while the Republicans were the party of money and the professional-managerial middle class. Now, we have two parties representing capital. One them (the Democrats) still draws votes heavily from the labor ranks and will occasionally stand up for labor's interests. But Democrats often shun the working people if the party's capital constituents insist upon it.

This is not the story either party tells the public. It is easier for both parties to portray themselves as being in fierce combat with the opposition and ask voters to join in their do-or-die struggles. One-third of the electorate no longer buys this story. They call themselves independent voters and try to choose the less bad option. Given the policy cross-dressing by both parties, voter suspicion of party labels is understandable.

Democrats, for example, do occasionally complain about the inequities and excesses of the financial system, but their criticisms are tempered. It was the Democratic Party, not Ronald Reagan and the Republicans, that deregulated the financial industry with the seminal 1980 legislation that abolished interest-rate ceilings and this law against usury, collapsed the savings and loan industry, and freed banks to engage in collusive, fraudulent accounting deals (think Enron) that led to extraordinary losses for hoodwinked investors.

It was the Democrats under Clinton who created the new megabanks—Citigroup, JPMorgan Chase, Merrill Lynch, and others—that have lately been disgraced by their own megascandal in mortgage lending. To create these financial conglomerates, Clinton repealed a piece of landmark New Deal legislation, the Glass-Steagall Act, that separated commercial and investment banking. Bankers in the 1920s mixed the two functions to sell dubious stocks issued by their corporate customers to innocent bank depositors and trust account holders. That scam had helped to fuel the stock market speculation that ended disastrously in the crash of 1929, the event that triggered the Great Depression.

Clinton's friends in banking (principally Robert Rubin and Sanford Weill, the founder of Citigroup) assured the president that with the safeguards built into modern banking, this sort of fraud couldn't happen again. Yet, within a few years, the very modern megabankers were back again with their own versions of double-dealing and fraudulent valuation of financial assets. When the housing bubble collapsed, so did the rotten securities. Investors and bank shareholders, including many pension funds, were stuck holding hundreds of billions of dollars in inflated financial assets. If Democrats were embarrassed, I have not heard any acknowledge their culpability. They could hardly blame George W. Bush or Ronald Reagan. The party of the working class had engineered this fiasco on behalf of its Wall Street friends.

The party is marooned on the wrong side of myriad economic issues. For the credit card industry, leading Senate Democrats championed the bankruptcy bill that tightened the screws on debt-soaked consumers. Prominent Democrats likewise pushed legislation for insurance companies and investment brokerages to protect them against lawsuits by defrauded investors. Democratic legislators have been regular participants in corrupting the tax code by inserting ludicrous loopholes for corporate clients. Like Republicans, Democrats also claim that allowing capital holders to avoid paying taxes helps the economy and lets money trickle down to the little guys.

★　★　★　★　★

Growing income inequality is not simply a social injury bemoaned by bleeding-heart liberals. When it reaches an extreme, inequality can badly damage the overall economy. A generation of the federal government favoring wealth over workers has unhinged the normal relationships in the economic system. A Federal Reserve governor expressed his puzzlement over the "global saving glut."[5] But isn't that what you would expect if every lever of governing power were tilted to encourage the accumulation of capital and to undercut wage incomes?

To put it crudely, the United States has too many rich people awash with surplus wealth, but not enough healthy consumers with incomes that allow them to both spend and save for the future. This imbalance helps explain the financial system's recurring frenzies and crises as overconfident wealth holders bid up prices in financial markets until the speculative bubbles of overvalued assets collapse. It explains why the US savings rate fell to zero while the very, very wealthy went on a spending spree.

Neither conventional economists nor politicians seemed to recognize this deformity, but some Wall Street observers did. In 2005, the global analysis team at Citigroup dubbed the United States a "plutonomy"—a top-heavy economy "where economic growth is powered by and largely consumed by the wealthy few."[6] The imbalance works fine, as Citigroup analysts see it, though they grant that the United States may be ripe for "labor backlash."

"At the heart of plutonomy is income inequality," the Citigroup report explained. "Societies that are willing to tolerate/endorse income inequality, are willing to tolerate/endorse plutonomy." By Citigroup's reckoning, only the United States, the United Kingdom, and Canada qualify. "We project that the plutonomies . . . will likely see even more income inequality, disproportionately feeding off a further rise in the profit share in their economies, capitalist-friendly governments, more technology-driven productivity, and globalization." A follow-up report in 2006 asserted, "We think the rich are likely to get even wealthier in the coming years. We like companies that sell to or service the rich—luxury goods, private banks, etc."[7]

Citigroup fell victim to its own excessive optimism. When the collapse of mortgage securities unfolded, the megabank lost tens of billions of dollars, its CEO was fired, and the impact spread like cancer through other financial markets, injuring innocent others. *Fortune* magazine, usually a cheerleader for financial titans, published on its November 26, 2007, cover a rogue's gallery of disgraced bank executives along with the question "What Were They Smoking?" Lending froze at many financial venues because suddenly no one could trust the debt paper the megabanks were selling. The chief executive of an embattled private-equity fund told the *New York Times* he had weathered similar financial crises in 1982, 1987, 1990, 1994, 1998, 2001, and 2002, but this one was "'the most disturbing.'"

These disturbances in economic stability are a natural result of dumping regulatory rules and supervision. No one thought to blame economic inequality, but this is what happens when the government manages the economy on behalf of plutocrats and financial firms. Both the Federal Reserve and the Bush White House focused on serving the plutonomy described by Citigroup's analysts. After the stock market bubble melted down in 2001, Bush delivered his massive tax cuts to the wealthy to stimulate a recovery by boosting their consumption. The Fed, likewise, cut interest rates to near zero to revive the stock market and encourage the wealthiest 10 percent to invest.

This worked in a twisted way: A recovery occurred, though not for the working people in the real economy. But the lopsided stimulus also generated a new bubble in asset prices—another giddy run-up for overconfident investors, this time centered in real estate. When the housing bubble collapsed, the Fed introduced some rules to enforce honest lending practices, but it was too late to protect anyone from the predatory bankers selling fraudulent loans that were sure to bankrupt the borrowers. The fallout for the economy continues.

This crisis reveals more fundamental problems than just corrupt practices in the unregulated banking industry. The Federal Reserve, which is supposed to maintain order in the financial realm, lost control of events as its lopsided policies destabilized it. It's like a small boy playing in the bathtub, pushing the water with his arms and feet. Pretty soon, the water is sloshing back and forth on its own momentum, and soon it surges out of the tub and onto the bathroom floor. Roughly speaking, this is how the central bank destabilized the financial economy. First, it allowed price bubbles of financial speculation to form and spiral out of control. Then it rushed to the rescue when the bubbles collapsed. The central bank cut interest rates drastically to rescue the economy from the mess it had created. That response jump-started new asset price bubbles and set up the national economy for another disaster down the road, one that has required massive emergency lending.

The political lesson is simple and rather obvious: When government policy is extreme, the society experiences extreme results—giddy instability and the eventual collapse of illusory prices. Unfortunately, the victims usually are not the same people who inspired and benefitted from the extreme measures. Instead, millions of home owners lose everything while the CEOs fired from Wall Street banks walk away, comforted by extraordinary severance pay packages worth as much as $160 million.

This kind of extremism in high places is unlikely to occur if a country has an authentic two-party system and a fully functioning representative democracy. It is more likely to happen when both major parties are feeding at the same trough.

★   ★   ★   ★   ★

Some social wounds go deeper than money and cannot be measured by economic statistics. The conservative order shifted the balance of power in American economic life, but it also damaged the moral fabric of the country by skewing our shared understandings of right and wrong. That accusation may sound odd since Republicans portray themselves as the party of traditional values, but I think many people will recognize my point.

Liberating business and finance from public obligations and government discipline ratified many forms of behavior that violate ancient principles of moral conduct. Children learn these rules of fair play and decency from their parents or at Sunday school or on the playground. People recognized that these moral tenets were being violated. Yet, how could isolated individuals object to what authorities described as smart new ways to do business? Feeling alone and powerless, many Americans kept their objections private.

Janet Krueger was a software developer for IBM who regularly put in eighty-hour workweeks at the company's laboratory in Rochester, New York. An IBM employee for twenty-three years, Krueger got a notice in the mail announcing changes in the company pension plan. The fine print was impossible to understand. When she went online to see how the changes affected her, the IBM pension calculator was no longer there. The company's 800 number was constantly busy. Weeks later, after collaborating with colleagues, Krueger figured out that her benefits had been cut by $100,000. IBM was targeting loyal older employees like her.

"'It felt like the rug had been pulled from under me,'" Krueger said. "'There's no way I could retire on the new, lower pension.'"[8] What hurt especially was the sense of betrayal, she told David L. Madland, a graduate student at Georgetown University who was examining the collapse of corporate pension funds. "'It's probably hard for people who haven't worked in a corporate culture like IBM's to understand how much we had trusted the company,'" Krueger said. "'IBM always told us that our benefits were secure. We might not have been getting the highest salary, but our benefits were supposed to make up the difference. It wasn't supposed to be this way.'"

"Do unto others as you would have them do unto you." IBM was not breaking the law. It was trashing the Golden Rule.

Mutual respect, honest dealing, trustworthy commitment—these values were cast aside by corporate America in the name of boosting shareholder value. By reneging on old promises, corporate managers legally misappropriated the assets of workers and delivered the money to stockholders in the form of higher profits.

In Madland's PhD dissertation, entitled "A Wink and a Handshake: Why the Collapse of the US Pension System Has Provoked Little Protest," he estimated that some 10 million Americans had experienced the same sudden loss of wealth during the previous five years. Many millions more had earlier lost pensions, health insurance, and other benefits. Krueger and her colleagues organized and managed to win a reversal from IBM, but most victims did not. Among the factors that discouraged many worker protests was workers' correct expectation they had little chance of winning. Unless they were represented by a labor union, most workers had neither the expertise and resources nor the political clout to defend themselves.

Even then, companies developed a legal way to break their union contracts. They declared bankruptcy and got the bankruptcy judge to set aside the company's obligations to workers. Union members were stripped of the hard-won rights and benefits they had secured through collective bargaining by making concessions on wages.

Government and law, as well as business and finance, had embraced a new moral principle, famously articulated in 1974 by conservative economist Milton

Friedman. "So the question is, do corporate executives, provided they stay within the law, have responsibilities . . . other than to make as much money for their stockholders as possible? And my answer to that is, no they do not,"[9] Friedman declared. His libertarian logic was broadly appealing because it promised to liberate individuals and their money from social obligations and government rules. His popular bestseller was called *Free to Choose*. To put it bluntly, Friedman's new moral order amounted to this: Every man for himself.

Greed and gluttony—two of the seven deadly sins enunciated many centuries ago by the Catholic Church—have made a spectacular comeback in our time. You can see it in the glossy advertisements in high-end magazines that define taste and beauty for the wealthiest consumers. How rich must one become to qualify for this lifestyle? It turns out that there are no practical limits on avarice in Milton Friedman's world.

In 2006, Mark McGoldrick was a top employee at Goldman Sachs, where he managed the special-situations group, investing the firm's own capital and yielding billions in profit. McGoldrick was paid $70 million a year—nearly $200,000 a day—but grumbled that he and his staff were being shortchanged. He resigned to run a private hedge fund where his talents would be more appreciated, his income more in line with "market reality." McGoldrick had a point. The year before, two hedge fund managers had earned more than $1.4 billion—each.[10]

"Thou shalt not steal." On some occasions, the eager pursuit of greater wealth crosses the line into what is arguably criminal behavior. Spectacular scandals involving famous corporations—Enron, WorldCom, and hundreds of others—that used duplicitous accounting schemes to defraud shareholders and deprive them of their wealth provide the evidence. Their actions amounted to grand theft on an epic scale. A few CEOs were prosecuted and went to prison, but most corporate executives were allowed to settle with cash, paying fines or restitution to the victims so modest that it amounted to pennies on the dollars that were stolen.

Leading megabanks like Citigroup and Merrill Lynch collaborated in these crimes as the financial architects who designed the felonious deceptions. But their lawyers went to federal court and claimed they were merely advisors who could be not be blamed for assisting clients who were crooks. The courts agreed with the bankers.

In the aftermath of the scandals, Congress enacted a rather mild reform based on one of the Ten Commandments, "Thou shall not bear false witness." CEOs would now have to sign off on the company's annual reports to shareholders, attesting that what they reported was in fact true. In other words, the executives could be held personally accountable for telling lies to the company's putative owners. Business and finance were outraged by this intrusive measure. It was an impractical burden that added unreasonable costs to doing business, they complained. The major lobbying groups immediately organized a campaign to repeal or dilute the provision.

Their political efforts were complicated by the fact that "false witnessing" by corporate management did not stop. Some 130 corporations, including celebrity executives like Steve Jobs of Apple, were caught in another lucrative lie. They or their staffs backdated executive stock options in ways that added many millions more to the already swollen compensation packages of corporate executives. A few were prosecuted; most pleaded innocent error and promised not to do it again. The *Wall Street Journal* suggested that when so many CEOs had made the same "mistake," it could hardly be thought of as a crime. Warren Buffett, the billionaire investor, expressed a darker view, "The five most dangerous words in business may be 'Everybody else is doing it,'" Buffett told his Berkshire Hathaway managers.[11]

The gravest blow to the common morality, in my view, was the repeal of the federal law against usury. When financial deregulation abolished the legal ceilings on interest rates, the legislation explicitly eliminated a moral prohibition grounded in Judaism, Christianity, and Islam. The definition of usury has evolved over the centuries, but its essential meaning has remained intact: Usury is the rich exploiting the poor. Throughout history, usurers have been seen as evil figures who prey upon the misfortunes of others, ensnaring the poor with unpayable debts and eventually seizing their property. Societal protections against usury have long been in place, thanks to the core understanding that people and institutions of great wealth must be prevented from exploiting the weak. But in 1980, Congress declared usury to be a victimless crime, like gambling or prostitution, and predatory lending was made an acceptable transaction between consenting adults.[12]

As a result of this action, usury is now commonplace—30 percent interest credit cards, "payday loans" for the working poor, the notorious subprime mortgages that lured home owners into debt contracts that guaranteed their failure. The victims are not solely the poor. The debt industry also turned middle-class families into anxious prey. As more and more Americans began to default, the banking industry, with bipartisan support, enacted the new federal bankruptcy law that further punishes debtors.

The cumulative effect these moral wounds have had is to coarsen society, and that is reflected in the popular culture. Human sympathy has been devalued, displaced by fashionable indifference. Anyone who expresses a bleeding-heart concern for "losers" risks looking weak. The harshness of the moral climate reminds me of a literature professor I had years ago in college. He grew tired of listening as his students offered opaque, wooden explanations for the death of a novel's tragic hero. He finally cut us off and asked, "Doesn't anybody feel sorry for the poor bastard?"

I do not believe Americans have succumbed to Milton Friedman's conception of moral order—it still feels wrong to most people—but many have certainly been intimidated and silenced. After all, Friedman's hard-nosed doctrine of me-first economics is taught at the leading business schools and economics departments of all the best universities.

It may surprise people to know that Adam Smith, founder of modern market economics, was on the side of compassion. Economists revere him for describing "the invisible hand" of the marketplace. But Smith actually taught that "moral sentiments"—human acts of "fellow feeling"—are the guiding forces that govern economics and prevent markets from injuring society. Empathy for others, self-interested mutuality, and other moral verities—these are the things that Adam Smith taught (and most economists continue to ignore), and they sound a lot like the Golden Rule.[13]

When Friedman died in 2006, he was mourned and celebrated by his profession, and his memorialists ignored the cruel side of his legacy. But Art Hilgart, a retired business economist, remembered a lecture from 1991. Friedman briskly called for closing down Medicare, the postal system, Social Security, welfare, and public education. The audience was aghast. A young woman finally asked what this would mean for poverty. "There is no poverty in America," Friedman answered. A voice from the back of the hall called in response, "Bullshit." The audience cheered.[14]

★　★　★　★　★

Beneath the choppy waters of politics, a deeper tide runs against the nation's prospects, demanding a profound change in how we live. It is not just that the United States' economic system and federal governance must be reformed, cleansed of many disorders, and restored to an equitable balance. The transformations affecting our economic life and social relationships are going to be more fundamental than cyclical crises and recurring scandals.

This is not a matter of political desire, but of practical necessity. As I suggested at the outset of this book, the forces bearing down on the United States will transform American life, for better or for worse. How we live, the social fabric, our shared expectations and faith in the country's future—all of these are in play. We will change because we have no choice.

These converging forces are no longer secondary issues consigned to the inside pages of newspapers. The evidence is now too strong to dismiss. Ecological destruction—the encroaching degradation of nature and its life-supporting systems—is most dramatically reflected in global warming, but the irreparable ecological threats from industrial production and consumption extend across a far broader field of the natural world.

Similarly, the approaching scarcity of oil is like a ticking clock—or time bomb—for modern economies based on hydrocarbon fuels. As more poor nations achieve industrialization and older oil fields are depleted, the rising demand for fuel threatens to outstrip the world's capacity to produce it. In the meantime, oil prices are driven still higher. The critical moment—when world oil production peaks and either levels off or begins to decline in relation to consumption—is evidently much closer than conventional opinion had assumed. It won't happen fifty or a hundred years from now, but more likely during the next twenty or thirty years. The *Wall Street Journal,* not normally given to spreading alarmist theories, reported that leading oil companies think the world may hit the practical ceiling on increasing production as early as 2012.[15]

US oil reserves peaked in 1970, and the nation has become steadily more dependent on imported oil ever since. The US energy strategy, in essence, is to burn America's oil first instead of saving it for the day when world supplies become scarce or run out. This policy is dictated by the profit-seeking goals of the US oil companies, but it does not serve the long-term interests of the nation. Wouldn't it be wiser to hold on to the last of the dwindling US reserves? The oil in the ground steadily becomes more valuable as scarcity approaches. Husbanding the reserves would provide us with a cushion for use during the great transition to alternatives. Other countries have founded national oil companies to manage their energy resources in line with their long-term national interest. But the US government turns its oil assets over to private companies to exploit right now.

These two forces—ecological destruction and the end of oil—together pose a fateful imperative for everyone in the world, but especially for the United States. As the largest and most dependent consumer of oil, it has the greatest and gravest incentive to shift to alternative sources of energy. The most profligate and wasteful consumer of material goods has the most awesome need to change its ways. We literally have to give up our carefree habits, which are powerfully seductive yet self-destructive.

A culture of mass consumption accompanied the fabulous cornucopia of goods and pleasures that "democratized" American abundance during the twentieth century. It cannot survive as presently practiced. There is simply too much jumbo-size waste and breakage, too much industrial poison dumped on the earth and in the air and water. The US economy literally must be transformed, from top to bottom, to eliminate the harmful consequences of our highly inefficient production and overindulgent consumer appetites. The nature and content of goods must be altered in large and small details. Like it or not, mass consumption will be altered either by these economic and ecological imperatives or by purposeful decisions that ensure better quality and longer-lasting value in consumer goods, as well as a more equitable society.

For some years now, ecologists and other advocates have been explaining that it is technologically feasible to accomplish these systemic changes. Every production process, every product's constituent parts, and the recovery and reuse of spent materials in new products—all these elements can be redesigned to stop the ecological destruction. It is entirely possible to do it. Oil scarcity and global warming provide the motivation to institute the deep reforms that have long been advocated but never achieved in the absence of visible crisis. The bad news—crisis is upon us—may turn out to be good news.

The hard part is the politics. Political awareness of the problem is rising rapidly, and Congress has launched important initiatives to encourage development and use of alternative fuels like ethanol and to compel manufacturers to build more fuel-efficient vehicles. But these are only the initial steps in the process, and the United States is way behind. Leading corporations are belatedly turning their politics "green" and acknowledging the necessity of reform. But they also want to control the design of the reforms and the pace of change. The costs of transition are formidable and involve every aspect of private enterprise—production, profit, investment capital. Will corporate power allow the political system to act fast enough? Can politics finally break the oil industry's hold on US energy policy? The history surrounding these issues does not encourage optimism.

Resolving the cross-pressures will be an epic test of character for Americans, a reckoning that may be as unforgiving as war. What are our true values? The industrial reforms, while doable, are going to be very difficult and will inevitably divide us. The easiest way to absorb the burdens of adjustment is to shove the pain downhill onto those who are too weak or unorganized to resist. Taxing carbon emissions, for instance, looks like a logical solution, and it is widely endorsed by governing elites as a discreet way to discourage oil consumption. Tax gasoline and people will drive less, cars will get smaller and more efficient, they reason. Perhaps so, but taxing gasoline and other types of hydrocarbon consumption is guaranteed to deliver the severest blows to those with less income and limited personal options. The affluent will keep driving outsize vehicles because they can afford it, while others will be literally "taxed out" of these forbidden pleasures.

The truly tough political path involves developing a new economy and governing principles that can sustain the good life for all while eliminating reckless consumption and enforcing more prudent use of nature's resources. This option seems out of the question, given the political system's lopsided priorities and unequal distribution of power and influence. People can change this reality, but to do so they have to explore deeply their own values and behavior—their own understanding of what matters most in life and how they themselves might have to change.

In the reckoning ahead, Americans are going to find themselves rethinking the meaning of "onward and upward." We will be compelled to redefine "progress" and "plenty." The core challenge will be to develop a new national culture and economy that yield more from less by producing more human satisfaction from less wasteful excess and destruction, as well as less greed and extremes of wealth. The processes of capitalism are equipped to do this, but they are not likely to deliver unless society demands it.

Since the earliest settlers arrived, Americans have always put their faith in undifferentiated economic growth as the cornerstone for national prosperity. That faith is failing us now. We have to start making hard choices about what kind of economic growth is healthy and desirable, and what kind is no longer tolerable. The bottom line is this: The "good times" are not coming back, not as we once knew them.

We have to create a new, more fulfilling version of "good times" that is truly sustainable—an economic system that works for our grandchildren. Our national options are narrowing. So is our ability to always have things our way. Americans can no longer tolerate bloody adventures undertaken by egotistical leaders. Nor can we continue to indulge the casual pleasures of consuming and discarding without regard for the consequences. That's over. To get the life we want, Americans will have to grow up—learn to make wiser choices about what we want for ourselves and our country, and then somehow force the governing classes to do the same.

Can we learn to do this? Or, like an adolescent throwing a tantrum, will we stubbornly resist? You may write me off as a hopeless optimist, but I am excited about the reckoning ahead. We are on new ground, in a place where Americans have never been before, facing adversities very different from those of the past.

I sometimes find myself telling young people that I am a little envious of them. Their generation is bound to live through exciting times, a tumultuous era in which some fundamental questions about our country and our character will be decided. The country faces converging adversities, and we do not know what the outcome will be. The young will have a lot of influence on the answer, there is no way to avoid it. These may sound like lines from a graduation speech, but young audiences seem to know what I mean. They are not intimidated by the message. They feel empowered by the unique moment they will have in history. That is what I envy.

I am among the incautious optimists who insist on believing that our country can emerge as a far better place. The competing pressures may even lead the nation to resolve social and economic contradictions—the paradox of poverty amid great abundance, for instance—that it has evaded in the past. America the Possible: What would that look like? This reckoning gives us the opportunity to ask.

Americans can do this, not easily or overnight, not without painful adjustments, mistakes, and false starts. But tragic consequences are not inevitable. After all, we are not going to become a poor and pitiful country. The United States must give up some of its inflated presumptions, but it is certain to remain very rich and bountiful in comparison with other countries, as well as vastly talented and inventive. Americans are capable of accomplishing great change, as we have proved in the past, if we summon what is within us—ingenuity and nerve, the creativity and risk taking that have always been our most distinctive qualities. We can change the country if we find ways to reengage the power of citizens, if we are mature enough to understand that we must change ourselves.

The following chapters will take us deeper into the layers of complexity, not to exhaust the issue with more discouraging detail, but to attempt to visualize the dimensions of our great reckoning and to ponder possible resolutions. I offer some ideas of my own to illustrate how some of these redeeming reforms might work.

The people will decide the shape of America the Possible. Then we must find practical ways to make it happen, that is, to develop our untapped power as sovereign citizens to push politicians further than they intended to go. Does that sound farfetched? I embrace the audacious notion that ordinary Americans are fully capable of envisioning a different and better future for the country. As citizens of a democracy, we are entitled to participate fully in designing that future and in making it happen. These large matters cannot be left to the authorities. People don't need to wait for Washington. Washington must learn to wait upon us.

CHAPTER ELEVEN

AMERICA THE POSSIBLE

I have been brooding about these matters for some years, and as I gradually got a better understanding of our circumstances, I grasped the enormity of what the country faces. I wasn't alone, of course, since many others were voicing similar alarms. I used to assume—somewhat naively—that sooner or later the political system would listen and decide to deal with the problems. Instead, it became clear that I was seeing a convergence of adversities that neither governing authorities nor most of the nation recognized. That felt a little lonely. Was I perhaps wrong about what I saw happening? For many years, I played the lonely Cassandra, warning of dire economic consequences ahead and being mostly ignored. I began to feel like a bag lady on the street corner, waving a placard at the passing crowds.

The hard facts did not go away. They became more obvious and ominous, and, for me, more convincing. How would the United States get out of this mess? I kept asking that question, trying to reconcile my stubborn American optimism with the mounting evidence of negative forces. The more I saw the situation deteriorate, the harder it was for me to imagine plausible solutions. I began to appreciate that solutions to the American dilemma may lie at a level deeper than politics or anything the political system is likely to deliver.

Thinking about these things led me to conclude that America is in much deeper trouble than is generally realized and that restoring national well-being will require profound change—a historic transformation in how we live and work as well as in how we are governed. Strangely enough, the conclusion brightened my thinking. I began to envision how the country could change itself—first to get out of the ditch, then to restore the noble promises Americans make to themselves about who we are and how we can live together equably as one nation.

Americans know how to do this, I told myself, or at least many Americans do. One way or another, throughout the history of our country, ordinary people have worked to change their circumstances and reinvent themselves. Many still do, imaginatively and in every sector of American life. Imagining that we can change the future requires an incautious optimism, but also heroic patience. It means pursuing large goals that cannot be met in one season or maybe even in one's lifetime. Start where you are and do what you can, then pass it along to the next generation. Historic change is not a sentimental endeavor. It involves great risks, and the very real possibilities of failing and looking foolish. To get anywhere, people first have to see themselves clearly, free of false pride and patriotic evasions.

This is a task for risk takers and optimists, people who are willing to take a leap of faith into the future to make our nation a better place. America the Possible requires relaunching the country in a more promising direction, reenvisioning a society that is more fulfilling for all. The United States is a very rich and capable nation but, from my perspective, we have not yet learned how to live with our great wealth—not wisely and well, with respect for our deeper values. The drive to accumulate economic gains has instead pushed aside what we hold to be essential, damaging and even precluding life's precious qualities. America is incomplete, far short of realizing its possibilities.[1]

I think this is part of what ordinary people are feeling when they express doubts about the future. The fabulous expansion of American wealth no longer leads reliably to the greater contentment that was promised. The climb to prosperity seems steeper, more costly, and precarious. Glimmering notions of personal fulfillment recede into the hazy distance. Material abundance has not made us "free," just as awesome military power has not made us feel secure. If we are so strong, why are we so scared?

If you think the American story is essentially complete and triumphant, my proposition makes no sense. Why would we want to change anything basic when the United States is the world's great success story? But if you believe instead that the national saga is ongoing and that important qualities are missing from American life, then my perspective might sound exciting. The national drama is entering a challenging new era, ripe for new departures. The status quo may seem mighty powerful, but it is not set in stone. This new situation empowers

Americans to envision ambitious change and pursue it. Basically, I am suggesting a better foundation for American optimism. We will need it.

As I wrote earlier, to change our future, we have to change ourselves. One of the toughest things to change is how we see our world—the thoughts and assumptions we have inherited from the past. We must reconsider and revise our idea of progress because economic growth, as we have known it for generations, is not only endangered, its terms must be changed for our good. The implications of such a change are momentous since growth in standard economic terms is the glue that has always bound Americans together in common pursuit. Expanding production capacities and wealth has been the vital thread running through the American experience from the very beginning.

The expectation that the economic engine will increase output more or less continuously and distribute the bounty widely is the bedrock of American faith in "onward and upward." As a people, we are deeply committed to hard work and self-improvement, and we expect to be rewarded with better lives. What happens to the country if the promises and assurances are proven untrue?

Economic growth is failing as the lodestar for our society. The US economy is losing its capacity to sustain economic expansion in the ways people have come to expect and need to maintain their faith. At the same time, circumstances are compelling the economic system to undergo the wrenching changes of an industrial transformation to save the planet, and these changes are sure to redistribute the costs and benefits to the disadvantage of many, especially the less affluent. The culture of mass consumption that consolidated popular aspirations across class lines during the twentieth century is breaking up into rival camps—those who can afford the luxury of deep ecological reform and those who can't.

Economic growth is unlikely to be stopped cold, at least as far as official statistics reflect it, but the normal business cycles of recession and recovery no longer deliver general prosperity in the familiar terms. Experiencing an extended period of sputtering stagnation seems hard to avoid as the United States struggles to work off the effects of indebtedness, diminished domestic production, and the financial system's breakdown. Other nations may continue to prop up the ailing Goliath in their own self-interest, but that will not heal what ails us.

In the worst case, a climactic financial unraveling might arrest growth like a stopped clock and leave the economy stuck in recession, unable to regain the energy to recover. In reality, many millions of Americans are already living with the absence of economic growth. Over the last seven years, working-class families and those even lower on the economic scale have experienced the equivalent of a low-grade depression. It was not akin to the full-scale catastrophe of the 1930s, but rather more like the agony of slow bleeding, and its existence has gone largely ignored or denied by financial reporters, who assured readers that the economy was sound and even robust.

But here is why ordinary people have felt otherwise. Throughout most of the "Bush recovery," the average wage for all nonsupervisory employees—more than 80 percent of the workforce—was flat, or, when wages were discounted for price inflation, actually falling. The median income for households, which always falls during recessions, normally regains its previous level and rises to a higher peak. But this time, it stalled out as economic growth resumed and indeed looked robust. In later stages, the wage average did begin to rise modestly in real terms, but the trend didn't last. By 2007, when the Dow Jones Industrial Average achieved its historic high, real wages were declining again. The median income, after finally having regained lost ground, began to decline again.

Incomes were weak for another basic reason—less work was available. The moderate unemployment rate suggested otherwise, but the erosion of work was reflected in the industrial measure of weekly hours worked. It declined steadily throughout most of the recovery for broad ranks of employees. Less overtime and shorter workweeks meant smaller paychecks.

Naturally, families borrowed more to fill the gap. In August 2005, for the first time since 1933, households spent more than they earned in disposable income—$101 billion more—an ominous event known as "dissavings." This ought to have been a wake-up call for the establishment. Instead, myopic economists again reassured consumers and told them to keep spending. The economy would tank if they stopped.[2] Three years later, it did.

Democrats piled on George W. Bush for creating this lopsided recovery—and he deserved it—but the pattern did not start with his presidency. Over the last three decades, the same trend has played out after each recession, and each time it has been more pronounced: The economy would regain momentum and begin expanding again, but the growth rate compared to earlier cycles was lower and slower to restore prosperity to the ranks of working people in the form of job growth and rising wages. The new profile of economic growth meant working people were the "last hired, first fired."

A lot of people blamed presidents (Reagan, Bush I, Clinton, and Bush II) for allowing "jobless recoveries" to occur on their watch, but the true culprit was the Federal Reserve. Its conservative monetary policy, combined with globalization's erosion of US wages and jobs, guaranteed that the good times would be delayed and less "good" than usual for working families. The Fed achieved this by deliberately holding back the natural expansive energies of the economy, delaying a vigorous recovery, to ensure that price inflation was subdued. It worked for capital, but not for labor.

Four presidents in a row went along with the central bank's antilabor strategy, though none thought to reveal this to the working people. If elected politicians take on the Federal Reserve, the wrath of Wall Street is unleashed upon them, so most have remained silent. So long as that is true, the erosion of middle-class incomes will continue, and the falling living standards families have struggled to forestall will be unavoidable.

★ ★ ★ ★ ★

Faltering economic growth is a formula for political upheaval. Politicians used to assure the public that "a rising tide lifts all boats." We don't hear that expression much any more because it is obviously no longer true. But the statement never did accurately convey the full reality. The tide did not rise evenly for everyone, but instead lifted the big boats much higher and made them more powerful. It sounds like a gentle process, but the "rising tide" of growth has always been destructive in ways the government has largely ignored, and now it is quite treacherous for little boats.

The unbalanced economy might not seem like a problem for business and finance since they have chugged along profitably during many years when the economy underperformed for working people. But this lopsided condition poses an economic risk that elites have largely ignored—the implosion of US domestic demand. Who's going to buy all this stuff when consumers lose their capacity to sustain economic growth? Corporate leaders once assumed that global trade was the answer—they would sell their surplus output to the new consumers in developing nations. But quite the opposite has happened. Foreign producers are selling their surplus output to the United States.

If nothing fundamental about this picture is changed, the failure of "growth" could sooner or later derange American politics. Personally, I hope for a small-d democratic rebellion—a nonviolent uprising of citizens that breaks through the political barriers and forces insiders to incorporate their views in decisions. But also plausible is an era of even uglier politics in which confused people are drawn into irrational conflicts or futile nostalgia for the "good times."

Either way, the issue of economic inequality will be back at the center of politics in the absence of reliable growth. As astute politicians have always understood, economic growth is the magic potion that allows the political system to avoid facing some of the nation's deeper contradictions, especially the great inequalities in wealth and income. So long as the rewards of an advancing economy are widely distributed, however unequally, the promise of growth muffles dissent. When the promise fails, neglected questions come into sharper focus. This can be good for democracy, but dangerous for the governing order.

"Growth is a substitute for equality of income," the late Henry Wallich explained many years ago. "So long as there is growth there is hope, and that makes large income differentials tolerable."[3] Wallich, a moderately liberal economist and Federal Reserve governor, was defending the system against ecologist critics who emerged three decades ago to describe the limits of indiscriminate economic growth.

George Monbiot, a columnist for London's *Guardian* newspaper, recently offered a harsher version of Wallich's point. "Governments love growth because it excuses them from dealing with inequality," Monbiot wrote. "Growth is a political sedative, snuffing out protest, permitting governments to avoid confrontation with the rich, preventing the construction of a just and sustainable economy."[4]

In other words, when growth fails, the political system loses its cover. The safety valve is off. The comforting mythology about growth loses its power to distract the public from anger and to discourage critical inquiry into how the system actually functions. People who are pushed around by the blind forces of economic life start to ask why this is happening to them, their families, and their friends—why are they working harder, yet losing ground? Stripped of security, harassed by anxieties, feeling bad about the children's future, people begin to feel that "life, liberty, and the pursuit of happiness" is an unaffordable luxury.

If we are living in the richest country on earth, why does it have to be like this? That's an excellent question. When people ask it, they are taking the first small step toward political engagement by connecting their private pain to larger public troubles and getting beyond feeling guilty for failing to prosper in this very prosperous country.

It is not people who have failed. It is the system that has failed people. The awkward secret about the American growth engine is that it thrives by wantonly wasting the noneconomic "assets" of people's lives, the lost potential of their time on earth. These are "priceless" because they cannot be bought or sold. Their true value is unknowable, even to the individual. The growth engine wastes the future—the full range of possible experiences that ought to be commonly available in this very wealthy nation. When people look around, they see that vital elements of their surroundings have also disappeared or crumbled, and these things are not just the roads and bridges, but also essential public assets like the grace notes of community life and common verities trashed by the manic competition for growth and profit. Why must we live like this if we are so rich?

Ecologists look at the natural world and ask essentially the same question. The most dramatic and threatening price paid for economic growth, they argue, is the systematic destruction of nature. The finite capacity of the natural world to sustain life—human and otherwise—is endangered by the relentless encroachment of the industrial system. This threat means that there are indeed limits to growth, at least to growth as it is presently practiced. To put the point crudely, you can only pave over so much of the earth before nature begins to lose its life-supporting capabilities. Most mainstream economists dismissed this idea originally, but now they are more respectful, since global warming has provided frightening evidence of the collision between nature and the industrial system.

Images of the Arctic ice cap receding and polar bears stranded on floes have been seared onto our consciousness. Oceans and mountains, topsoil and rain forests, water, land, air, and the natural diversity of living things have all been laid waste. These are the things that sustain existence for all species, including ours. There are limits to growth and the world is bumping up against them, especially now that industrialization has spread to some very poor societies. Like wasted human lives, the losses to nature are not factored into the economic accounting, nor are they redeemable.

It may seem odd to accuse US business and finance of wastefulness since they are obsessed with efficiency. But the intense competition for returns among companies and investors focuses their managements on reducing their own companies' costs, not the costs to society or nature. The gross domestic product is essentially the total of all of a country's economic activities—the money transactions of producers and consumers and the performance and profits of enterprises and investors. Everything else is left out—human lives, society's needs and values, the well-being of nature. In this system, even obviously negative events—a train wreck or an earthquake—are treated as positive since they will stimulate more economic activity.

Worse than that, the growth engine actively damages anything it does not itself value. Companies know how to enhance their own growth and profit by dumping their production costs onto innocent others, such as the workers stripped of their pensions and the rivers destroyed by pollution. Then the government must clean up the human injuries and environmental wreckage left behind. Some of the collateral damage businesses cause is no doubt accidental, but most of it is deliberate. In numerous ways, companies develop careful strategies for extracting profit from the assets of others. Someone does pay eventually for this antisocial wastefulness, but usually it is not the perpetrators who gained wealth from their irresponsibility.

This is more than an accounting problem. It is a deep disorder in the values that govern our country. The economy keeps output—production and consumption—expanding as measured in dollars. But the process of growth simultaneously creates a political illusion by concealing the net negative loss to society. Politicians do not have to face this contradiction since the government conveniently does not look at growth in these terms.

Herman E. Daly, a rare economist who endeavors to see the world whole, set out to unmask the illusion. He calculated the full consequences of growth by combining various indicators of social and ecological gains and losses with the standard economic measures of output and wealth creation. Daly and his collaborator, John B. Cobb Jr., called it the Index of Sustainable Economic Welfare, and its stunning results were a rebuke to narrow-minded economics.

In *For the Common Good*, Daly and Cobb explained that for many years, although US growth had been officially reported as positive, it was actually negative for the overall society when these other factors were included. Economists quarreled with Daly's method of calculation, but other researchers have since confirmed his point by using different ways of weighing the losses and gains.[5]

The great American economic icon—gross domestic product—is in trouble, especially as more Americans discover the truths that ecologists have been explaining for years. The familiar measure for defining progress no longer makes much sense, not for people or for society. Progress as it has been traditionally defined feels dizzying instead, like running in place, faster and faster, without getting anywhere, and even sliding backward without realizing it. Americans need to rethink the meaning of progress in broader, more realistic terms that are more consistent with the human condition. Demanding an honest accounting of reality represents a major step toward straightening out our future.

Think of a talented young athlete—a track star or competitive cyclist—who decides to take steroids. The drug does enhance his or her performance and chances of winning races and trophies. But it also harms the body and shortens the life span. Above all, it corrupts the contest and cheats everyone else.

The US economy is something like a drugged athlete in the way it functions. It gains short-term growth based on false pretenses and pretends not to see any negative consequences. It burns up the foundations of future development. It denies or ignores competing social values that are ultimately more important to the lives of citizens and society. This denial shrinks the country's possibilities and compromises the search for greater fulfillment.

The operating premise of the American system is "growth before justice," as author Lew Daly once put it.[6] To maximize economic gains in the present, the system leaves the collateral damage for future generations to resolve. The inequalities and injuries generated by growth can be dealt with later, it is assumed, once new wealth has been created and the country has achieved a higher standard of living. This mentality is widely shared by political elites and citizens as an article of faith that has been deeply grounded in the American experience going all the way back to our national origins.

In earlier times, when the country was young and undeveloped, this mindset seemed morally acceptable. Living conditions did improve dramatically with growth and new wealth. But that moral justification no longer works for the country. In a very wealthy nation that proclaims the opposite values, inequality, the result of powerful interests imposing their choices on the nation, has been revealed as morally wrong.

We have seen the social problems and environmental wreckage of these choices left to fester for generations. When the government does eventually address the social and environmental consequences, their cost is much greater, as is always the case when correcting things after the fact. Taxpayers pick up the tab, spending billions to try to remedy past neglect and repair the wounds. These efforts frequently fail. Once lost, some things of value cannot be restored.

★　★　★　★　★

My larger point is this: The United States is still behaving like an impoverished developing country that thinks it must pursue "growth before justice," sacrificing people, society, and the environment in order to climb still higher on the ladder of wealth accumulation. In the raw, early stages of America's story, when most Americans were poor and struggling immigrants and others were enslaved laborers, people typically accepted such abuses. Wasteful, inhumane practices were tolerated during those stages of US development, just as similar abuses are tolerated today in very poor nations struggling to industrialize. Americans of conscience are understandably appalled by the inequities they see elsewhere.

But what is our excuse? Despite great wealth and sophistication, the United States remains underdeveloped in these terms. The political system and economic engine continue to behave as though social equity and sustainable industrial practices are obstacles to prosperity that are too costly unless the cost–benefit ratio looks favorable to business. Other nations, both rich and poor, are puzzled by this behavior. They admire our fabulous technological advances and love America's inventive culture, but they wonder about our wisdom.

When I talked earlier about the United States being an adolescent still short of maturity, this is what I meant. We seem to be stuck in our development, yearning for something better but not sure how to get there. Acquiring more stuff doesn't seem to do it, and it may even makes things harder.

Comparing a mighty nation to a confused teenager might sound demeaning, but it fits the facts. Compared to many older societies and less fortunate countries, we are still young and full of energy. We are vibrant, inventive, and cocky about our place in the world. We remain unfinished and are still adjusting to grown-up realities. Adolescence is the critical juncture when young Americans begin to realize that their parents do not know everything and are flat wrong about some stuff. A child has to get smarter about things, become more independent. The challenge in this process is to hang on to the idealism and purity of thought that are natural to childhood without giving in to the cynicism characteristic of jaded adults. A country seeking maturity faces the same hurdle.

In *Steady-State Economics,* Herman Daly invoked a similar analogy. To grow, he pointed out, is defined as "to spring up and develop to maturity." People do not grow physically bigger and bigger throughout the life span (they would look like freaks if they did). At a certain point, they level off in physical size, but continue to develop the skills and qualities they need to sustain and enrich their lives. At a certain point, he suggested, wise and wealthy nations must do the same.[7]

The steady-state economy described by Daly and elaborated by others is radical and uncompromising. It rejects growth as we know it as a fixation on expansive accumulation that does not discriminate between good and ill consequences. This does not mean an end to "progress," however. In terms people can recognize, the steady-state society continues to improve itself, developing and redeveloping internally, perfecting the social conditions that promote the public welfare and more fulfilling lives. The United States has the wherewithal to achieve this if it has the nerve to try.

Daly's "steady state" is an economy in dynamic equilibrium that fulfills human needs without destroying the planet. It is an economy fully reconciled with nature's limits and in harmony with the country's abiding values of equality, freedom, democracy, and "life, liberty, and the pursuit of happiness." Daly's pioneering insights have gained a lot of ground among economic and social theorists in the intervening years, despite the hostility of orthodox doctrine. His perspective has been popularized as a foundation for sustainable development (though the meaning of sustainability is often corrupted in practice).

A concrete expression of Daly's thinking is popularly known as the ecological footprint—a measure of how much humanity and industrialization have encroached upon and diminished nature's capacity to replenish life. Even some leading corporations now promise to reduce their corporate "footprint." The footprint of human activity—including the spoiling of natural resources like air, land, and water—is already overshooting nature's carrying capacity by an estimated 25 percent, according to the Global Footprint Network. Biologists have called our era the Sixth Great Extinction, with thousands of species doomed by the shrinking habitats and failed ecosystems.

"Humanity is living off its ecological credit card," said Mathis Wackernagel, the group's executive director. "While this can be done for a short while, overshoot ultimately leads to liquidation of the planet's ecological assets."[8]

These are social and ecological wounds whose existence can no longer be evaded. They are defining realities that Americans must face and accept if they are to think clearly and honestly about transforming how we live and are organized as a society—the dream I describe as America the Possible. Reconstructing a promising society from the wreckage of the past is possible, though every aspect is difficult and lies beyond the usual expectations of what seems possible in politics. Failure is also possible. I won't dwell on the consequences of failure because it means genuine decline—we would become a country that was past its best days and resigned to a dispiriting future. That is not where we are, nor where we want to go.

★　★　★　★　★

Instead, let us reimagine America's future and explore what a mature and balanced society might look like. What would we need to put in place to sustain general satisfaction and to open wider paths for individual fulfillment? Above all, we have to devise a new understanding of "progress" that does not rely on the economic measures of wealth, but instead is based on commonly shared values concerning life itself. Do children get what they need to feel that they are at home in the world and free to explore its infinite wonders? Are families equipped to nurture them? Do people feel secure in their ability to experience the wholeness of their own lives?

These soft questions are truer measures of equality and freedom than tallies of personal financial wealth or material possessions. We will never all wind up with identical bank accounts and luxury goods. The right test for progress assesses things that people can judge from their own experience. Are they free, given their circumstances, to make big choices and lead self-directed lives?

Regardless of income, talent, or inheritance, can they explore and experience life in the terms or ambitions that are meaningful to them? Americans are not utopian dreamers; they fully understand practical realities. They know that it's possible to fail in life or get sideswiped by bad luck and bad choices. What they want (and deserve) are better odds, a fair shot at securing the joys of mortal existence and the distinctive pleasures of being American.

This could be the proper goal for any decent society, and it should certainly be attainable in a society as wealthy as ours. Everyone ends life at the same juncture—mortality is the great equalizer—but life in these United States does not need to be a river of sorrows or a confusion of riches. Americans might ponder this: How well does our society enable people to fulfill their commonsense expectations? Is the country moving toward or away from this goal? We do not need expert answers. Most economists do not appear to understand the question.

The transformation I envision requires government to step up and act forcefully on important matters it has neglected for at least a generation. Put aside for a moment the improbability of this happening: Events are creating necessities that cannot easily be brushed aside by Washington. New political leaders will either rise to the occasion or find themselves quickly discredited. The real force for change, in any case, must come from the people—citizens who decide to step up and take responsibility for our country.

The government can construct a new framework for American life, but the real objective is to liberate people and empower them, not government. The goal is to have a restored society that ensures that people have the security and freedom they need to invent their own lives. Collectively, ordinary citizens can shape the national destiny by redefining the good life in terms that are more equitable, and also sustainable for the future. To achieve this, the economy obviously must be reordered, which is a daunting challenge in hard times. But the political order can draw upon the famous strengths of Americans—their inventiveness and adaptability, their self-confidence and courage.

I propose six large imperatives that can guide transformation and restore the country's well-being. It is not easy to imagine either of the major parties embracing these, not without having to renounce their familiar behavior of recent decades. Movement to fulfill these guidelines will have to be driven by the people, who can reclaim their rightful power and force themselves upon a reluctant political system.

The first imperative is to restore moral principle and public obligations to the financial system and to corporations. This means writing tough new rules of behavior that will govern financial markets, banks, and investment houses, commandments that will go beyond the components of the old regulatory system that both political parties gutted or repealed. The list of reforms is lengthy and complicated, but two examples illustrate the thrust. Restore the federal law prohibiting usury to eliminate the predatory lending practices that exploit and bankrupt millions of the working poor and middle class. Then force the major banks and financial houses that now are treated as if they're "too big to fail" to become a lot smaller and to have a narrower purpose and less power. In other words, cut Wall Street down to size so it serves the real economy of work and production instead of acting like its master.

Second, government can replenish our battered social reality by reversing the forces that for three decades have depressed wages and destroyed work for broad ranks of Americans. This profound task requires making fundamental shifts in economic policy—creating a rising floor under wages, starting from the bottom up—and it will take years to restore and stabilize wage equity. But America will not get well until ordinary people regain confidence in their incomes and are freed from the harsh effects of swelling inequality.

If government gets it right on work and wages, people generally can take care of themselves. Elected politicians can start by confronting the imperious Federal Reserve and forcing the central bank to abandon its narrow-minded bias that favors capital over labor, financiers over producers. Likewise, the United States must abandon its losing role in the global economy, which results in the exporting of good jobs and the importing of mountains of debt, to reduce downward pressures on wages (as described in Chapter Seven).

The country also needs a large and permanent public workforce—a job for anyone who is ready and willing to work—to help do the work of rebuilding the nation. Public workers are needed to tackle our huge inventory of unmet needs involving everything from redeeming blighted neighborhoods, to modernizing the public infrastructure, to launching innovative new businesses in the fields of energy and ecology. These are the tasks private enterprise has ignored.

Third, people need and deserve to have a sturdy platform under their everyday lives that will ensure them access to the "essential needs," ranging from good health care to schooling, from guarantees for a comfortable old age to affordable transportation and decent, well-heated homes. Given the complexities of modern industrial life, these are not luxuries, but necessities. In this very rich nation, it seems immoral that so many Americans must constantly struggle to attain the basic requirements for life. Government can relieve their anxiety significantly by filling the gap with permanent guarantees that reduce the cost of living for families while also ensuring that people have the time and freedom to explore life's other possibilities.

Some goods and services are too essential to let their availability be governed by the narrow pursuit of profit making. Health care is the most obvious example. Fundamentally reforming that system means not only making sure good care is available to and affordable for all, but also breaking the industry's monopoly on prices to curb the relentless cost inflation that can overwhelm even prosperous families.

The collapse of the private pension system feeds another form of unnecessary desperation. Government can rebuild a platform for comfortable old-age security by creating a new national pension system alongside Social Security. The pension would be similar to that given to federal civil servants and Congress, and it would be financed largely by workers themselves through compulsory payroll deductions. A government-guaranteed system, unlike privately managed pensions, would be dependable, less costly, and tamper free.

For some essential needs, government will have to charter limited-profit or nonprofit companies to operate like regulated public utilities in providing electricity or communications services, and even manufactured products like the personal computers that everyone, even the poor, now needs to function in our technological society. If private businesses will not make these essential goods at affordable prices, then government can find other people who will.

The fourth imperative is to reinvent American capitalism by literally reforming the values and operating assumptions within business and finance so the economy functions with less wasteful destruction and more responsiveness to society at large. This reform will necessarily go beyond the old regulatory goals of prohibiting fraud and predatory behavior. It also has to include a fundamental overhauling of the obsolete economic valuation that enables companies to extract profit from the carefree destruction of nature or ripping off of workers and communities. In the new corporation, the traditional top-down management will have to share power with all of the other contributors to the firm—workers, investors, suppliers, shareholders, communities—who will have the right to participate in decision making, influence corporate strategies, and oppose scandalous excesses.

Employees from the front office to the shop floor need labor laws that protect their right to collective representation and democratic voice, but workers should also have preferred rights to ownership of the firm. Worker–owners have the power not only to reshape the company's corporate culture, but also to take personal responsibility for their own performance. The democratized workplace respects and protects social values, and also produces more effectively and efficiently. This does not eliminate the need for executive authority, it ensures that everyone has the right to participate in the direction of the firm. Government can assist by offering various incentives for cooperative work relationships and by embracing this goal as capitalism's next great advance toward human self-realization for all.

A comparable set of reforms is needed for the financial system. Investors large and small likewise need to have a voice and legal protection in the financial firms where they park their savings. Wall Street is awash with conflicts of interest in which the managers of money funds abuse investors and depositors in order to serve their larger corporate customers. Communities need to have the power to block reckless subsidies that cities and states are compelled to offer companies to attract jobs. The list of the irregular and often criminal abuses is lengthy.

A significant reform movement has grown up around these issues in recent years, though it has mostly been ignored by regular politics. Movement proponents include major unions and public pension funds, environmentalists, and conscientious financial managers who know how to invest for the long-term without sacrificing profit or social obligations. Their goal is to make capitalism responsible by democratizing it. Creating a trustworthy system will require years of patient experimentation and tough-minded agitation, but the current Wall Street crisis improves the prospects for serious reform.[9]

The fifth imperative is the federal government has to yield some of its own power in order to encourage a new era of social and economic innovation. Dispersing resources and decision making to state and community governments brings these issues closer to the people and gives them greater leverage to devise solutions. This proposal is a hard sell in Washington for obvious reasons, but decentralizing power will lead to freewheeling experiments and departures. The center is paralyzed by encrusted webs of private interests, and its inventiveness is being held hostage by hoary political alliances. Americans at large need the freedom to redefine what the "good life" means in their own lives.

Bringing these decisions closer to home could foster healthy competition among different places and regions to determine what works and what doesn't, what priorities should come first. Some local projects will surely fail or waste money. But others may become working models other people can adapt to their own surroundings. The federal government, meanwhile, can regain credibility by doing well the things that only it can do. Creativity rarely starts at the top.

The sixth and most important imperative is to thicken our democracy. This idea is reflected in all of the above suggestions. By "thickening" I mean giving citizens active influence. They need informal powers and governing mechanisms that permit many more opportunities to advise and consent, to kibitz and object or even to place a temporary hold on public decisions. They need to have the ability to make elected officials listen to them on the people's terms, not the government's. Citizens need to be able to strengthen their relationships with the people who supposedly are representing them.

The American system assigns citizens a very weak role in politics, one that limits them mainly to being spectators who have the occasional chance to vote on something. This weakness may have mattered less when political parties were stronger and more coherently connected to their popular constituencies. But people now are distanced from the action and treated like a lumpish mass. Enabling people to insert themselves into decisions more effectively definitely complicates life for those in power, including those who govern private enterprises. Despite the rhetoric of democracy, American society is still largely organized as a top-down operation. In the workplace most obviously, but also in the public square, people are expected to follow the leader, whether or not they like the direction. There are often severe penalties for individuals who resist. How can Americans learn to become active citizens in a functioning democracy if their everyday lives remain governed by command and control?

★ ★ ★ ★ ★

The possibilities for renewal and transformation of American life collide with the obvious question: How can we afford any of this? That is the usual objection whenever citizens propose major projects serving the general welfare. Economists and other authorities begin poor-mouthing. Their silence was noticeable, however, when the government quickly found something like a trillion dollars to rescue the banks and financial houses in crisis. Nor do elites object when the military machine needs many additional billions for its war plans. The US indebtedness is stark reality, however, and it forces the nation to make hard choices. Our margins for error and waste have narrowed dramatically.

My answer to the cost question is simple: The American people cannot have everything we might want, but we can afford anything that other advanced nations have, from guaranteed health care to modern high-speed rail systems, because we are a lot richer than the others. We can afford anything they can afford—if the American people choose different priorities.

That answer won't satisfy gimlet-eyed budget accountants, but it ought to help people reconsider national priorities. Different choices can be made and, in these tougher times, should be made. In the end, the choices we make depend on our values as a people—what we think matters most.

The simplest measure of our preeminent wealth is income per capita—the total national income divided by the population. The United States has a per capita income of $41,890. That is one-third greater than Japan's per capita income of $31,267. France's is $30,386; Germany's, $29,461; Sweden's, $32,525; and Kuwait's, $26,321. At the bottom of the ladder, scores of poor countries get along with a per capita income of a few thousand dollars or even a few hundred.[10]

I don't want to start an argument about which nationality makes the best use of its money. My point is simply that other rich societies have successfully arranged themselves to ensure that their citizens have comfortable lives with many benefits US citizens lack, even though those nations are far less wealthy. When Americans recognize that money is not the issue, they can consider the real question: What kind of society do we want? What do people need to lead satisfying lives?

Self-assured assumptions of America's superiority—that we live in the best of all possible places—are complicated, even contradicted, by comparisons with other nations. Poverty, for instance, and especially the poverty of children, is a universal yardstick for judging a society's condition. By that measure, America does not look so rich. In the United States, 21.9 percent of children live in "relative poverty"—households with incomes more than 50 percent below the national median. In this regard, the United States is a little bit better off than

Mexico. Portugal, one of the least wealthy of the European Union nations, has a lower rate of child poverty than the United States does—15.6 percent. In Canada, the rate is 14.9 percent; in Germany, 10.2 percent; in France, 7.5 percent; and in Denmark, only 2.4 percent. It is not surprising that poor nations have large populations of children in poverty. But people are shocked by the child poverty in America.

Inequality, as Americans know, has a direct impact on how people live, on which choices they are able to make. Inequality in a nation can be measured by the distribution of income from top to bottom. How much of the nation's total income reaches the poorest 10 percent of citizens? To put it another way, how generously does the country share prosperity with its least fortunate? Among the richest industrial nations, Japan does the best: Its poorest 10 percent get 4.8 percent of the total income. Sweden's poorest get 3.7 percent; Germany's, 3.3 percent; France's, 2.8 percent. The United States shares only 1.8 percent of its national income with the poorest 10 percent of its people. We rank eighty-fifth among all nations—behind even China.[11]

Other nations make very different choices about society's needs, not just in relation to the poor, but also to the broad ranks of citizens, the working people. The political goal in virtually all other advanced economies is to provide a reliable floor for families and children so they have what they need to maintain secure and comfortable lives. The US system looks quite stingy in that regard.

"Americans remain remarkably unaware that generous work-family reconciliation policies operate successfully—and with widespread political support—in many other rich countries," Janet C. Gornick of City University of New York has observed.[12]

The ignorance of Americans can be partly attributed to the major media. When the US press writes about European social systems, for example, it typically depicts them as extravagant failures, burdens that drag down economic growth. For two decades, US media commentators have been predicting the demise of European social protections, echoing the views of both American and European elites. It has not happened. Because the political resistance is so fierce, only modest changes have been made at the margins of these policies. Meanwhile, the economies of the European Union are flourishing compared to that of the troubled United States.

For starters, every advanced nation in Europe has a nationalized system that guarantees to all citizens universal health care that is cheaper and usually more effective at sustaining health and longevity. European governments likewise provide national pensions, plus myriad other laws to protect families, women, children, and workers from raw market forces.

The precious commodity that matters more to Europeans is time—time to live their lives—and government measures actively free up people's time. Employees are guaranteed paid leave from work to take care of family duties, for childbirth and attending to the illnesses of relatives. National laws limit the number of working hours and ensure parity in benefits and wages for part-time workers. High-quality and affordable child care is available to working parents.

France provides a family allowance that essentially compensates mothers and fathers, single or married, for the work they do in rearing children. The écoles maternelles are France's much admired universal preschools, and these neighborhood institutions are used by families of all classes.

Germany provides a monthly child allowance for each child, and substantially larger benefits for low-income families. German children are supported in this way until they are sixteen years old, or until the age of twenty-seven if they are attending college or vocational school. German parents continue to draw their pay for up to twenty-four months if they stay home to rear infants. Their jobs are guaranteed for three years.

The United States, Gornick reported, is one of only five countries in the world without a national policy of paid maternity leave. The US child care system is among the least developed in the industrialized world. Ask any couple about the ongoing tensions of arranging day care for small children while both parents are working. Many families cope by doing split-shift parenting—one parent leaves for work when the other comes home to tend the kids.

The stress is compounded by the fact that Americans work longer hours than their counterparts in competing industrial nations, longer hours than even the hardworking Japanese. Nearly two-thirds of US couples work more than eighty hours a week combined—that's an unthinkable burden in any European country. The average US worker is on the job 1,824 hours each year. For a German worker, it is only 1,426 hours, about the same as in France. The four-hundred-hour difference is equivalent to nearly ten weeks. A worker in Japan is closer to one in the United States at 1,789 hours a year, but Japan's companies also grant protective guarantees that in some ways go beyond Europe's.

Leisure time is simply valued more highly in Europe than in the United States. The decision to grant employees paid vacations is largely left to companies in the United States, not addressed by law. In Europe, all workers are legally entitled to vacations that are roughly twice as long as the American average. When vacation time is combined with public holidays, workers get twenty-eight days off a year in the Netherlands and Britain, thirty-two in Germany and Sweden, and up to thirty-six in France. In the United States, everyone gets ten official holidays, whether paid or unpaid, but beyond that, it depends on where they work. Medium and large firms on average grant fourteen paid vacation days after five years of employment, and a couple more days after ten years. Part-time workers, including many working mothers, have no paid vacation time.

The social guarantees of other nations reflect each country's collective values—their national consensus about what matters to people—and they are embedded in law. This approach automatically leads to greater equality in how people live, despite differences in income and wealth. In these countries, if white-collar employees get long vacations, so do the factory workers.

One crucial reason for these differences between Europe and the United States is the presence of strong labor movements and high union membership in workplaces. In Germany, 68 percent of workers are covered by collective bargaining agreements. In France, 90 percent are. Even in conservative Britain, 30 percent are in unions. In the United States, only 14 percent of the workforce has union representation, and that figure is only 9 percent in the private sector. Polls consistently indicate that more than half of American workers, about 55 percent, would like to become union members if they could. But they are effectively blocked from doing so by corporate antilabor strategies, such as firing key workers who are trying to organize unions, in violation of labor law. Employers illegally threaten other workers with reprisals if they attempt to exercise their rights.

The highly developed social contracts in Europe were created by generations of political conflict—usually left versus right—but they also originated thanks to strong support from conservative churches, both Catholic and Protestant. In defense of family and society, the churches were and are leading advocates for social protections, while left-wing labor organizations are aggressive watchdogs that make sure the rights of families and workers are honored.

I am not proposing that the United States copy Europe or Japan. Americans have to work out their own versions of solutions. Nor do I suggest that somehow

Americans are in competition with other countries to be "the best." My point is that American political ambitions look quite timid and incomplete in comparison with what many other nations achieved long ago. It is simply fraudulent for governing elites to insist that the United States cannot afford any of these social rights and benefits. The reality is that some powerful interests who do not want them have the ability to block them, no matter what the people may want.

America's competition is not with the rest of the world, it is with ourselves. Who gets to decide what our society should look like in the future? And who has the power to make it happen?

CHAPTER TWELVE

MACHINE POLITICS

If Americans were to embark on instituting an agenda of deep reform, they would run into a huge log across the road—the heft and girth of corporate America. Major corporations and the Wall Street finance system are the modern equivalent of those old urban political machines that once exercised such great influence, especially over the Democratic Party. The big-city machines sometimes obstructed progress, but they also played an important role by speaking for working-class voters, new immigrants, and scorned ethnic groups.[1]

A corporation speaks for itself, though it claims to represent shareholders, employees, and the communities it operates in. A corporation finances both political parties, but especially the Republicans. It manages the nation's mainstream political dialogue by supplying a steady flow of expert opinion, ideas, and propaganda. When the largest and most sophisticated corporations work together in lobbying alliances, as they regularly do, their collective influence acts like a headlock on democracy.

This behavior is so commonplace that it is widely accepted as normal. Most politicians will not talk about it. Occasionally, one might assail a particular company that has behaved roguishly or publicly deplore the influence of big money on his or her colleagues, but conventional politicians rarely discuss the systemic problem of corporate power because it might sound radical. It also might provoke corporate retaliation in the next election cycle.

The dominating power wielded by business and finance is a central reality in our deformed democracy. Government is a profit center that private enterprise feeds off of and corrupts while it simultaneously blocks action on achieving goals that the citizenry strongly desires. Companies and their front groups have a very wide wingspan, and they use their many skills to undermine existing laws and veto popular reforms, to manipulate politics and government in ways that are unavailable to ordinary citizens. Corporate power could have been a lively topic for debate during the presidential nominating process, given the abundant evidence of insider deals and other scandalous behavior. Save for honorable exceptions like John Edwards and Dennis Kucinich, most candidates wouldn't touch it. The closest they got was deploring the influence of unnamed lobbyists (though many candidates' campaigns were managed by lobbyists). This was occasionally embarrassing for politicians who failed to understand the public's distrust of Washington insiders.

Consider this sampler of corporate outrages the candidates might have discussed but didn't.

General Electric, one of the country's most admired companies, is admired especially for its tax accounting. In 2002, GE earned $12 billion in profit but paid nothing in corporate income taxes. Indeed, it collected a modest rebate of $33 million from the federal government. GE is a champion at harvesting tax breaks. From 2001 to 2003, the company collected $9.5 billion in so-called tax incentives that are supposed to encourage greater US investment by businesses. During those years, GE reduced its US investment by 40 percent.[2]

Other famous names also took the money and ignored the purpose of the tax incentives—SBC Communications, IBM, Microsoft, AT&T, Verizon, and many others. Robert S. McIntyre of Citizens for Tax Justice examined the years 2001 to 2003 and found eighty-two Fortune 500 companies with profits totaling $102 billion that paid zero taxes in one or more of those years. Instead, they harvested $12.6 billion in tax rebates. The 275 companies covered by McIntyre's study produced $1.1 trillion in profit, but instead of paying the statutory rate of 35 percent, they were able to shelter more than half of their profits and paid an effective rate of 18 percent—roughly what working people pay on their incomes.

The corporate income tax used to be a major component in the financing of the federal government, but no longer. Between new tax breaks and rate reductions enacted by the Bush administration, the corporate income tax in 2003 fell to 7.4 percent of all federal tax revenue. In the 1950s, corporate income taxes provided 32 percent of all federal revenue—one-third of the cost of government. The corporate burden has been steadily whittled away ever since.

When companies get out of paying their taxes, the burden naturally falls on other taxpayers. Business lobbyists continue to assert that US corporate taxes are higher than those in competing countries, but this hasn't been true for many years. Nations that are members of the Organisation for Economic Co-operation and Development (OECD), representing the advanced economies of Europe and Asia, where the average tax rate on corporations is one-fourth higher than in the United States.

Before it went bankrupt, Enron was a leading user of offshore shelters and off–balance sheet "entities" designed to avoid taxes and conceal the company's debts and losses. Before its collapse, Enron had 881 subsidiaries in tax-haven countries (692 in the Cayman Islands alone) and had paid no taxes in four of the five years from 1996 to 2000, when the company's reputation for dynamic innovation was at its peak.

Wachovia, one of the nation's highly regarded megabanks before its collapse, specializes in leasing deals that shelter profits from taxes. At one point, Wachovia pretended to own a German town's sewer system. This allowed it (don't ask me how) to avoid paying any federal income tax in 2002, a year when the bank told its shareholders its profits were $4 billion.

Boeing, the jetliner manufacturer and defense contractor, is another major winner thanks to tax avoidance. In 2003, it collected a tax rebate of $1.7 billion— $700 million more than its profits. But Boeing is better known for manipulating the government in less than reputable ways.[3] Boeing obtained proprietary documents from its rival, Lockheed Martin, with the illegal assistance of an Air Force procurement official who steered Pentagon business to Boeing. The company used the purloined information to rig its bids on major contracts. The Air Force's second-ranking acquisitions official, Darleen Druyun, was rewarded with a $250,000 job at Boeing. She subsequently confessed and went to prison.

But Boeing negotiated a "deferred prosecution" agreement for itself. (AOL Time Warner, Merrill Lynch, KPMG, and other large firms have also arranged such gentlemanly understandings when faced with criminal prosecution.) The Justice Department promised not to charge Boeing or its top executives with any crimes in exchange for a payment of $615 million. Government lawyers originally sought $1 billion, but were told by superiors to be more forgiving.

At the settlement, Boeing announced that it had worked things out "in a constructive way." The Pentagon restored Boeing to good standing as a defense contractor; it was not eager to have its second-largest defense contractor and the maker of "smart" bombs, F-15 fighters, Apache helicopters, cruise missiles, and parts of all three of the military's new advanced fighter planes convicted of a felony.

Like the best and biggest corporate machines, Boeing is staffed to be politically versatile and intimately connected with both parties. To achieve this, it recruits from the government. At one time or another, Boeing has had General John Shalikashvili, retired chairman of the Joint Chiefs of Staff, on its board; former deputy secretary of defense Rudy de Leon (a Democrat) heading up its Washington office; and three members of the Pentagon's Defense Policy Board, neoconservative Republican advocate and former assistant secretary of defense Richard Perle, Air Force general and former Air Force chief of staff Ronald Fogelman, and Navy admiral and former vice chair of the Joint Chiefs of Staff David Jeremiah. Retired senator Bennett Johnston of Louisiana lobbies Democrats, and former representative Bill Paxon of New York does the same with Republicans. Longtime US ambassador Thomas Pickering looks after the interests of foreign customers in the market for weapons.

Wal-Mart, the retail giant, figured out how to save money on state taxes by renting its buildings to itself, using a tax-exempt real estate trust as the middleman. "The strategy is complex," the *Wall Street Journal* reported, "but the bottom line is simple: It has saved Wal-Mart from paying several hundred million dollars in taxes. . . . And Wal-Mart is far from alone."[4]

Pfizer, the major drug manufacturer, transferred ownership of valuable patents to Britain, where the royalty income would be taxed at a lower rate. Stanley Tools moved itself offshore to achieve similar benefits. Offshoring was authorized by law as another way to improve American competitiveness. Wealthy people do the same. The Tax Justice Network estimates that rich people around the world hold some $11.5 trillion in offshore assets. Americans hold a significant share of that.[5]

More than 115 companies have been caught backdating stock options for senior executives (including celebrity CEO Steve Jobs of Apple) to inflate the value of their bonuses. But the *Wall Street Journal* pleaded their innocence: "Were all of the CEOs, CFOs and general counsels at *all* of these companies greedy and corrupt? Seems unlikely," an editorial insisted. The right-wing business paper blamed Congress for allowing "ambiguous option accounting standards."[6]

In 2004, the Democratic presidential candidate, Senator John Kerry, came up with a nifty answer to one of the popular complaints about globalization. It was a way to help American workers without hurting US multinational corporations. Kerry proposed granting a one-time tax holiday to the companies. The multinationals could repatriate hundreds of billions of dollars in overseas profits and pay taxes at a sharply reduced rate so the capital would be invested in creating jobs at home. Republicans liked Kerry's idea so much that they swiftly enacted it into law, even before the presidential election that Kerry ultimately lost.[7]

Many multinationals did bring their profits home—more than $200 billion—and it was taxed at a reduced rate of only 5.25 percent, instead of the average effective rate of 25 percent (which is what companies pay after claiming deductions and exceptions). What most companies did not do was invest their windfall in US jobs. Eli Lilly, the drugmaker, saved more than $2.3 billion in US taxes while also reducing its American workforce by 22,000 jobs. The drug industry in general, the *New York Times* reported, repatriated about $100 billion in offshore profits and paid trivial taxes while laying off tens of thousands of American workers.[8]

In high-tech and other sectors, the money freed up by the tax amnesty was mostly used for other purposes—stock buybacks, dividend payments, regular compensation, even advertising and marketing, the *Wall Street Journal* reported.[9] Some tax analysts warned that granting this amnesty to large and profitable international companies was a dangerous precedent: The multinationals would again store up their overseas profits, then demand another amnesty to bring the money home—then another and another.

"Corporate welfare," a label used by critics on both the right and the left, takes many forms. The contracting out of government functions to private, for-profit firms doubled under the Bush administration and now stands at $400 billion a year, according to the *Multinational Monitor*.[10] The public became more familiar with the process because of the many scandals involving supplying services in the Iraq war zone. The army paid Halliburton nearly $2 billion for work that officials could not prove was done.

Similar contracting abuses have proliferated for years in the domestic government, ever since Vice President Albert Gore embraced the idea in his Reinventing Government initiative. Does it save taxpayers money or increase efficiency? Evidently not. A 2004 study by George W. Bush's Office of Management and Budget found that federal employees are more efficient than private contractors 90 percent of the time.[11]

Deregulation also created new profit centers for private business. Electric utilities used to operate with limits on their profits that were determined by the rate-setting regulatory agencies. The companies typically enjoyed a monopoly in the markets they served. Since they produce an essential need that people must buy, their profit levels were held to limited rates of return. But under deregulation, the staid old utilities have become high fliers that deliver an average annual return to shareholders of 22 percent, according to the industry's Edison Electric Institute.[12]

Deregulation created a rich opportunity for financial players. As *New York Times* reporter David Cay Johnston explained, Wall Street hedge funds developed a very lucrative market in buying and selling utility companies and power plants, quickly doubling or tripling returns to their investors. Each time ownership was flipped, hedge funds took their profits and left the electric companies deeper in debt—forcing them to raise their rates for customers.[13]

Deregulating the utilities did not benefit household consumers, as had been promised. Electricity bills did not decline with more competition or improved efficiency, as Johnston pointed out. Customers in western states were fleeced with a series of spectacular price-fixing scandals. In many cases, electricity bills are rising rapidly—faster than the price of fuel—because customers are saddled with monthly surcharges put in place to pay off the debt accumulated by the ownership swaps.

Where is the outrage? Ralph Nader, the legendary public advocate, keeps asking that question. Back in the 1960s and 1970s, Nader employed an effective method for enacting major reform laws—expose the shocking facts, arouse public anger, and then lean hard on Congress to respond. But Nader-style reform has broken down. The shocking facts are still regularly exposed, often by leading newspapers, but nothing much happens afterwards. People figure this is how the system works and it is not going to change.

There is plenty of outrage, however, even if the scandal exposures do not stir Washington. Robert Weissman, editor of the *Multinational Monitor,* collected polling data and observed that Americans have "shockingly low regard" for big business—even worse than the dismal ratings they assigned to Congress and President Bush.[14]

A 2007 Harris Poll asked which industries, sector by sector, people regard as "generally honest and trustworthy." The highest rated sector was supermarkets, approved of by only 32 percent of the people. Other sectors did poorly: oil companies, 3 percent; health insurance companies, 7 percent; telephone companies, 10 percent; drug companies, 11 percent; electric and gas utilities, 15 percent. People know these companies from personal experience.

When the Harris Poll asked a broader question, 84 percent of the people said they think big corporations have too much power in Washington.[15] This is not news. It is also discussed very little in politics. Polls have been reporting overwhelming public discontent with corporate power for more than two decades. People also don't expect the government to do anything about it. An entire book could be filled with stories about illegitimate, even illegal corporate behavior and the public's rage about it. My sampler of outrages is just a snapshot of how the corporate machine performs in the governing process.

A corporation feeds on the government like a predator. It harvests vast profits from the tax money collected from other taxpayers while working with other corporations on other fronts to stymie the governing system. The corporate machine writes laws for itself (the tax code, for example) and disables existing laws to undermine their original meanings (such as labor rights and environmental protections). Through trade associations and think tanks, corporations collectively block legislation that might intrude on their interests—think of universal health care, trade reform, environmental reform, pension reform, and workplace reform, to name a few.

Corporations collaborate to seduce or capture the regulatory agencies that oversee their sectors, often by getting corporate hacks appointed to run those agencies (the FDA, the FTC, the FCC, the SEC, the Interior and Agriculture Departments, the Federal Reserve). They further disable the regulatory agencies (such as the EPA) with endless legal challenges and political manipulations. Corporations harvest subsidies and major contracts from departments (like the Pentagon) that, in turn, become their advocates and protectors before Congress. When a corporation breaks the law, it has the option of settling in cash or talking its way out of criminal prosecution. In this era of recurring corporate scandals, fraud has been largely decriminalized.

The major corporations also shape new priorities for the government, developing policy initiatives that ostensibly serve some higher public purpose but also generate cash flow for the companies. For obvious reasons, these proposals are a lot easier to enact than genuine reform measures. When Bush legislated Medicare drug benefits for the elderly, he created a multibillion-dollar bonanza for the drug and insurance industries (their lobbyists helped write the legislation). Democrats had tried to pass Medicare drug benefits for more than thirty years, but they were always thwarted by the industry. But Bush's plan blocked Medicare from negotiating lower drug prices from companies.

When Congress enacts a new environmental law that corporate interests oppose but cannot stop, their lobbyists focus on the fine print and get legislators to plant "poison pills" in the enforcement language—loopholes that let companies evade compliance for many years, or even decades. One of the most powerful antipollution laws, which requires companies to disclose annually their releases of toxic chemicals into the air, land, and water, was enacted in 1986. It had no enforcement penalties, but making this information available to the public enabled citizens and communities to fight back and they did, quite effectively. The EPA gutted the law in 2006. It was "streamlined," the agency claimed, to make the reporting process less cumbersome for companies. Twelve state governments have sued to restore the law's original meaning.[16]

Above all, corporations have walked away from their obligations to society. They routinely inflict injuries upon common social values, employees, communities, and the ecological imperative. Corporations receive enormous benefits from government, yet they tenaciously resist paying their fair share to support the government. Sometimes, companies are the open adversaries of government. At other times, they pretend to be social partners.

Corporations, all in all, are "free riders" on the system. Like the US multinationals I discussed earlier, corporations have abandoned the unwritten social contract of commitments to people and society. Yet, they still demand and get preferential treatment from government. They extract wealth and favors from the public sphere, but do not reciprocate; this one-sided exchange defines the illegitimacy of the modern corporation in politics.

★ ★ ★ ★ ★

But not all corporations act like irresponsible free riders. My description accurately portrays most of the largest and most aggressive corporate organizations, but not all of them. The generalization is unfair to a virtuous minority that behaves quite differently. These exceptions are profitable companies, but they do not take the low road, in either influencing politics or their corporate performance. They do not insist on maximizing profits by gaming the tax code with extreme gimmicks. In general, they obey environmental laws and sometimes go beyond what federal standards require. They maintain equable relations with their employees, union or nonunion, and with their local communities and suppliers.

On the whole, these corporations are good guys, not predators. For whatever reasons, these firms resist the fierce pressures from financial investors and withstand the price competition from low-road rivals. Contrary to market propaganda's teachings, these well-performing companies do not sacrifice profits by adhering to higher values. Many of them are market leaders in their sectors. They do better because they are better run and their employees take pride in beating the competition.

The contrasts among companies in corporate behavior are not widely understood or appreciated, partly because business lore generally ignores these distinctions. Business schools tend to celebrate the cold-blooded titans whose slash-and-burn tactics produce such good numbers for investors. The "good guys" do not make a big deal about their distinctive differences since that might alienate other managements they may someday need as allies. Environmentalists, however, have identified dramatic differences in corporate behavior and documented how eco-friendly companies perform better in business terms.

Innovest, a financial advisory firm, measured high-performance companies by using hundreds of concrete indicators on ecological and social behavior. It found that several hundred companies that earned high marks financially outperform lower-rated companies, winning better credit ratings and higher stock prices. Even within notorious sectors like oil, chemicals, and electric utilities, there are vast differences. The "good" companies enjoy a performance premium in the stock market—higher valuations that range on average from 12 to 17 percent.

These corporate differences may reflect not so much the CEO's personal values as the caliber of the management. The smartly managed company thinks ahead and prepares for long-term consequences, avoids lawsuits and potential liabilities, solves problems promptly, and cuts operating costs by improving efficiency instead of using rip-and-run tactics. A low-rated company tends to cut corners and frequently gets in trouble with lawsuits and unexpected losses. It ignores the collateral damage caused by its operations and goes for quick-hit profits rather than long-term development.[17]

These differences suggest that society and government have more leverage than they realize to compel significant changes in corporate behavior—if we are willing to, so to speak, separate the sheep from the goats and treat them differently. This approach, forcefully applied, can lead companies to align their behavior more closely with what the country wants. To put it simply, why should taxpayers subsidize miscreant companies that are actively damaging society or plundering public resources? Why not redirect the flow of government's rewards and penalties to support the good guys and make the bad guys pay a price for antisocial behavior and recurring offenses?

Making such distinctions is an important bridge to making other reforms. The tragedy of American economic life is that the exemplary corporations are in the virtuous minority that is largely unheralded. In an earlier era, there were many more of them. But a lot of companies that had good intentions were eventually pushed into adopting harsher, short-term strategies by overbearing financiers who demanded higher returns right away, with no thought for the future. And financial firms and markets are blind to collateral consequences, though financial firms could be changed, too, if government made distinctions among them.

Leveraging corporate differences is a promising idea, but it requires the government to change first. Politicians would have to stand up to their patrons and turn against machine politics. They would have to discard old habits and reform the practices that distribute public largesse to private interests. Neither lobbyists nor most members of Congress will have much enthusiasm for that idea.

★　★　★　★　★

At the risk of upsetting some old friends, I must point out that the corrupted values and undisciplined routines of modern government probably had their origins in the great liberal reforms of the New Deal. Fundamental changes enacted in the Roosevelt era live on in the ethos and structure of the federal government, but many of those achievements have atrophied or been debased over the years. The honorable legacy of an activist government that is willing to intervene in the private sector to advance social justice and the general welfare was gradually transmuted into something very different.

Big government in Washington became like a grand bazaar. It is as if the gleaming marble shrines to democracy are surrounded now by tents and stalls. It is a place filled with deal makers and the noisy commerce of buying and selling. Noble intentions have been sidelined in a government system that lacks serious planning and self-discipline, that dispenses generous public favors without demanding much in return, that cannot distinguish between the national interest and the many grasping hands of private interests. Leading corporations are naturally the dominant players in this place because they have been the working partners of government since the New Deal's dramatic days.[18]

I am not making an argument for small government or against a government that intervenes aggressively in the private economy. I do not intend to second-guess the New Dealers and their decisions. I am in awe of what they accomplished in very difficult circumstances—a fundamental reordering of government and society. But that was then. We live in a different country now.

If modern reformers simply try to recreate the New Deal model, the results are likely to disappoint the expectations. Unless new principles that close down the bazaar of buying and selling are introduced, the federal government will again fall short of its promises, from universal health care, to restoring prudent financial regulation, to creating a stronger enforcement system that deals promptly with the causes of global warming and other threats. If Congress appropriates the financing for such major reforms, the grand bazaar will find ways to spend the money, but that does not mean the results will reliably serve the public interest.

In the crisis of the Great Depression, the federal government learned both how to manage the national economy while focusing on broad social objectives and how to intervene confidently in the marketplace. The New Deal began a much more precise and vigorous policing of the behavior of finance and business. But it also worked cooperatively with the private sector to revive prosperity and advance public welfare. While Washington regulated businesses, it also nurtured their success. The government supplied public financing to build a vast infrastructure and create millions of jobs. It developed supportive rules and the business conditions that companies needed. Government recapitalized many firms ruined by the Depression and subsidized the development of many new industrial sectors. Government spending force-fed market demand, especially for the armaments needed for the approaching world war.

Conservatives bitterly opposed all this on principle. By expanding the reach of government enormously, the New Deal permanently buried the old conservative order of a small national government with limited purpose, free-market economics, and the long-standing constitutional doctrine that property and wealth are honored before people and society. The Supreme Court fiercely resisted this shift for many years, and some injustices embedded in legal doctrine were not entirely corrected. But the New Dealers fashioned the basis for a more equitable, egalitarian society. The right-wing justices who currently sit on the Supreme Court are laboring to undo Roosevelt's victories and restore the primacy of property over people.

Conservative resistance to the New Deal in the face of popular support for it consigned Republicans to minority status in Congress for several decades. But the Republicans eventually came around. Instead of futilely trying to repeal the big-government system Roosevelt had created, a new generation of conservatives decided in the 1970s to use the New Deal's tools for their own purposes—directing subsidies, tax breaks, gross spending, and irregular market interventions to serve their clients and, not coincidentally, to reward property and capital before the broader society. Since liberal Democrats were the authors and inheritors of the activist government, they could not object to conservatives aggressively using it as a tool, but only to the Republicans' choice of preferences.

In other words, both parties gradually became comfortable with big government's undiscriminating excesses. The convergence is what led to the mess I call the grand bazaar. With the two major parties competing to dispense rewards to differing causes and clients, nobody is left to enforce self-discipline or to apply orderly principles for achieving national priorities. Instead, Washington tries to do a little of almost everything. Democrats on occasion have tried to impose fiscal discipline, but at other times they have whooped it up and joined in the bidding. Republicans still preach the small-government line, but that is not how they govern.

The country, it seems, is stuck with the worst aspects of both parties—Republicans' lost sobriety of judgment, and Democrats' abandonment of their historic commitment to social reform. Both parties share the faith in undifferentiated economic growth and subsidizing businesses as the best way to promote growth. The logic had direct relevance to overcoming the massive suffering during the Great Depression. In our affluent times, however, it has become the tax accountant's version of pork-barrel politics.

The New Deal left behind another debilitating legacy that contributes to the confusion and paralysis typical of modern governance. It is the business–government partnership that formed during the crises of the 1930s and World War II. Despite Republicans' loathing for Roosevelt and his mocking disdain for them, business leaders collaborated with government in a cooperative relationship that functioned successfully for many years. This relationship effectively ended a generation ago, when corporate America unilaterally resigned from the partnership. One by one, famous corporate names declared they were no longer going to honor long-standing commitments to the social contract, and instead they launched a broad counterattack on the federal government's power and reputation.

Yet, despite this rupture, the original collaboration has endured, and so has business's privileged position. In Washington politics, business continues to enjoy a priority claim on public resources. Most politicians act as though business and government can solve the largest public problems by getting together and working out the terms. But the experience of recent decades suggests the opposite is true.

Whether the reform issue is health care or pensions or global warming, deferring to corporate preferences puts a noose around reform ambitions. Corporate strategists get to insist on a solution that is acceptable to them, or else they mobilize to kill it. The result repeatedly is a safe solution that does not disturb the corporate world, but also does not solve the problem. This confronts politicians with a cruel choice—support a solution that actually may work, or keep the business interests pacified by enacting halfway measures that are sure to fail.

In New Deal days, the political dynamics were utterly different. American manufacturing was on the rise and the leading industrial corporations became virtual partners of the federal government, cooperating in crucial ways with New Deal reforms. These major companies, along with a handful of progressive investment banks, lent their prestigious support to landmark legislation like Social Security. They collaborated with the government more substantively on social programs and the economy's conversion to wartime production.

Progressive corporations were important actors in the New Deal's social order because, as employers, they were the agents who provided such benefits as health insurance, pensions, equitable labor relations, and other social advances associated with the New Deal. Typically, these new benefits for workers and families were not government programs in the usual sense, but rather voluntary private arrangements worked out in wage bargaining with labor unions. Government blessed the arrangement and discreetly financed it with tax subsidies.

The philosophy of that era, improbable as it sounds now, was known as corporate liberalism. General Electric was the leading exemplar of the progressive-minded companies. Starting in the 1920s, GE was a pioneer in developing workplace and community relations that defused the harsher conflicts of labor versus capital. Before government became a social activist, General Electric was already experimenting with innovations like profit sharing and worker councils. Its CEO even articulated a vision that someday workers would become the company's owners as the majority shareholders. Cooperation, GE argued then, enhances efficiency and sustains profit and long-term prosperity.

Other big names—Kodak, DuPont, General Motors, even US Steel and Standard Oil—also supported various progressive measures. This enlightened relationship between business and government was encouraged and kept honest by the vigorous and growing labor movement. Collectively, these three elements fashioned the informal understandings known as the social contract. Companies would provide their employees with job security; industrial wages that rose in step with productivity; and health insurance, pensions, and other benefits, and inclusive bargaining would be the means to settling disputes. Not everyone in the country benefitted, but the industrial arrangement became the core model for the postwar economy and helped create the large and stable American middle class.

Then it fell apart. In the 1970s, major companies began to break their truce with organized labor and also turned hard against the government. The Business Roundtable and other groups allied with hard-right ideologues who were taking command of the Republican Party. General Electric once again led the way, this time as the premier example of the harsh new bottom-line strategy that put corporations in conflict with workers and social values. Frank P. Doyle, GE executive vice president, acknowledged in retirement, "We did a lot of violence to the expectations of the American workforce." Thanks to the civil rights movement that broke racial segregation in the South, major national companies were free to relocate plants and jobs in southern states, where they could give nonunion workers lower wages and fewer benefits. Next, they began moving the jobs overseas.[19]

The corporations' rightward political shift was driven by real distress. Stagnation and inflation in the 1970s undermined corporate profits, and brilliant new competitors emerged from Europe and Asia. The regulatory system created by the New Deal—particularly for the financial industry—could not cope with the new conditions. Inflation undermined the regulatory ceilings on interest rates, and they were gradually abandoned. A fabulous new industrial era was being born—technology based on computers and semiconductor chips—but rigid industrial-sector regulations stood in the way of innovation.

At that point, liberal Democrats might have reformed the regulatory system to make it more flexible. Instead, they retreated. With the election of Ronald Reagan in 1980, the old liberal order was over.

My own political education, I have to acknowledge, proceeded roughly in reverse through the great ideological transition of the 1970s and 1980s. Having grown up Republican and conservative in the managerial middle class, I shared the lingering hostility toward the Roosevelt era. I began to understand and admire the logic of the New Deal only belatedly—just as it was crashing. The joke was on me. At the very moment I was embracing the core principles of economic liberalism, the political system discarded them.

My wrong-way conversion was grounded in real experience—what I learned as a young reporter traveling around the country. I encountered the highs and the lows of American life—degrading poverty amid fabulous wealth, rank injustices and contradictions generated by the economic system and tolerated or even supported by most of the political order. As an adult, I saw the country whole for the first time, including the rugged, sometimes cruel realities many people routinely face that contrasted with the comfortable circumstances of my own sheltered upbringing. It seemed wrong to me, as well as unnecessary. New Deal economics, I discovered, spoke to the broader, more complicated America that I wanted to be part of. I retained a good measure of conservative skepticism, but it was sweetened by liberalism's thirst for justice.

Instead, government's obligation to the general welfare became enmeshed in fierce ideological combat that usually results in the corporate interests prevailing. It would be nice to think that a business–government truce that revives the old cooperative spirit could be negotiated. I have heard this yearning expressed many times by businesspeople, men and women who are aware that their companies used to operate with greater respect for and responsibility to the larger objectives of society and their own employees. The story of corporate liberalism tells these people that it should be possible to restore the relationship. Personally, I suspect that it is too late for reconciliation.

The corporate institution has not fulfilled its lofty potential. It has regressed. It has returned in many ways to the brutish practices that were the rule before the New Deal—intensely pursuing returns over the interests of both society and its own employees and supporting communities. Companies promote the conservative ideology of a smaller government, but they do not live by it. They have developed the machine politics that steadily adds to the privileges they first enjoyed in the New Deal.

After having broken the social contract and manipulated politics to harvest more rewards, the corporate world can hardly be trusted to keep its word or collaborate in good faith with government. Yet the government remains deeply entangled with corporations and cannot easily break free of the corrupt relationship. When major reforms are on the table for consideration, discussions in Washington essentially ask two questions: What approach will work best, and will it be good for business. Those two goals often are incompatible, so government decides to drop the best solution and do something less effective that business will accept. Roughly speaking, that is how lobbyists trump the public.

If America is ever to develop a mature system of sustaining social protections and guarantees, the government somehow has to break free of the partnership and stop giving in to the private needs of business and finance. In other words, the government has to clearly separate the public and private spheres, then decide that on some important matters it must act in the best interests of the people instead of sacrificing the social objective to the demands of private corporate preferences.

The US system is incomplete and often dysfunctional because private partners have repeatedly effectively vetoed sound ideas or threatened to withdraw from the long-standing partnership. Corporate leverage in these matters relies on the unusual premise of the original New Deal arrangements: that corporations' participation is voluntary. In political bargaining, if companies do not like the terms being offered, they not only can use their clout to rally political opposition, they can also decide as employers not to play. Business–government bargaining, therefore, is often influenced by the threat, and employers have used it again and again to persuade government to water down legislation to whatever solution they prefer.

Washington will never be able to solve large problems like universal health care or guaranteed universal pensions unless it breaks the business–government partnership in order to pursue an uncompromised public solution. Many Americans recently have been shocked to learn that their employers are free to cancel long-promised benefits, including health care insurance, pensions, and other social contract assurances. There is no contract, it turns out.

Even union members who, in hard bargaining with companies, had given up wage increases in exchange for improved benefits have found themselves mouse-trapped by corporate business decisions. Companies discovered that they could generally break union contracts by declaring bankruptcy and asking the judge to relieve them of their contractual obligations to employees. Workers lost out, and without recompense for what they had given up in the original bargaining.

The essential choice in any major reform is whether government will step up to its responsibility and, with full authority, deal with the public problem, not the business problem, to further the general welfare instead of private interests. This means enacting programs that are mandatory, not voluntary, and that subordinate the private sphere to the common good.

Social Security is a living example of the necessity of making programs mandatory. It succeeds as a trustworthy system of social insurance because it covers everyone and neither workers nor employers can opt out of it. "Mandatory" is an unpopular word, but it often is the key to practical success. Social Security is a monopoly, but its administrative costs are much lower—dramatically so—than privately operated pension plans. A profit margin is not part of its overhead.

The strong political support for universal health care, for example, founders in the face of this public–private question, which explains politicians' reluctance to resolve the conflict. The sensible solution, as other nations have demonstrated, is a system of nationalized health care covering everyone that is financed and supervised solely by the central government, which can control the rapacious inflation of costs that the private, profit-making system produces. Politicians usually describe the health care crisis in terms of the number of Americans who lack health insurance—almost 50 million, nearly one-sixth of the population. But that is the symptom, not the cause, of the rising costs.

People don't have health insurance because they can't afford it. The country can't afford it either. With each passing year, the health care industry swallows larger and larger chunks of the GDP. Comparisons with advanced nations that have nationalized health care systems demonstrate that Americans pay much more for health care and get far less in return, judging by indicators of good health. Administrative costs account for 31 percent of all health care spending in the United States, but only 17 percent in Canada's single-payer system. Administrative costs for Medicare, the nationalized health care program for the elderly, are only about 3 percent, compared to 13 to 15 percent for private insurers.[20]

None of the leading presidential candidates in 2008 were willing to propose a national solution. Only also-ran Representative Dennis Kucinich endorsed a single-payer system, sometimes known as Medicare for all. Most 2008 candidates proposed halfway approaches involving variations on a public–private system that maintain the current system of employer-provided plans underwritten by private insurance companies, but tack on government-provided alternatives and subsidies for insurance costs for low-income families.

The trouble is that less radical approaches have been tried again and again by state governments over the last twenty years and have failed. Six states—Massachusetts in 1988 and again in 2006, Oregon, Minnesota, Tennessee, Vermont, and Washington—have vowed to cover every citizen with affordable health insurance. Every state has failed to deliver, according to David U. Himmelstein and Steffie Woolhandler, Harvard Medical School professors and longtime advocates of a nationalized system.[21]

Back in 1994, Hillary Clinton attempted to implement a more ambitious reform plan, essentially by buying off different sectors of the industry. She bargained privately with a half dozen of the largest insurance companies and worked out concessions for the auto industry, hospitals, doctors, and other interests. The resulting plan was so nightmarishly complex that it overshadowed its true intent—controlling costs and prices. The plan failed politically, in any case, because the private interests involved, under pressure from their Republican allies, abandoned her. As a result, instead of government managing the health care system by attempting to control costs, the insurance industry did so through HMOs that approved or rejected each patient's treatment. Fifteen years later, the private approach is obviously a failure.

Nothing of significance was done to break up the private-industry source of the health care cost spiral—insurance and drug companies, doctors, and hospitals. Health care providers, as both liberal and conservative critics have observed, have strong incentives to keep upping their costs by overtreating patients, overusing expensive new diagnostic technologies, and overlooking irrational duplications within the system.

"Only a single-payer system of national health care can save what we estimate is the $350 billion wasted annually on medical bureaucracy and redirect those funds to expanded coverage," Himmelstein and Woolhandler wrote in the *New York Times*.

As the only customer and principal manager of health care for all Americans receiving Medicare, the federal government can use its market power to control costs and compel change—forcing down drug prices, reducing the overuse of exotic technologies, and eliminating the malfunctions that reduce efficiency in the delivery of care. As other nations have demonstrated, a nationalized system puts a lid on both prices and profits, the main sources of the perennial inflation. The US approach, in contrast, rewards the private sector and punishes the customers. Medicare and Medicaid are in financial trouble mainly because health care providers escalate costs faster than tax revenues can rise. Taxpayers are, in effect, hit twice. They have to finance the exploding budgets of government programs as well their own ever-rising medical bills.

This is an irrational approach, yet politicians turn their backs on the one practical solution that has been proven to work. Why? Because a truly nationalized system would be derided as "socialist" by the same people who insist that Social Security and the progressive income tax are socialist. The initial cost of conversion also carries a huge price tag, though it is less than the amount Washington quickly expended on rescuing Wall Street firms. The resulting savings would be huge—$30 billion a year. Most politicians simply do not want to mess with the corporate machine.

Halfway approaches would require companies to provide insurance for their workers while a government-run program similar to Medicaid would be open to all Americans. As Himmelstein and Woolhandler explain, this "rests on impeccable political logic: avoid challenging the insurance firms' stranglehold on health care. But it is economic nonsense. The reliance on private insurers makes universal coverage unaffordable." Smart politics leads to economic nonsense.

The collapsing pension system is a similar scandal. It, too, has an obvious practical solution that very few political actors are willing to touch. Meanwhile, this very wealthy nation lives with an extraordinary contradiction. In an era when financial wealth has grown explosively, millions of baby boomers now find themselves approaching retirement with paltry savings and no pensions. They will have to keep working in their old age or accept a sharp drop in their standard of living. Social Security, the bedrock insurance for the elderly, provides income equivalent to the federal minimum wage. The old-style corporate pensions that guaranteed retirement benefits are fast disappearing as companies shed them to boost their profits.

The new individual savings accounts—IRAs and 401(k) plans—have flopped as replacements. Fewer Americans are now covered by pension plans of any kind than were covered twenty years ago. Only 48 million families have individual accounts, and the median value of their savings is $27,000.[22] Even older employees close to retirement have a median account balance of only $55,000—enough to fund a monthly stipend of $398, far short of middle-class security. For the first time since the Depression, America's next generation of elderly are going to become poorer, many of them a lot poorer.

"The whole thinking [behind the 401(k) idea] was: Let's relieve the employers of this burden and empower individuals," said Karen Ferguson, director of the Pension Rights Center in Washington. "The problem is, it has failed—and failed miserably—and no one wants to say that."[23] One reason the 401(k) experiment failed is that corporations acted like the fabled grasshoppers that failed to save for winter. Corporate managements have gamed the pension system for years with clever accounting methods, using pension capital to boost their profit reports. In the fat years, companies failed to fully fund the plans. In the lean years, they complained about the burden and, in extreme cases, dumped the whole mess on the federal government for a bailout. Companies could get away with this because they wrote substantial portions of the pension laws, creating many escape hatches for themselves.

"The bottom line is that the companies always have the upper hand, even though they've gotten huge subsidies and tax benefits," said Ferguson. "The system is voluntary, so companies can always opt out."

The Pension Rights Center hosted yearlong discussions on solutions for the pension crisis that brought together the relevant players: major corporations, unions, Wall Street finance firms, and insurance companies. To get their participation, however, the center had to promise up front that mandatory solutions would not be discussed. The group proposed doing a lot of tinkering with the failed system of 401(k) plans, but was barred from exploring a genuine solution—a new, inclusive national pension that, alongside Social Security, would require all employees to save in exchange for guaranteed portable individual pension accounts that would pay up to 70 percent of preretirement earnings.

As it happens, there are many successful models that use this approach and provide stable, reliable retirement benefits, including for low-wage workers. The savings and investments are managed by low-overhead, nonprofit administrators with no game playing and no profiteering. Examples include the mandatory TIAA-CREF pensions for college professors, the construction trades' multiemployer pension plans jointly managed by labor and management, foreign systems like Australia's new national pension system, and the US government's own Thrift Savings Plan for federal employees. These arrangements all produce what they promise—the security that comes with being able to count on a comfortable retirement.

But would workers be willing to support a system of forced saving in order to ensure the security of their future retirement? If they knew the facts, I think they would. Evidently some labor leaders agree, because they are exploring the idea. Maybe somebody should ask the workers themselves what they think. In a functioning democracy, serious discussions start by asking people to consider their options and make some informed judgments about their own lives.

The political system, I fear, is heading into a similar trap with a particular proposal for addressing global warming—the so-called cap-and-trade solution. Government would issue a limited number of certificates that allow the emission of carbon pollution, the chief source of global warming, then companies could buy and sell these carbon certificates to each other. That presumably would create an incentive for companies to reduce their pollution levels so they can profit by selling their surplus emission rights to other companies that fail to make improvements. Business and environmentalists endorse this market approach.

The theory sounds elegant, but in practice it converts carbon pollution into a tradeable commodity and as Europe has learned, the system would be extremely vulnerable to corporate manipulations. When government inevitably tries to reduce the overall levels of pollution by withdrawing more and more of these valuable certificates, companies would be at the center of negotiations and could hold the political system hostage, either demanding more money or slower progress. Thus, the great imperative of confronting global warming could end up as muddled as health care or pension reform.

The confusion between serving public and private purposes is the debilitating reality of American democracy. It was expressed most dramatically in the recent financial bailout for Wall Street that committed something like $1 trillion in public funds to save the villains at the expense of the victims. There is more to come. The corporate–financial establishment has organized its allied forces to promote the parallel objective of cutting the federal entitlement programs that serve the people—Social Security, Medicare, and Medicaid. Just when the political system ought to be expanding its support of ordinary citizens, governing elites are instead pushing Washington in the opposite direction. The problem, they claim, is that the federal government simply cannot afford these social programs. Cutting the costs of social guarantees can help make up for the public wealth that has been transferred to Wall Street in the bailout. This amounts to bait-and-switch taxation. Higher payroll taxes collected from working people to support social security would be diverted to other uses.

On one flank, billionaire financier Peter Peterson launched an extravagant propaganda campaign to persuade presidential candidates to create what he calls a "fiscal responsibility commission" to recommend reforms. Peterson published a two-page ad in the *New York Times* to sound his battle cry on the very day the federal government was announcing another sweeping bailout for financiers.

On another flank, economists at six Washington think tanks allied with corporations produced a political plan for cutting the people's benefits while also evading their predictable wrath. Sixteen economists from the Brookings Institution, the Heritage Foundation, the New America Foundation, the Urban Institute, the Progressive Policy Institute, and the Concord Coalition collectively suggested a "bipartisan" gimmick that would let politicians broadly reduce Social Security benefits and other entitlements.[24]

Congress, the economists recommended, should authorize a special commission to design the "reforms" and have an up-or-down vote on the package, with no amendments allowed. This technique takes the issue out of the realm of politics and is modeled after the base-closing commission that decides which military bases to eliminate. It cleverly disables the democratic process and suspends the rights of citizens in order to accomplish what the elite interests think is best for the nation.

Follow the sequence of events: Washington uses public money to replenish the losses of premier banks and investment houses, then it turns to the task of stripping the taxpayers of vital government benefits that working people have already paid for. How much would the people lose in this sleight of hand? The elite sponsors, naturally, won't say. They are hoping not to upset anyone. This deal will be done behind closed doors.

★　★　★　★　★

From social partners to free riders: It took corporations a couple of decades to complete that transformation. It should not take that long to undo it. The government has ample leverage for persuading corporations to surrender certain privileges and accept their obligations to society. The prospects for reform have been greatly improved by the cascading scandals, one after another, in which Americans have seen reality exposed and their skepticism confirmed. The manic profit seeking of corporations has adverse consequences for the economy, and for shareholders. Wall Street's fraudulent financial valuations have triggered a historic reckoning for the US economy. Even some complacent politicians are trying to sound like reformers.

Government can advance the effort to reform corporations by using a powerful tool—imposing taxes on their behavior as well as their profits. Government can make concrete distinctions between companies that adhere to society's broader values and goals and those that consistently trash the public interest. The bad guys could be taxed at a higher rate, while virtuous companies could be rewarded with a lower rate. This performance-based approach has many advantages, including the fact that it speaks to companies in a language they all understand—the impact on their bottom line.

Here is a simplified version of how the performance tax might work. The corporate income tax—now a corrupted shell of its former self—would be refashioned both to restore to the government the tax revenue it has lost to loopholes and to enforce corporate obligations to society. The statutory rate would be set higher—perhaps at around 45 percent—but companies would have ample opportunities to pay far less by adhering to higher standards that promote the public good. These standards would rely on measurable results, not subjective judgments. Does the company raise wages in step with rising productivity? Has it persistently violated the lawful requirements for protecting the environment? Does it have a criminal record on matters like financial fraud? Is it a repeat offender?

Positive measures could reward progressive companies that go beyond what's required by law and set higher benchmarks for what is possible. Is the company increasing its US workforce instead of offloading value-added jobs to foreign locations? Is the corporation's ecological footprint being steadily reduced? Does the company maintain equitable relations with its employees by supporting two-way communication and democratic participation? Employees could be asked what they think about that, and for confirming evidence, perhaps the IRS could require a periodic vote of confidence in which workers would judge the managers by secret ballot.

Companies would be free to ignore the performance standards, but they would have to pay dearly for their evasion. Profit losses incurred due to neglecting social obligations would show up in the annual report as market signals to shareholders and consumers that the company's management was in trouble. Corporate tax ratings—white hat or black hat—could inform investors about a corporation's credit worthiness and serve as a public label signifying exemplary or shameful behavior.

The reformed corporate tax would add new muscle to the currently eviscerated regulatory enforcement. Corporate miscreants that were able to capture or compromise regulatory agencies would also have to deal with the IRS, where tax fraud is still regarded as a serious crime. The regulatory agencies also would need reforming to do away with the overbearing influence of the industries they regulate. Outside voices should be given formal leverage inside the regulatory agencies by being kept informed of corporate manipulation and abandonment of public obligations so they can blow the whistle or exercise temporary vetoes of proposed actions. A permanent council of six or eight randomly rotated state governors could serve as a watchdog keeping tabs on the feds.

Unlike other ideas I have offered, the concept of linking corporate behavior to taxation has found a modest beachhead in regular politics. The Patriot Corporation Act has been introduced by a handful of House and Senate Democrats led by Representative Jan Schakowsky of Illinois and Senator Sherrod Brown of Ohio (then-senator Barack Obama was among the original cosponsors). The measure offers rewards to companies that demonstrate loyalty in their performance, but it does not suggest any penalties for those who don't. That is the hard part, of course.

Still, the basic principle is advancing. The government can prescribe terms for individual corporate behavior that go beyond the dos and don'ts of regulatory law. The House version would give tax breaks and preferences in federal contracting to firms that produce 90 percent of their goods and services in the United States; comply with federal laws on workplace safety, the environment, and consumer issues; invest in domestic research; and provide workers with adequate pensions and health care. The Senate bill adds a 1 percent credit on taxable income to companies that pay a "living wage" and maintain or increase their US employment compared to their overseas workforce.[25]

This is a small, wishful beginning, to be sure. Reforming the corporate tax code is one among many fronts on which the grand bazaar can be challenged. Congress also has to clear away the notorious loopholes and exceptions that disfigure the tax code and outlaw the accounting gimmicks that allow firms to hide their debts and profits in off–balance sheet "entities." Congress can start by repealing the perennial boondoggles in which taxpayers "pay" corporations to do things that boost private profits but have no obvious value to the public. Likewise, political reforms will have to shut down the pork-barrel spending that rewards the free riders and demands little or no accountability.

The stable is piled high with rotting manure. Beneath the carefree deal making, the integrity of government is drowning. In an earlier time, when the United States was flush with rising incomes and new wealth, the drain on public resources might have seemed tolerable. But when the country is mired in debt and facing bleak prospects, the pork-barrel deal making begins to look like criminal waste.

Numerous steps could be taken to impose discipline on deal making in the bazaar. These steps don't need to be radical, but instead merely commonsense measures that follow the standard rules for business accountability. Get everything in writing, and don't take anything weaker than hard-nosed contracts with enforceable penalties. Nobody in business or finance would lend money—much less give it away—without carefully negotiating a contract that described the transaction and is enforceable by the courts. In other words, you need to get hard, clear terms. Why does government simply put the money on a stump and leave it for any private interest that wants to claim it?

For instance, if tax concessions or subsidies are enacted as incentives for business to do something in particular, the recipients should be required to prove that the money was spent for the intended purpose. If it wasn't, the government should sue to recover the public funds with penalties and interest. As my earlier examples illustrated, corporations cannot be trusted to fulfill commitments that are based on what's said in press releases or what lobbyists promise to legislators. Since the government cannot be trusted to enforce its own laws, other parties—including the citizens—should have legal standing to sue the corporations and recover the money on behalf of the people.

As is the case in business affairs, government relationships with individual companies develop a history that should be relevant to all future transactions. The government is not just swindled now and then. It is often swindled over and over again by the same companies. (Boeing comes to mind.) There ought to be a choke point—well defined by law—that essentially bans certain companies from doing business with Washington.

Persistent antisocial behavior—not to mention criminal fraud—should render rogues ineligible for tax breaks and other favors. Lawyers are disbarred, priests are defrocked, and corporations should be able to be dissolved. Some companies deserve to die, especially those that persistently cheat their biggest customer, the US government and taxpayers.

If the government makes a deal to provide aid to a private enterprise, then the public—now investors—should do what private investors do and demand an equity share in return. Deborah Groban Olson, a Michigan labor lawyer, is campaigning for "fair exchange" legislation at the state and federal levels to require this. If a company that accepts government assistance subsequently prospers, the public deserves a return on its investment. "No matter what else is done to regulate the financial industry," Olson wrote, "we can't afford to let Wall Street put at risk trillions of public assets without clearly rooting those assets for the benefit of US citizens."[26]

No one should expect pork-barrel politics to disappear, or greed and corruption to be eliminated in the private sector or in human behavior. The species is fallible, not perfect. But there ought to be room in US politics for righteous anger that asserts an old-fashioned kind of fundamentalism—the demand for integrity, the insistence on honest dealing in public matters. Those qualities have been gravely undermined in the grand bazaar, so much so that many people regard them as lost forever. The United States is not yet like a corrupt third world regime where no one trusts anyone, but the country is on the same dangerous slope.

I can envision a political formation of "fundamentalists" marching with torches on the capital to clean out the stable. It would include conservatives and liberals who understand, perhaps for different reasons, that this cause is so important to the American future. Instead of dwelling on obvious targets, these angry patriots could coalesce behind a larger banner—demanding a cleansing amendment to the Constitution. Its objectives would be to restore the integrity of public purpose, to yank the governing system away from its complacent habits, and to insist on regular order. This integrity amendment probably would not be adopted, but it could serve as a galvanizing tool to organize citizens. At a minimum, it would stir up a very healthy storm of debate about fundamental principles. The amendment might say something like this:

> *Public money shall only be spent for lasting public benefit and defined purposes. Public assets cannot be transferred to private ownership except for recompense at fair value and with the explicit approval of Congress. Misappropriation of public resources for private gain shall be recoverable by citizens and their elected representatives. Violators are barred for life from public office and government service.*

Does the idea that public money should be devoted to public purposes sound naive? I am not suggesting putting an end to all forms of subsidy and government assistance or marketplace interventions. I want to see the corruption of democracy confronted with force. What public purposes does government have? Do myriad transactions with private interests serve those purposes in any real way? If not, why are taxpayers made to pay for them? If the sponsors cannot provide hard evidence of their lasting benefit to the general welfare, then they should be stopped cold. The generous favors that flow from Washington are an illegitimate distortion of democratic governing, not to mention a gross waste of scarce public resources.

Education, health care, the general welfare, civil order, and national defense—these and other well-established public purposes justify many forms of government aid to private entities and individuals. Anyone can easily make a case for them. But the governing landscape now extends far beyond those guideposts. The question of public benefit has become so murky and malleable that the question is not even asked. If the integrity amendment were adopted, it would generate a whirlwind of provocative lawsuits. That would upset the deal makers in the bazaar, but it could be good therapy for restoring an active democracy. The courtrooms could host the great public debate that Congress refuses to engage.

*   *   *   *   *

For the last one hundred years or more, the fundamental contest in American politics has been the power struggle between strong government and the private economic sphere—a tug-of-war for dominance waged by Washington and the political machines of big business and finance. Over the decades, controlling influence has swung back and forth between the two, from the New Deal's activist government to the business-first conservatism of the Reagan era. As a result of the present economic confusion, power is shifting back once again to government. Government versus private enterprise—that has always been the choice.

But something is missing from this power equation—the people. The people have been distanced from power under both liberal and conservative regimes, albeit in different ways. Citizens became spectators, further alienated from participating in the decisions that govern their lives. To be heard in the halls of democracy, one has to hire a lobbyist. To influence the private decisions of corporations, one has to become a major shareholder. Many Americans, not surprisingly, have become passive and resigned to their powerlessness.

Liberal big government delivered great gains for ordinary citizens, including the establishment of new individual rights. But the act of centralizing power in Washington inevitably shifted the decision making farther away from the people. Federalizing the big issues was necessary to overcome regional poverty and political resistance—mainly the South's racist caste system—but shifting power to Washington also disabled the capacities of citizens to act locally, where they naturally have the most influence and energy. Big government instead found itself resented for its bigness and its seeming indifference to the smaller voices of mere citizens.

The conservative order, while celebrating the entrepreneurial freedoms, concentrated power on its own terms. The big corporations got much bigger and more closely allied in their efforts to maintain their dominating power. By degrading and dismantling government's role, conservatives effectively turned governing powers over to business and finance on a mammoth scale. They freed private enterprise to adopt harsher, more confining terms for workers and greater indifference toward public objections. When corporate clout has no significant opposition in politics, when its influence over economic and social conditions becomes more concentrated and overbearing, the people lose again.

This is not the end of the story. What the country needs is a third front in the political power struggle, a counterforce to both government and the private sector. This new source of countervailing power can come only from the people themselves. That means they must learn how to reengage their sacred birthright by rediscovering the original meaning of "citizen" and then develop collective power that both checks and competes with the existing power centers of government and enterprise. In anger or sorrow, the people must step up to the challenging circumstances and find their voices, then find ways to make themselves heard.

This sounds fanciful, I know, given the long deterioration of democratic relationships over the last thirty years or more. I won't try to persuade skeptics with random bits of evidence. But I am encouraged to believe that this is possible to achieve, and I know many Americans—a fervent minority—share my conviction. I ask readers to keep their minds open to the possibility that I am right.

A new democracy beckons, if Americans have the nerve to believe in it. We are ready for a next stage that advances the meaning of the word "democracy" beyond where any society has taken it to before. This is the ultimate test of our maturity. Can people really handle their responsibilities as citizens? Or must our "betters," who claim to know what is best for us, forever lead us around like children? We need to cut through their fog and condescension. We must reclaim our sovereign powers as citizens. From what I know of Americans, they are capable of doing this for themselves. And I feel sure the country is in for terrible trouble if the people fail to try.

CHAPTER THIRTEEN

THE RECKONING

This may sound strange, but what the United States faces today is roughly the economic equivalent of World War II. In our predicament, Americans have to save themselves and the country—for the children, for the generations beyond. The first task is to get the nation out of the deep ditch. The second is to reshape the country in profound ways that, despite the present adversities, can lead to a more promising future. Just as World War II presented a chance to thoroughly reorder American life, this generation of Americans has the opportunity—the obligation—to envision a country very different from the one we have known for more than half a century. Likewise, the present challenge requires a great mobilization, a summoning of the collective energies of people, resources, and national purpose. Like the war, this will demand immediate sacrifices from virtually everyone, plus lots of changes. Generalized pain is an unavoidable first step toward making a better country tomorrow.

I do not bring up World War II for nostalgia. Nor do I liken our condition to war as a way to inspire the kind of unifying spirit that accompanies a great war. In fact, our present situation has some uncanny similarities with the country's economic condition during World War II and also calls for heroic responses. If full-blown economic breakdown does unfold, the necessity for large-scale emergency measures should become apparent. In the meantime, World War II provides a concrete illustration of what is possible—a great transformation can be achieved, swiftly and equitably, despite terrible circumstances.

The economic measures the United States adopted in the crisis of world war suggest the broad outline for what the nation could do now. What's required is a dramatic jump-shift in economic priorities and strategy that would abruptly depart from the prevailing views to overhaul the economic system and repair social conditions, much like the great changes the United States accomplished in wartime. The details then were controversial and disruptive, but most Americans recognized the need and accepted the wrenching adjustments. In return, people were promised a better life once the war was over. The government largely kept the promise.

We associate heroism and famous battles with World War II, but it was also an extraordinary moment of economic transformation. Washington pushed aside the failed marketplace that had led to the Great Depression and fashioned a vibrant new economy largely with government financing. The resonant date of that era was December 7, 1941—the day when Japan attacked Pearl Harbor. The shock of Pearl Harbor triggered a vast mobilization that amounted to a government-led industrial revolution.

In many ways, the American condition is a lot less promising now than it was in 1941. The United States is a debtor nation that is losing altitude as an economic force, not climbing toward preeminence as the world's leading economy, as it was in the wake of World War II. US debt and dependency on foreign creditors, the loss of manufacturing and value-added jobs, the economic inequalities and eroding middle class, repeated financial crises that destabilize the real economy, the reckonings ahead with oil scarcity and ecological crisis—these negative factors are beyond anything the World War II generation had to face. They seem even more threatening because the United States is no longer entirely in control of its destiny.[1]

On the other hand, we Americans today have so much more compared to what people had then. Our exalted standard of living cushions us from the extremes of suffering and insecurity that the earlier generation experienced. The fabulous abundance and routine entertainments of our time would probably look like royal luxury to them. In 1941, Americans had just come through the cruel decade known as the Great Depression, which involved real deprivation for millions, with unemployment as high as 25 percent. The standard of living in the 1930s was primitive compared to ours. Most families did not own their own homes, but were renters or tenant farmers. Millions of families still lacked electricity and telephones in their homes, and even indoor plumbing. The economic collapse was a searing test of character. In World War II, they were tested again.

Practically overnight, the government clamped down hard on domestic consumer goods. The production of new cars and houses was abruptly stopped (in my memories of childhood, chocolate ice cream and metal toys also disappeared). By 1942, auto factories were turning out bombers. Capital and labor quickly converted to producing planes, tanks, and ships for the war—thousands of them. Public investment turned to financing the research and development for new technological wonders like radar. Government procurement contracts force-fed the rapid development of new industrial sectors—a galaxy that included electronics, petrochemical synthetics, aircraft, nuclear power, modernized steel production, and shipbuilding—that would be the platform for America's postwar prosperity.

Emergency controls, meanwhile, imposed limits on personal consumption to strictly regulate excess and greed. Legal ceilings were placed on everything from corporate profits to interest rates (the Treasury bond rate was pegged at 2.5 percent for the duration of the war). Prices and wages were capped. The government rationed purchases of essential materials, oil and rubber, meat and sugar. Income-tax rates spiked, in particular for the very wealthy, who paid a top marginal rate of 90 percent. Federal borrowing spiked, too, as the government's spending exploded.

Amid the strains and sacrifices, amazing things happened in the US economy. Despite the restraining force of government controls, US economic growth took off, expanding by as much as 16 percent in a single year. From 1939 to 1945, the national economy virtually doubled in size and per capita income rose by 40 percent. Since families could not buy big-ticket items like cars or houses, they saved their money instead of consuming. While at war, the United States managed to achieve an extraordinary national savings rate of 25 percent of incomes. The government essentially borrowed money from the people and used their savings to pay for the war. The deferred consumption and swollen savings, in turn, became the pent-up consumer demand that would drive America's dynamic postwar expansion.

Roughly speaking, this jump-shift was accomplished on borrowed money. The federal government piled up staggering budget deficits throughout the war.

About two-fifths of federal spending was financed by debt, not tax revenue. The New Deal recovery programs of the 1930s had already run up federal debt to more than 40 percent of GDP; the war nearly tripled that debt-to-GDP ratio. By 1946, the accumulated government debt had reached 120 percent of GDP. This unheard-of burden naturally alarmed people. Many thought the nation was bankrupt and feared it would slide back into depression after the war.

The opposite occurred. The massive wartime borrowing was invested in productive ways—new factories, new technologies—that paid off for the country. The postwar economy expanded robustly for nearly three decades, spreading the economic rewards widely throughout the society and generating the broad new middle class. In the good times of the postwar decades, people generously turned their attention to the question of poverty and sought to include those Americans who had been left out.

The government-managed economy of World War II was a triumph for liberal economic principles and, in particular, the doctrine of British economist John Maynard Keynes, whose ideas are scorned by market conservatives. Almost everything Franklin Roosevelt did during the wartime transformation was denounced by the right as an illegitimate (or socialist) intrusion on the workings of free-market capitalism. The criticisms were disproved by the prosperity that followed.

Keynes's lessons are relevant to our modern predicament. There are some economic functions that only the national government can undertake, especially borrowing during a crisis to get the economy moving forward or to accomplish large public goals that private enterprise will not undertake. Debt itself is not the problem, Keynes explained, if the borrowed money is invested in creating a more productive future that generates jobs and incomes and creates the new wealth that will support better lives for the society. World War II and its aftermath essentially proved the Keynesian case.

Despite conservative worries, the wartime debt receded as a problem. For the next thirty-five years, the postwar economy expanded and the debt-to-GDP ratio steadily declined. At war's end, federal debt was 120 percent of GDP. By 1980, it had fallen to 35 percent of GDP. This occurred mainly because the US economy was by then many times larger and annual deficits were much smaller.

At that point, the virtuous trend was reversed not by free-spending liberals, but by the conservatives who espoused smaller government. The era that began with Ronald Reagan and ran through George W. Bush's terms introduced swollen budget deficits in peacetime. Republicans became spendthrifts and ran up the federal debt to wartime levels. It is now back up to 70 percent of GDP and rising rapidly.

Only this time, the borrowed money was not so well spent. The Republican deficits paid for huge tax cuts for business and the wealthy. It financed massive subsidies to older industries instead of investing in new ones. The nation's heavy borrowing paid for enormous trade deficits and the excess consumption of a country living beyond its means. It paid for still more armaments and foreign deployments. It funded a costly, ill-considered war in the Middle East.

Public investment, meanwhile, was allowed to atrophy in the conservative era. So did public infrastructure—roads, bridges, schools, and so on. The United States consumed at an exalted level, but fell behind on investing in the public goods that are necessary for a productive economy and livable society.

The current adversities are very different from those during World War II, but the United States once again faces the need for a dramatic shift in governance. We need big, new strokes in economic policy that can turn things around and at the same time restore equity and promise. This jump-shift does not require the same catalog of emergency controls applied during World War II, though some may be needed, but a similar kind of belt tightening is required to reshape the US economy.

If the political system came to its senses and recognized the enormity of our situation, what could it do?

In essence, government actions would suppress domestic consumption in order to replenish savings while shifting the government-led economy to make large-scale public investments in industry and public goods—everything from factories and highways to parks and hospitals. Investment would replace mass consumption as the dynamic driver that sustains growth, much like the shift in World War II. Public capital and federal spending would be redeployed to jump-start promising new industries and technologies that would better serve the future's demands for ecological living and substitutes for oil, for public services and public benefits, and for goods available to all regardless of status. Not coincidentally, these rising industries would generate millions of new jobs with good wages not tomorrow, but now. Government would use the taxpayers' money to nurture thousands of smaller firms put to work developing the numerous innovations needed to secure alternative energy sources, ecological balance, and economic equity. In hard times, government would become the reliable employer of last resort, hiring unemployed people to do the work the society needed done.

In every case, Washington would demand an iron rule be fulfilled if firms wanted to secure federal investment—new production would be done in the United States, and the jobs would be filled by Americans. The World Trade Organization might complain, but other nations do this routinely, either slyly or openly, on behalf of their national interest. The United States has the right to manage its own economy just as others do.

If US consumption were held in check for a time, people could replenish their savings. This shift could transform the global trading system, too. US trade deficits would decline as American consumers pulled back. Essentially, Americans would resign the role of "buyer of last resort" for the world's exports. Other trading nations, including China, would have to readjust their economic strategies to produce more goods for their own domestic consumption rather than relying on exporting to the United States. The period of transition would be fragile and tense, but it would be healthy in the long run. Along with instituting the other trade reforms described in Chapter Seven, the United States would gain an opening for negotiating new rules and international institutions that could sustain a balanced trading system. Our trading partners would have strong incentive to come to the table and work things out.

Obviously, a dramatic shift of these dimensions would be possible only if there were a change in public consciousness, with people grasping that the current predicament goes deeper than a brief detour from the usual prosperity. Instead of trying to run the world, the country's wealth and ingenuity would come home to concentrate on reconstructing our own embattled country. Instead of preparing for the next war, the United States would confront its interior deterioration and begin to rebuild. People would be free to reimagine the "good life" and how it can be accomplished with greater prudence and wisdom.

Painful adjustments are unavoidable. Government constraints on mass consumption would mean an interlude of austerity—perhaps four or five years long—in which people would be encouraged or compelled to forgo some expenditures in order to restore their savings, easing the debt burdens on themselves and the country. Consumption could be suppressed mainly by imposing legal restraints on access to credit, though millions of families in financial trouble will need no incentive. They are already tapped out as consumers. Instead, to get through this lean period they need help with measures like debt forbearance and government-mandated credit workouts for families who are underwater.

Reform measures, in effect, have to shut down the unregulated system of easy credit that has bankrupted so many families. People instead need the restoration of the legal prohibition of usury, the predatory lending by which wealth takes advantage of the less fortunate. Reform must also reorder the financial system, which has unhinged the real economy of production with the accounting gimmicks and fraudulent illusions manufactured on Wall Street. New rules would help to restore equity by restraining borrowers from recklessness while protecting them from impossible loan interest rates. National savings could be boosted further by creating a new national pension system alongside Social Security to replace the collapsed corporate pension system. Many workers would welcome the discipline of mandatory savings taken in regular payroll deductions if a government-supervised pension plan would ensure comfortable retirements for all, even the low-end wage earners.

Equality is an essential theme for any successful reconstruction. Government will not be able to impose the sacrifices that are in the national interest if people know the pain is not being shared universally. During World War II, "hoarders" caught with illicit stores of rationed sugar or gasoline were reviled and sometimes prosecuted, as were corporate profiteers. Now, various measures could ensure that the affluent participate in the belt tightening. To encourage solidarity, a stiff luxury tax could be levied on overconsumption to penalize the wealthiest families who insist on oversized mansions and six cars in the garage. An end to excess is one of the important new values that could emerge from this transformation, along with an end to the carefree destruction of nature.

For public investment, the nation can choose from an abundance of compelling, well-known opportunities. An ambitious agenda could be swiftly assembled. For instance, building high-speed passenger rail systems is the mass-transit alternative to having traffic-choked cities and suburbs. The burgeoning landfills of discarded cell phones and other modern artifacts could give way to the systematic restoration of vital ecosystems damaged by industry, agriculture, and careless consumption. The national backlog of deteriorating public infrastructure is a well-known scandal. Converting from oil to a post-hydrocarbon economy is a daunting, epochal challenge. After years of enervating political resistance, the impacts of global warming are upon us. Most of these imperatives are by now at least acknowledged by the political system, and some modest steps are being taken.

Of all the hard facts we face, the most frightening is the complacent pace of change in the United States. The last twenty years produced a lot of high-minded resolutions about mitigating global warming and implementing sustainable development, but not a lot more. The same can be said about dealing with globalization's detrimental impact on the US economic condition. At the present lazy tempo, there could be another generation or two of political haggling before concerted transformation is underway. Yet a lot of Americans outside Washington are caught up in the excitement of making over American life and pursuing the wise husbandry taught by ecological principles.

Buildings, homes, factories, farms, cars, consumer products—everything must be changed in this generation. That means designing into US products and production less destruction and waste and more efficient use and prudent reuse of nature's materials. That broad challenge describes the inventive edge needed in this new era, which will require translating the values of ecology into practical reality. Innovative people and firms are working on it, and they need help. Government can provide firms with capital and protection from predatory market forces so inventors have time to dabble and experiment with new ideas. Creativity, not consumption, can become the national preoccupation.

Fannie Mae, the government-chartered financial intermediary, has historically played an effective role as underwriter for affordable housing and home ownership. Now the country needs a Fannie Mae for environmental progress, for rehabilitating blighted towns and urban neighborhoods, for small businesses experimenting with workplace reforms like worker ownership, and for other capital-starved sectors that can lead the way on reforms.

But how could the government pay for all this? By borrowing the money from the American people, just as it did in the crisis of World War II. The money problem is real enough, but it can be solved by another dramatic jump-shift in political thinking. First, the government would have to restore the progressive income tax that was systematically dismantled during the last generation. Billionaire investor Warren Buffett observed that he pays a lower tax rate than his secretary; that pretty much tells the story. The tax code has been deformed on behalf of corporations and the people occupying the uppermost reaches of wealth and income. The tax rate on capital gains—the rate most important to those with great financial wealth—is about the same as the rate blue-collar industrial workers pay on their wage income. Restoring just taxation is a moral cause, but also a major step toward financing big changes in the society.

A direct tax on wealth is supposedly taboo in American politics because, it is said, it amounts to "confiscation" of private property. Yet home owners pay a "wealth tax" every year at the local and state levels—the property tax on their homes—and no one calls this confiscatory. Alternatively, the largest wealth holders and financial institutions could be offered a choice—either pay a modest wealth tax to the government or invest the equivalent in a list of innovative priority ventures or public improvements.

Tax reform would give billionaires another opportunity to express solidarity with the national agenda. Instead of paying the wealth tax, they could also be given the choice to invest in low-yield government bonds that would provide cheaper financing for whatever reconstruction projects the government hopes to accomplish.

The point is, the nation has to mobilize patient capital to undertake hundreds or thousands of large-scale, long-term projects. As in World War II, the federal government can raise taxes, but it still must borrow enormous amounts of the money that will be required to finance this effort. Despite our losses and debts, America remains a very wealthy place, and government can borrow from the people, not from abroad, and pay them back with the economic returns that follow. As World War II demonstrated, the crucial test is not the size of the federal budget deficits. It is whether the borrowed money is invested in the future.

When asked to support big changes, Washington politicians typically plead poverty, saying that there is no money to pay for them, but what they are really saying is they don't want to disturb the status quo. A decisive mobilization is unlikely to happen unless the political system takes the money away from hoary old interests—the oil industry and agribusiness, for instance—that no longer have any rational claim to federal subsidies and directs the money to transformation projects. The bloated military budget belongs on the target list of cuts, as does the catalog of egregious tax loopholes for corporations and financial investors. Reformers could also harvest billions from the wrongheaded subsidies granted for destructive "growth" activities that are not only wasteful, but also take the country in the wrong direction, devoting scarce public capital to the further destruction of nature.

I am not delusional. I know very well that these emergency measures and other provocative ideas are utterly unlikely to get anywhere unless the wrenching crisis disarms the prevailing concentrations of power. I think the country has reached such a rare moment and is on the brink of a new political dynamic that generates rapid changes and enables citizens to claim a decisive role in influencing the action. The old order is crumbling, fighting to hold on to its dominance. As the massive bailout of financial firms demonstrates, neither party has yet found the courage to break free from the old order, though Democrats are taking hesitant half steps in that direction.

Still, the financial crisis and other events may liberate democracy from its diminished condition and serve as an inspiration to citizens that opens the way for popular revival and a historic shift in power. As World War II demonstrated, big change is possible—and rather quickly—if the country knows what it needs to do and has the political will to try. The war taught a vital lesson that was widely forgotten afterward: Government—if it has not been degraded and corrupted—can play a central role in the rescue and rehabilitation of the society. Politics—if politicians have not been captured by powerful interests—can become a source of creative thinking, promoting ideas that lead the people to higher ground.

Think of the political daring and originality of that era, the courage it must have taken for politicians to act quickly and confidently on so many big ideas. The present era of politics seems pale and inept by comparison. Though protected from challengers in many ways, most incumbents seem insecure and always to be looking over their shoulder. They are skilled in self-preservation, but small-minded in their understanding of the public interest.

★ ★ ★ ★ ★

Franklin D. Roosevelt was one of the great presidents—second only to Lincoln in my book—but also a shrewd, audacious politician. Throughout the Depression and the war, common people loved FDR and forgave his mistakes and false starts. Despite his patrician upbringing, Roosevelt was on their side, able to know their minds and speak for them with high style and wit.

In the last years of the war, solidarity was badly frayed. Bitter domestic disputes broke out over wage controls, excess profits, and other matters. People everywhere were wearied by the sacrifices (and their casualties). Roosevelt took them to the mountaintop, so to speak, and made a grand promise. Americans would realize a better life, he declared, "after this war is won." He enunciated what he called "a second Bill of Rights." These rights, he said, belong to everyone who is American.

"We have come to a clear realization of the fact that true individual freedom cannot exist without economic security and independence," Roosevelt declared in his 1944 State of the Union message. "'Necessitous men are not free men.' People who are hungry and out of a job are the stuff out of which dictatorships are made. In our day these economic truths have become accepted as self-evident. We have accepted, so to speak, a second Bill of Rights under which a new basis of security and prosperity can be established for all, regardless of station, race, or creed."

With that, FDR enumerated a list of "rights" that would for many years be the textbook for political reform and social advancement. They included: "the right to a useful and remunerative job; . . . the right to earn enough to provide adequate food and clothing and recreation; . . . freedom [for businesses] from unfair competition and domination by monopolies; . . . the right of every family to a decent home; . . . the right to adequate medical care; . . . the right to adequate protection from the economic fears of old age, sickness, accident, and unemployment; [and] the right to a good education."

Roosevelt's words prompted sweeping thoughts in ordinary people and politicians. The country had been through years of sacrifice, but the president assured everyone that greater equality was at the top of the national agenda. He provided an everyday definition of what "equality" meant. The terms of his "second Bill of Rights" provided the floorboards for an active political agenda that would dominate the postwar years. The legislative accomplishments helped generate the modern middle class and transform American society. The opening of higher education to all classes of citizens through the GI Bill, broadening home ownership, Medicare and Medicaid, antipoverty programs, the protests for racial equality that became the civil rights movement—these and many other postwar achievements drew legitimacy from FDR's grand promise. Not every item on his list was fulfilled, but most were conscientiously pursued and at least partially realized. As political promises go, FDR's was kept, even long after his death.

In our present condition, the country needs something similar to help people get through the hard parts of what's ahead. Even with the best intentions, it will take years to fulfill the goals of greater social equity, to unwind the destructive habits in the financial system, to thrash out new understandings about consumption that distinguish "good" growth from "bad" growth and other difficult, controversial matters. At this point, people do not need hardwired promises so much as a plausible vision to understand the path that lies ahead. They need a road map that is clear and honest and beckons them to embrace big principles and goals or to change them if they think the ideas are incomplete. This is the hard work to be done by the people of a democracy, not governing elites, and it is the people who can turn great goals into practical realities.

If the road map originates in Washington, many people will be deeply skeptical of it, and justifiably so. Did anybody consult them? In a functioning democracy, the people would be actively engaged in the discussions, questioning the experts and offering their own thoughts about what goals the nation needs to pursue. Sovereign citizens would participate in the decision making. The authorities would learn to listen respectfully.

We do not know how to do that very well in this country, not yet. Except in rare moments, the governing system does not even try. The kind of free-flowing democratic engagement I just described represents a higher level of self-government than Americans have yet achieved. Try to think of a maturing democracy that has figured out how to give concrete meaning to the hallowed idea of self-governing citizens. That proposition has not been fully realized anywhere in the world. It is an alluring possibility, however, for Americans to work on.

★　★　★　★　★

As Franklin Roosevelt understood, Americans will postpone immediate gratification and endure hard sacrifices—if they must—so long as they are convinced the future can be better than the past. But we face a far more difficult problem at our moment in history. What do you promise people who have been told they can have anything they want, who are repeatedly congratulated for living in the best of all possible circumstances? How do you tell them the "good times" as we have known them are not coming back? Americans need a new vision that helps them deal with reality, a promising story of the future that helps them let go of the past.

The political system, for obvious reasons, finds it hard to talk about limits. The loss of American preeminence is taboo. Most influential thinkers and politicians are in denial about the US loss of economic power. Others, who should know better, attribute the faltering prosperity and foreign setbacks to "mistakes" made by the opposition party. Voters, it is assumed, will not listen to any criticisms of America, not in these fragile times. So media and politicians continue to espouse the old triumphalism, assuring everyone the United States is still number one. The 2008 presidential campaign was drenched in hyperpatriotism that scorned any candidate who said US power is deteriorating or failed to wear a flag pin in his lapel. Most Americans, nevertheless, figured out something is terribly wrong. The "extreme consensus" was pessimism.

The national purpose must envision the more fulfilling country that can emerge on the other side of adversity. Discarding patriotic self-congratulation requires honesty about our situation, but it also liberates the country from stale assumptions that are actually self-destructive in our new circumstances. We are at a historic turning point where ordinary people can stand up to the inflated self-esteem of the governing classes and reject the obsolete dogma of official America.

A deep collision in politics is underway between the old order, which is crumbling but clinging to power, and America the Possible. This argument between the past and the undefined future forms a fundamental clash beneath every large issue, and I expect it will be with us for many years to come. True patriots will not cling to old illusions based on the wastefulness of mass consumption, our dangerous overreliance on military power, or utopian claims made about globalization. Realists offer new directions for the country and ask whether we should we keep trying to "save" the world or instead focus on saving the country we know and love.

Unburdened of expanding foreign entanglements, Americans could turn to the interior landscape of American life and concentrate on reconciling some long-neglected contradictions, strengthening some abandoned national ideals, healing the injured, redeeming equitable relationships, restoring ourselves. I have no doubt that most Americans—if given a choice—would choose to focus on America first. That is not because people are isolationist or want to withdraw from the world. No one expects that to occur. But in our weakened condition, it makes sense to back away from overreaching global ambitions and tend to the large problems at home.

It was never America's destiny to run the world. That was not why waves of immigrants came to our shores. They came to be free, to make a better life for their people. Some came as slaves and struggled for freedom. Our global preeminence and power grew out of America's accumulated successes and gradual development, not the other way around. Our global posture is now actively undermining what made the nation strong in the first place, including those constitutional principles that have been corrupted in US efforts to prevail over other nations. Turning inward will actually make it easier for the United States to work out new relations with the rest of the world. Instead of dominating others, we can learn to live with the differences. Instead of attacking foreign governments that deviate from the US model, America can once again advocate self-determination for all nations.

Here is the grand vision I suggest Americans can pursue: the right of all citizens to larger lives. Not to get richer than the next guy or necessarily accumulate more and more stuff, but the right to live life more fully and engage more expansively the elemental possibilities of human existence. That is the essence of what so many now seem to yearn for in their lives. People—even successful and affluent people—are frustrated because the intangible dimensions of life have been held back or displaced in large and small ways, pushed aside by the economic system's relentless demands to maximize yields of profit and wealth. Our common moral verities have been trashed in the name of greater returns. The softer aspects of mortal experience are diminished because life itself is not counted in the economic system's accounting.

The political order mistakenly accepts these life-limiting tradeoffs as normal, as necessary to achieve "good times." At earlier periods of US history, the sacrifices demanded by the engine of American capitalism were widely tolerated because the nation was young and underdeveloped. The engine promised to generate higher levels of abundance, and it did. But what is the justification now, when the nation is already quite rich and the engine keeps demanding larger chunks of our lives?

Getting more money is an inadequate solution and, in any case, it is not an option for many millions of people. What families, even those who are well-off, typically lose in the exchange are the small grace notes of everyday life, like the ritual of having a daily family dinner with everyone present. The more substantial thing we sacrifice is time—time to experience the joys and mysteries of nurturing the children and other fulfilling obligations. People forfeit the small pleasures of idle curiosity, of learning to craft things by one's own hand, and of the vital satisfactions of friendships and social cooperation.

These are made to seem trivial alongside wealth accumulation, but many people know they have given up something more important and mourn the loss. Some decide they will make up for it later in life, after they are financially well-off. Still others dream of dropping out of the system. If we could somehow add up all the private pain and loss caused by the pursuit of unbounded material prosperity, it might look like a major political grievance of our time.

More important than all the other losses is that people are also denied another great intangible—the dignity of self-directed lives. At work, at home, and in the public sphere, most people lack the right to exercise much of a voice in the decisions governing their daily lives. Most people (not all) are subject to a system of command and control over their personal destinies. They know the risks of ignoring the orders from above. Not surprisingly, many citizens are resigned to this condition and accept subservience as "the way things are," and their lives are smaller as a result. Many find it hard to imagine that these confinements could be lessened, even substantially removed, if economic organizations were informed by democratic principles.

What's needed in American life is a higher definition of "life, liberty, and the pursuit of happiness." Given the nation's great wealth, people are entitled to engage more fully and freely in the circumstances that shape their lives. Every citizen, regardless of status or income, deserves this since, for most people, the ancient threats of scarcity and deprivation have been eliminated from American life. Yet people remain yoked to economic demands despite wanting something more from life—freedom to explore the mysteries and bring forth all that is within them. Collectively, Americans need to take a deep breath and reconsider what it means to be rich.

The challenge, as John Maynard Keynes wrote many years ago, is "how to

live wisely and agreeably and well" once desperation and deprivation are no longer the driving forces of our existence. As the British economist predicted, the old
economic problems of scarcity and survival have been solved, at least for developed nations. People should put aside the old fears, Keynes suggested, and learn
how to enjoy life. Free of want and worry, the new challenge is to discover what
it means to be truly human.[2]

That wondrous pursuit is what I recommend as the alternative to our old
definition of progress. In the years ahead, Americans will suffer unavoidable
losses of familiar pleasures and be compelled to alter some deeply ingrained habits of material consumption. These painful adjustments can be endured if the
people are confident the country is progressing toward a more fulfilling transformation. The essential trade-off could be playfully expressed on a bumper sticker:
Smaller Cars for Larger Lives.

To accomplish this sweeping change, people need power—more power to
say what they think without getting fired and to make choices that are more in
line with their personal values and aspirations. They need more security—the
self-confidence to explore options in life without dooming their families to poverty. People need more philosophical space—the room to decide what "success"
is in their own terms and to make their own "mistakes."

We should start thinking of living larger lives as a fundamental human
right and begin throwing off the confinements imposed on us by the old order.
Since scarcity has been vanquished, the collateral suffering manufactured by the
economic system should also be declared unnecessary—even immoral—in a
healthy and wealthy society. A minority of Americans, people blessed with special talents, wealth, or status, may already enjoy this level of freedom. But, as
rich people can attest, wealth does not exempt one from the human struggle, the
search to find one's groove in life, to draw forth one's unique purpose and
strengths. That treasure cannot be bought. It has to be earned.

Government can do many things, but it cannot transform the society. Only
the people can accomplish that. They change the fabric of society gradually and
in unannounced ways with their behavior and creativity, guided roughly by their
enduring moral values. If government set out to impose transformed values on
the rest of us, the results would be oppressive and wrong. During the last generation, the coarsening pressures of the market system did a lot of damage to our

society, but they did not succeed in stripping Americans of what they believe. Most people still know the difference between right and wrong and, despite the obstacles, they struggle to live accordingly.

What government can do is construct the rules, legal premises, and supportive platform that enable people to pursue social transformation more aggressively. Our inventive popular culture—the marvel of the world—does this in freewheeling ways. With a little help and less interference from Washington, Americans can similarly reinvent the society. An era of innovation and random experimentation would draw upon this same spirit, the life force of Americans, the people who are both practical and idealistic.

One important precondition government can provide is the platform of "essential needs" (described in Chapter Eleven) that will give everyone more security, and therefore more confidence to explore new and different choices. We could dust off Roosevelt's "second Bill of Rights" and address its unmet goals. Likewise, the thick backlog of legislative proposals that have been blocked by powerful interests during the last generation should be revisited in order to establish concrete rights and protections for families and children, workers and employees. The extensive family-centered social systems in Europe (also described in Chapter Eleven) suggest opportunities for US reforms. Reversing national economic policy on work and wages is, likewise, a necessary step toward healing the society. If government constructs a rising floor under wage incomes, starting from the bottom up, people at every level will be liberated to pursue creative social invention. In the face of deep recession and rising unemployment, there is not much anyone can do to boost wages. But government can make a promise for the future. When the economy recovers and unemployment declines, the minimum-wage floor will rise in step and other work-improvement rules will kick in. Congress can enact the laws in advance and time their effective date to economic conditions.

Beyond these essential steps, there are taller mountains to climb. We can envision loftier goals that require social imagination and then practical testing before gaining broad agreement and political implementation. This is where we get to dream a little. Can we imagine, for instance, a country that is virtually without poor children? A nation in which every child grows up entitled to explore life's possibilities, free to go anywhere in this diverse country and feel at home? Can we imagine an economic system that is not organized on the principle of command and control, on the few giving orders to the many? Can we envision an economy designed to serve the society rather than the other way around?

Some will say this is idle daydreaming. I say it is our birthright, our inherited privilege. We are Americans. We get to think larger thoughts about our country and ourselves. Daydreams are a seedbed for the possible. We can argue later about how to achieve them.

To encourage people to free up their imaginations, I add a radical proposition: Instead of asking what will be good for the economy, government should start by asking what will be good for our people and society. Instead of thinking first about how to help businesses flourish, ask instead what people need to flourish in American life. Essentially, I am suggesting a reversal of the usual process employed by the political system. In its efforts to take care of business, the social question is often never asked. Here are three big ideas—favorite daydreams of mine—to illustrate what it means to put the people first.

First, every American who is able and willing ought to have the right to work a job that pays a livable wage. If the private sector will not provide these jobs, then the public sector should do so as the employer of last resort. Franklin Roosevelt described the goal—the practical equivalent of full employment—in his "second Bill of Rights," and the public has overwhelmingly endorsed the principle ever since. In recent decades, the US economy drifted even further from the promise, creating in its place a broad labor market of the underclass—temporary jobs paying unlivable wages and often filled by illegal immigrants. Guaranteed public jobs paying more than the minimum wage would permanently and automatically stabilize the economy, swelling the ranks of public workers in recessions and shrinking them when private jobs become more abundant. Instead of punishing the working poor most severely in downturns, as the system now does, it would redistribute the costs to all taxpayers to share as a public obligation.

The social consequences of a change like this could be profound: It would be a direct assault on the poverty and hopelessness of inner-city precincts and decaying rural towns where the same pathologies ravage families and young people without regard to race or ethnicity. Real jobs would mean reliable incomes would flow into those communities, providing a concrete basis for economic development and neighborhood restoration as well as the redemption of damaged lives.

If the job slots included school-age young people, men and women in the bleakest circumstances would suddenly become valued members of their families and the communities in which they would go to work producing real improvements while gaining for themselves a foothold on the economic ladder. If eligibility were linked to continuing their educations, young people would get practical, on-the-job training and a strong reason to stay in school. I can imagine the American military providing its expertise and maybe its active-duty personnel or veterans in these public works projects. Old sergeants know how to take unpromising kids and turn them into highly competent and disciplined young people. Isn't that what society wants and needs?

Obviously, permanent public employment—jobs for all who need them—would be enormously expensive, but the fulfillment of large goals begins with smaller steps. The government might set some guidelines, then sponsor one hundred or two hundred projects around the country and invite impoverished communities to compete for them. What work needs to be done? What skills and equipment are required? People can answer those local questions for themselves. Some initial efforts will fail, but the country will learn from the mistakes and from the successes.

The second idea is that everyone who works, whether in the front office or on the assembly line, deserves to "own" their work, that is, to exercise personal responsibility for what they do and enjoy mutual respect and the right to contribute and collaborate in important decision making within the firm. These elements of individual voice and status are critical to personal satisfaction in one's work—the best companies encourage the cooperative spirit from top to bottom—but democratic qualities are largely missing from American workplaces. When most people go to work, they submit to a master–servant relationship in which a few people determine everyone else's behavior and most employees are denied a voice in the matter and have no right to object or criticize. These confinements are especially strict for lower-wage workers, but often extend far up the occupational ladder to include middle mangers and professionals.

Breaking free of this rigid top-down system and liberating workers to enjoy the rights of being human would represent a profound change for our society, a great leap forward in our social development as a people. As it happens, the shift to more cooperative and respectful workplaces can also yield economic gain for the nation. As numerous academic studies have shown and outstanding companies already understand, collaborative relationships between top management and the workforce are more productive and profitable. Instead of being ruled by fierce conflicts, the different elements within these companies share information constantly and steadily improve by learning from their mistakes. The profits are shared because the workers are also the owners.

This reorganization of employment and ownership cannot be commanded from afar because it requires everyone—workers and bosses—to change, to put aside old hostilities and begin trusting in more open communications. That change is very difficult for people to achieve in any setting. Government can encourage the pursuit, however, by setting out some incentives and loose guidelines for reforming work. One of the most promising routes to change is the employee stock ownership plan that invests everyone as co-owners with the same economic incentive—sharing the returns from self-improvement. Some 11,000 companies—mostly smaller businesses—are now organized this way, and workers accumulate capital savings in addition to their pensions. Employee-owned companies, however, must also make internal reforms to establish mutual accountability and honest communication if they want to gain the full benefits of having worker–owners. The concept may seem alien to many, but its core assumptions are very American: a practical belief that both equality and liberty can be present in our daily lives.

The third idea is that, to lead the way for social values, the economy needs a new, reform-minded business organization—call it a social corporation—that competes with old-line corporations adhering to their narrower values that enforce the supremacy of profit over society. The social corporations could be chartered by government and given certain benefits and exemptions from the usual rules, but most of them would be independent and private. They would produce needed goods or services the private sector won't provide and sell them at a price most people could afford. They might, for instance, fulfill the market for very cheap computers and other high-tech devices that are stripped of the bells and whistles that run up the price tags. The social corporation would be a working model for how the social imperatives—environmental values and equitable relations with workers and communities—can be integrated into firms and efficient production processes. Business lore and economic dogma say this is impossible. Social corporations would set out to prove they are wrong.

The purpose of this competition is not to replace orthodox companies (though eventually it might), but to put real market pressures on them to change. Social corporations will be successful when they go out of business because their superior methods and social qualities have been copied and coopted by the business world. Creating social enterprises, including nonprofit cooperatives, can liberate us from the political vetoes business interests exert over promising new ideas. As the system now functions, innovations are either stymied by existing forces or taken over and shut down by larger corporations anxious to eliminate competitors that might undercut their monopoly profits.

The social corporation will need some protections in its infancy and perhaps modest start-up subsidies, but another crucial objective is to limit the size of business organizations, including social corporations, in line with E. F. Schumacher's famous dictum "small is beautiful." The bloated scale of America's leading corporations has become a major impediment to freewheeling innovation and experimental reforms, not to mention a corrupting influence in politics. Americans are learning anew from the financial crisis why it is a mistake to let private firms concentrate more and more power under one management. The failure of megabanks that the government helped create threatens our general well-being and then government bails them out with taxpayer money because they are "too big to fail." Revived antitrust laws could simply prohibit the concentration of economic power as a threat to social values as well as to healthy competition.

Economic power must be dispersed in this broad nation, especially in banking and finance. We need many more financial intermediaries to allocate capital and credit and demonstrate more respect for society's needs. That includes regional banks, which are naturally closer to the customers. It means supporting and protecting the small and adventurous financial firms founded on commitments to social responsibility. They put capital into companies that have embraced environmental concerns and equitable dealings with workers and communities and practice high-road behavior. On many fronts one can now see the gradual advance of "social responsibility" in US capitalism. The pace is too slow to attract much political respect, but the current crumbling of the old order will clear the way for more dramatic progress.

These are three reform propositions among many people can consider. The ideas may seem distant from the usual chatter of policy thinkers, but they offer viable paths out of the losses and disruptions visited upon innocent Americans. They are alternatives to an economic system that has abused rather than served American life. I know a lot of smart people around the country are pursuing these ideas in different ways—they are our social pioneers. They and others constitute the beginnings of new formations of citizens that can disrupt inert politics and overcome the timidity of incumbent politicians. These agitators are engaging political action for the long run obviously and the fainthearted need not apply.

CHAPTER FOURTEEN

THE UNDERGROUND RIVER

"Democracy begins in human conversation. The simplest, least threatening investment any citizen may make in democratic renewal is to begin talking with other people." When I wrote that some years ago in *Who Will Tell the People: The Betrayal of American Democracy,* I meant the words literally. Democratic conversations do not start with presidential campaigns or issues or abstract assessments of "what's wrong with politics." People begin them by talking about themselves, their lives and circumstances. This doesn't happen in some big public hall, but rather among family and friends who are willing to listen sympathetically. Americans need to go off somewhere quiet and talk among themselves.

They can tell stories, talk about the children or grandchildren. They can air some of their dreams and everyday worries, whatever keeps them up at night. They can talk about the past, where the family came from and what their grandparents recall about early struggles. They may decide to share their semisecret fantasies about what they would really like to do with their lives. Or they may express their pain and frustrations, confess to the shame of falling short in life. What people know about themselves is the raw material of democracy.

"The world as it is and the world as it ought to be." The resonant tension in that phrase is the tension of authentic democracy. People who absorb its meaning are taking the first tentative steps toward reclaiming their status as citizens. You don't need a doctoral degree. Everyone can talk about the contradictions that fill their lives and draw evidence from their own experiences and values. Once they take it up, some people find they cannot drop the subject, but instead are compelled to dig deeper.

I borrowed the phrase from friends who are active in a nationwide network of vibrant community organizations loosely allied under the umbrella of the Industrial Areas Foundation (IAF). Some 57 interfaith groups bring people together across the dividing lines of race, religion, and class for political action, pursuing "the world as it ought to be." IAF groups win some of the battles they undertake and they lose some, but generally these faith-based organizations have endured because the participants can see that their work has meaningful results in their communities. The IAF approaches its projects from the perspectives of its members' personal experiences, and its agendas are based on what they know. The talk is respectful, concrete, and self-critical, lofty in spirit but down-to-earth in discipline. The IAF's Iron Rule is "Never, never do for others what they can do for themselves." People tend to stay engaged in these organizations because, unlike groups that play regular politics, the results seem real. People feel empowered.[1]

I have hung out with these IAF groups for some twenty years, mostly to listen, sometimes to talk. I suspect their meetings are the closest thing to a genuine democratic dialogue that I am ever likely to witness. Certainly, it is rare to see members of the middle class and the working class and the poor—white, black, Hispanic, Asian, Christian, Jewish, Muslim—working together in politics as if this is normal in American life. They do not take roll calls or hold elections. They might talk about how to pin down local politicians on unkept promises, or they might discuss the mysterious link between "power and love," which the IAF philosophy casts as complementary aspects of all relationships, be they personal or political. They have leaders who emerge from the ranks and full-time paid organizers, but they have no elected officers who hand down instructions. The IAF organizers include Catholic nuns and priests, black ministers and rabbis, schoolteachers and housewives—everyone who develops the listening skills to draw others out of their isolation.

IAF meetings are not very exciting because they are not about verbal combat or winning and losing. But I keep going back for more, and I always learn something. Their talk confirms for me that an authentic democracy is still possible in this country. They confirm my conviction that Americans have the capacity to govern themselves. Like most participants, I come away feeling good about the future.

I have no grand plan for reconstructing American democracy. It would sound ridiculous if I did. The people will find their way, or they won't. Their strategies are unlikely to come from books I or others have written. But I can offer some insights that may be helpful—understandings that I have accumulated over years of tramping through the political system as a reporter. Years ago, I was one of those "boys on the bus" covering the presidential candidates. I know quite a lot about congressional politics and how Washington works (or doesn't work). But as a reporter I was increasingly drawn to the politics that is distant from the formal machinery of elections. I became intrigued by the people who have no power but are trying to get some by organizing to break through the snares and obstacles and somehow get the system to respond to their demands.

I learned, among other things, that people can be ennobled by democratic engagement. I saw this happen again and again, especially in people of humble circumstances who lacked status or influence. They were told all their lives to accept their fates. When, for whatever reason, they decided to act, these people discovered that they were larger human beings than they had realized—more capable and ambitious, more self-confident and respected. One of the mysterious aspects of democracy is that people become empowered when they decide to act like they are empowered, when they choose to believe in their power despite all the evidence to the contrary.

Politics, almost by definition, is a group activity, and it involves the collective action of people who come together to work for shared goals, to change or defend what is. But democracy is anchored in the self, not in political parties or elections or policy ideologies, because it always begins with personal self-discovery. Can I do this? Dare I stand up and challenge the official version? The deeper transaction of people trying to engage power requires them to take themselves seriously as individuals. They accept responsibility and even demand it, acting like adults even though the system treats them like children. They are liberating themselves from the self-doubt and fears that tell people to keep their heads down and stay out of it. The decisive act of claiming the full rights of citizenship is an act of personal consciousness that resembles maturity, and it requires a measure of courage. Many Americans, maybe most of them, have never gotten there.

I want this book, in whatever way it can, to help Americans recover their self-confidence, and in the service of this, I have taken readers over the difficult terrain of lots of complicated subjects, I hope with clarity. But my real purpose is to convince people that they are already well equipped and capable enough to act once again like citizens. They must bring their common sense and practical experience to the table. They know things about the country that learned experts cannot see. They can challenge—even ridicule—the "crackpot realism" taught by distant authority figures who, from their lofty positions, have no concept of what citizens' lives are really like.

Some Americans naturally have this ability to stand apart from the crowd and take on the reigning wisdom. But many Americans are unable to do so. They may be pinned down by the daily obligations of their lives or intimidated by strong cultural pressures to conform and keep quiet. Standing apart can be uncomfortable, even a little scary, especially when your economic security seems endangered. Even people whose circumstances are failing may want to hang on to the status quo that is identified with success. Dissent risks exclusion. Rebellion does not come easily, even for people who are angry and despairing.

The confusing part, as many discover, is clearing their heads of other voices—the official noise that tells them how to think. Americans are drenched in and distracted by political, cultural, and commercial messages that crowd out the everyday realities that people know firsthand. Modern politics crudely uses the sophisticated techniques of commercial marketing, so that electing senators and presidents is not so different from selling cars or toothpaste. Citizens are studied like lab rats in a psychology experiment, they're tweaked and tested to find out which words or "hot button" images produce the desired responses. The messages organize Americans into herds of consumers, spectators, or voters who can be driven to buy, cheer, or vote for the correct agenda.

This system of communication generally works for the politicians since political marketing usually insulates them from the possibility of defeat. It does not remotely resemble a democracy of self-governing citizens. "Citizen," you may have noticed, is a term that mass-market politics seldom uses.

The failure of electoral democracy is grounded in the two-party system. One-third of the electorate rejects both Democrats and Republicans, yet these so-called independents have no comparable privileges in the system. People need to stand free of both parties to think clearly for themselves, and they also need to get a little distance from institutions that try to connect citizens with the higher realms of governing power. I say this with sympathy, but many representative organizations operating in Washington, from organized labor to environmentalists, are caught in the middle and compromised by their proximity to power. Because they have a seat at the table with the insiders, major groups typically temper their agendas so they won't lose their access to powerful figures. As a practical matter, these representative groups censor out or edit the full-throated opinions and aspirations of their own rank and file. The people are, therefore, distanced from power by those they chose to speak for them.

In rough outline, the United States has two parallel political systems. The official one, expertly equipped and in charge, produces and distributes political opinions and ideologies from above and delivers agendas fashioned from the top down. The "other" America, weak and largely unorganized, scattered, and passive, is the broad landscape of ordinary people whose yearnings are silenced, ignored, or easily manipulated. I suggest (dream, some might say) that this other America can find its voice—not one voice, but many, many voices—to become a nation of active citizens. In their varied ways, people would express the full, rich, complicated texture of what most Americans want to believe about our country, what truly matters to them, what they imagine is America the Possible.

From a grounding of self-knowledge, people can change the nation. They can use their well-formed convictions as leverage to destabilize the official system and open the way for deep reform. But first, people have to "own" their conversations—they have to get free of propaganda so they can talk coherently about the circumstances and values of their own lives. My hunch is that Americans of diverse political views and stark social differences would be surprised to find themselves much more in accord with each other on fundamental matters than we are led to expect.

I have occasionally cited opinion polls that confirm the overwhelming majorities and even extreme consensus on overarching questions like war and peace, the economic order, and the government's obligations to the general welfare. Ordinary Americans are disposed to believing in "the world as it ought to be." But they have very little confidence that regular politics will alter "the world as it is." It is not that the people are out of touch. The problem is that they cannot be heard.

The country's great challenge, as I have suggested, is not national decline, but our need to mature as a society. Because we are so young, especially compared to older societies, we are still developing, still growing up, still finding out who we wish to be. Just as I believe the nation can get through the current adversities if it develops a deeper sense of itself, I believe this progress depends largely on the people.

Governing elites, it's clear when you think about it, cannot do this for us. They are by nature locked into "the world as it is" and reflexively defensive. Only people who are distant from power have a clear view of what's wrong and are free to imagine "the world as it ought to be."

What Americans need, I suggest playfully, is a "club" of our own—a place where we can talk freely among ourselves. This club should have no officers, no dues or bylaws, and no affiliations with those in the existing power structure, such as the weak and tattered political parties. This approach, a very old tradition in American politics, needs to be revived so people can participate on terms that they define. These "clubs for America," which anyone can start, would be where people could discuss their convictions and vent their grievances and also dream audaciously about the future. We need 10,000 clubs, maybe 10 million, where people learn once again how to talk as citizens.

★ ★ ★ ★ ★

American democracy is confused and stunted, in part, because the history of the nation is taught backward. We learn from an early age that the United States was born of the wise brows of the Founding Fathers, the men who produced our sacred texts, the Declaration of Independence and the Constitution. The dogma holds that the nation proceeded ever after as a beacon of liberty and justice for the world, and the shrines in Washington are temples of worship to the "more perfect union" those men created. The ever-popular biographies of the founders celebrate the majesty of our immaculate conception.

This much-loved story line is basically false; it's heartwarming, but not what happened. Conventional history stresses the virtue inherent in our national intentions, but the country's true story is about the promise, not the delivery. The founding principles were visionary. They described the possibilities of what we may yet become as a nation. But lofty promises are rarely attained without great political struggle and bloodshed.

The sins of white supremacy and slavery, which treated African Americans as property, were formally authorized by the US Constitution. The confinements imposed upon working people, including children, were less severe than those of slavery, but they still stripped poor people of rights guaranteed by the Bill of Rights, such as freedom of speech and of assembly. The list of constitutional failures goes on, many still relevant to the American condition: the denial of voting rights to women of all colors and male citizens who did not own property, the continental conquest and decimation of indigenous peoples, the enshrinement of the rights of property as superior to those of human beings. The political system was designed to limit popular participation and reduce the ability of citizens to influence the governing authorities. These scars and blemishes tend to be overlooked on the Fourth of July. American democracy is a self-improving process, but improvement comes tortuously slowly and is as yet incomplete. Resistance to reform has often led to bloodshed, including officially sanctioned terrorism launched against those who protested the incompleteness. A terrible Civil War—which saw 600,000 killed—was required to end slavery. It was the equivalent of a second revolution that confronted grave crimes committed against African Americans in the first revolution.

Seeking a more authentic democracy inevitably requires politics built for the long run, because these struggles can last for decades, generations, and even centuries. One relatively simple example is how US senators gain their seats. Originally, the Senate was an American version of England's House of Lords—a parliament of landlords. Senators were selected not by the voters, but rather by state legislatures, which were often heavily influenced and bribed by those with wealth. It was not until 1913 that Americans were finally allowed to vote directly for US senators. At that point, women still did not have the right to vote. That finally was achieved in 1920. At that point, despite the passage of the Fifteenth Amendment in 1870, state restrictions (especially in the South) still prevented millions of black citizens from voting. They finally triumphed in the 1960s after another bloody struggle. Americans need not dwell guiltily on the historic failures. But they might exercise a little more humility when lecturing other nations on the virtues of our democracy.

The contradictions and imperfections of our democracy are well known enough, but their relevance is suppressed by the continual self-congratulation and deference to the myth of perfection. Patriotism itself is used as a weapon to suppress dissenting opinion. Any political candidate who declines to wear a flag pin in his lapel will be accused of disloyalty to the myth of "number one."

In the early days of the republic, the need for self-congratulation was easier to understand. The United States was new and insecure, eager to establish its distinctive strength as a freshly invented democracy. It did indeed become a model for the world, gradually discrediting monarchs and emperors. But it was never all that the patriotic cheerleaders claimed. The drumbeat of self-congratulation in modern times suggests a lingering insecurity, at least among those in authority. Exaggerating and falsifying America's democratic purity serves a purpose—to protect the status quo against popular demands for change. With very few exceptions, the established powers in government and the private sector have repeatedly resisted the continuing efforts of ordinary people to advance our society, to make it one that would share power more equitably and come closer to the original idea of self-governing citizens. "Not yet," the governors said when people demanded greater freedoms, "chaos might follow." "The people are not ready, neither sufficiently educated nor Americanized, to be trusted with a share of power," it was said. Law and the apparatus of government, including the force of arms, were (and are) regularly used to put down the complaints of unruly citizens seeking fundamental changes in their condition. Sometimes, the people have prevailed, but often they have not.

This suspenseful, long-running struggle to bring real meaning to those original promises is the true drama of American history—the story line Americans can celebrate if they are honest with the facts. Our great redeeming quality is not perfection, but possibility. America is a human society with all the usual human fallibilities, but this country makes possible great changes generated from the bottom up by those who resist and sometimes overcome the objections of those who hold the power. That is our true inheritance.

Seeing the nation as a still-unfolding saga of a people still struggling to fulfill their promise brings the national drama in line with our human experiences, similar to the stories we all know of individuals and families developing and changing (or failing to) over time. People strive and struggle, but sometimes they get things wrong and then they try again, perhaps with greater insight into themselves and their ambitions. Thinking and talking about America as an active process of maturing, a continuing struggle for human fulfillment, provides a shared language and a common platform for democratic conversations. Anyone can bring something to the table since everyone has experienced, in good ways and bad, the processes of maturing and developing greater accountability and wisdom.

Are we, in fact, the still-developing teenager I have described? Or is this wealthy, powerful nation already over the hill, too set in its ways to change any important aspects of its character? You already know my answer to this fateful question, but many Americans will reject my stubborn optimism. If the skeptics are right, it means that the nation is not just in decline, but also losing something more valuable than wealth and abundance: the promise of all that is offered by democracy. Obviously, I don't believe that. The force that drives striving Americans who are discontented with what is is the source of our loose and creative spirit, our willingness to explore the next chapter in the belief that it will be better than the past.

★　★　★　★　★

I have from time to time tried out the theory of our national maturation on people and found that the subject provokes intrigue and usually fresh optimism. At an informal seminar at the Southern New Hampshire University School of Community Economic Development, I watched sophisticated graduate students put aside dreary arguments about economics and plunge confidently into discussions of human development: What leads people to grow up? How do they mature without losing their idealism? What compels a young adult to let go of prolonged adolescence and embrace an adult perspective? Having a baby, one professor suggested; the experience is both frightening and exalting, as any first-time parent learns. Life's questions abruptly shift from "What do I want?" to "What does this child need?" Young parents, as Lee Halprin put it in one of my seminars, discover "the delight of responsibility." Family trauma—the death of a loved one or a sudden economic crisis—may teach similar lessons.

The preoccupation with children and young people frustrated a grad student from Mongolia, whose culture is steeped in ancient learning. "You talk about the teenager," she complained, "but who are your parents—your mother and father? Where did you come from?"

Her interjection reminded us that Americans are typically fixed on the present moment and have a very weak sense of the past and the continuum that connects human existence past and present to the future. Do Americans understand this story line? Can we find comfort and honor in our obligations to the future? The seminar reached no grand conclusions, but thinking this way may itself be an act of maturation—accepting what ancient cultures have already understood. Each generation inherits the knowledge of the past and discovers new things that it hands on to future generations. Life is not a foot-race where people declare victory at the finish line. Life continues on, with or without us.

The singular struggle of African Americans is the core narrative of our national experience because it encompasses all that is tragic, triumphant, brutal, and beautiful in the American story. The great victories that secured their eventual freedom unfolded not as blessings from the citadels of power, but from the desperate struggles of the most marginalized citizens in the land. They figured out how to move power out of their way. Their story has not ended. Black people, despite forcing great progress, are still digging through contradictions and confronting the remnants of white supremacy in new forms.

Patriotism has a distinctively different twist for black Americans. Roger Wilkins, a historian and leader in the civil rights movement, wrote a compelling inquiry, *Jefferson's Pillow,* that examined the Founding Fathers from his perspective as an African American scholar. He found himself admiring George Washington, who freed his slaves and in that sense was a more authentic small-d democrat than Thomas Jefferson, who did not. Jefferson gave us the words, but he did not live those words, Wilkins wrote.[2] I sent him a playful note thanking him for not completely destroying my hero, Jefferson, who authored some of our nation's noblest expressions. Wilkins wrote back, "I would like to have Jefferson as my speech writer. But I wouldn't want him in the same foxhole."

During the second half of the twentieth century, the nation experienced a great period of truth telling about the past. A new wave of historians came along and uncovered the facts behind many sordid chapters in our national history. They gave us the real story—the ghastly contradictions and injustices and the stories of the various people who struggled to overcome them. Highbrow critics complained that this version was disillusioning and potentially damaging to patriotic faith, but it actually helped many people come to terms with the facts of who we are.

These more truthful accounts of US history accompanied and helped inform an era of liberation politics. African Americans, women, the poor, gays and lesbians, Native Americans, and other marginalized minorities uncovered their own histories and mobilized themselves to fight for—and in some cases win—full rights and recognition. Despite enormous frustrations and setbacks, these mass social movements helped the country progress. They literally changed the prevailing values and demonstrated that people at large were ready to change. By dramatizing the moral contradictions of past and present, agitators made visible what others felt but could not bring themselves to admit.

★ ★ ★ ★ ★

Authentic mass social movements are very difficult to start and even more difficult to sustain. Successful movements can transform lives, even change the country. But they also fail regularly and often seem to disappear. Then, years later, new movements may arise composed of different people and strategies, yet focused on the same yearnings and grievances. The mystery is why people do this. Why do they persist in running into brick walls? Where do they find the nerve to rebel when the outcome seems predictable? The short answer is that people believe in the democratic promise.

I learned much of this from historian Lawrence Goodwyn in his magnificent account of the Populist revolt of the late nineteenth century, *The Populist Moment*. Desperate farmers in the South and Midwest rose up to challenge the banking system that was turning independent yeomen into debt-burdened sharecroppers. The Populists confronted not only the bankers, but also the federal government, which was allied with the bankers and deaf to the Populists' cries of distress. Goodwyn's account redeemed the Populists, who had been disparaged by conventional historians, and showed how their self-taught political mobilization revealed the modern weakness of formal democracy. The farmers started with nothing—no allies and few resources. Out of that, they built a muscular movement of powerless people, many millions strong, who taught one another how to think clearly about larger economic forces. They sent out traveling lecturers and started scores of newspapers to inform the populace about how and why they were being ruined.[3]

Eventually, they formed an independent political party that captured state governments and seats in Congress. Their rise was deeply frightening to those in the establishment, who saw unwashed hayseeds reaching for real power. In the end the Populists were defeated, yet they changed everything. They left behind an astonishing agenda of sophisticated solutions—radical new ideas about reorganizing government and the economy in the age of corporate industrialism. Their thinking informed progressive reform for the next fifty years, especially the legislative triumphs of the New Deal era.

They could not save themselves, but they helped to change the country. The legacy seems bittersweet, but the substance of what they said and did should inspire us in the present. If lowly, poorly educated citizens could accomplish that much, can contemporary Americans, with our many obvious advantages, do something similar? As Goodwyn explained, the agrarian movement drew its strength and creativity from within, producing the thrill of self-reliance.

"Out of their cooperative struggle came a new democratic community," he wrote. "It engendered within millions of people what Martin Luther King would later call a 'sense of somebodiness.' This 'sense' was a new way of thinking about oneself and about democracy." Surrounded as they were by hostile forces, they hardly had a choice. They talked with one another and learned how to spread the word. They debated big ideas in grand alliance meetings. They drafted their own policy proposals and enunciated what Goodwyn called "unsanctioned ideas."

Mass social movements, Goodwyn explained, begin with individuals who, for whatever reason, have "managed to attain a high level of personal political self-respect. They are not resigned; they are not intimidated." They dare to believe that they can spread this confidence to others. At every stage of the Populist mobilization, the decisive quality was their autonomy—they were independent and self-directed people. They created "an autonomous institution where new interpretations can materialize that run counter to those of prevailing authority," Goodwyn wrote. Scorned and isolated, the Populists were free to think for themselves.

This is what I am looking for now—the unacknowledged power of ordinary people who see things as they are, not as they have been interpreted for them by abstract theorists and learned authorities. This capacity draws upon the informal knowledge that people accumulate in their everyday lives from their families, their forebears, the Bible, or other revered texts. Some of this gets passed down from generation to generation. Some popular wisdom is reflected in the common sense that Americans know in their guts, regardless of their educational status or income level. They understand power from the perspective of those who don't have any.

The people's common understandings and political judgments are not always correct, of course, but they ought to be the foundation for politics and government. Their exclusion from the political process reflects the pretensions of our sophisticated era as well as the uses of power. The evidence is clear to anyone who is willing to judge it fairly: Again and again in many large matters, what the people "knew," though it was belittled and brushed aside, turned out to be right, while governing elites were terribly, disastrously wrong.

Reading Goodwyn's words about democratic culture and the humble people who create it led me to a revelation. This was what I had been hearing from ordinary people, I realized, during all my years as a reporter. I had heard fragments of their unfashionable wisdom. I had learned of their spontaneous insights about power that seemed radical, yet basically right. I had encountered common-sense ideas expressed with startling clarity but were unsanctioned in the larger debates. The ordinary people I had interviewed over the years were living evidence of Goodwyn's analysis. Many have the same uncommon self-confidence he saw in the Populists. More than that, these people affirmed for me that the pulse of democratic promise remains alive in the body of American life, despite the barriers and intimidation.

These thoughts led me to an entirely different understanding of America and how it works. I put aside the conventional history and conventional news that chronicle the top-down accomplishments of presidents and regular politics. Underneath all that, I glimpsed a more promising story about the country, one that is more realistic because it is closer to what we know and experience; more suspenseful because it suggests that the country is still becoming, learning, and changing. We don't know yet how this story will come out, whether for better or for worse. Nothing is decided yet.

The people play their own enduring role as torchbearers in generation after generation as they carry forward unfulfilled yearnings, keeping alive the promise of a more genuine democracy, even when their voices are weakened or unheard. Their role is conservative in the sense that they act as conservators of old values that others may regard as obsolete. Yet the people are likewise the recurring source of progressive advancements.

★　★　★　★　★

I began to think of this deeper current in American life—the pulse of democratic promise—as an underground river. It flows along beneath the surface of everyday events, largely ignored and seemingly impotent. The current is sometimes diverted or temporarily blocked. The flow of people's yearnings may at times be reduced to form a minor rivulet. It may seem exhausted, gone.[4]

Yet suddenly—once again—the unseen river regains its strength. The pulse of the promise surfaces anew. It breaks through to visibility with a burst of power that shocks the status quo and changes America. That is the true drama in our national history. You can see this pattern in most of the pivotal advances and liberating reforms—the abolition of slavery, the liberation of women, the rise of the labor movement, and the struggles for economic justice and triumphs of the modern civil rights movement, among others. After generations of failure, citizens break through, make themselves heard, and gain power. The pattern can be traced back to the origins of the republic and even before. The river has surfaced in good times and in bad times, nearly always coming as a threatening surprise to the governing powers.

I love the suspense in this story. Nobody knows when the next eruption might occur or can say exactly why it happens at one time and not another. I enjoy the unscripted chaos ordinary people can provoke for the authorities by suddenly reordering the landscape in ways no one anticipated. For official America, the event is the democratic equivalent of whiplash. Where, they wonder, did these people come from? Why weren't we told?

Knowing these subterranean currents exist and can be nourished and replenished even in unpromising times is what gives me my permanent sense of optimism about the country. It also requires patience with history. You can be part of something larger than yourself—the democratic continuum—even if within your lifetime you cannot know whether your efforts will have tangible results. You operate on faith and patience.

Years ago, I decided I wanted to be part of this story. I would contribute by writing for the vast, undefined audience of people who sustain the current rather than for those movers and shakers who hold the power aboveground. I thought I might be able to help people understand what they need to know, maybe even nudge them to another breakthrough. Just as likely, I knew, was that nothing much would happen. I would simply contribute to keeping unsanctioned ideas alive for the next generation, passing them forward to whoever inherits the democratic faith. Either way, I can report the work is deeply satisfying.

★ ★ ★ ★ ★

When I ask myself why I believe in this river, my thoughts fill with flashes of memory—the faces and voices I have encountered over the years. I can still see them and hear them and remember their fragments of self-taught knowledge. Many of the people I met were struggling in unpromising, even desperate circumstances. Others had comfortable lives, but were angered by the immorality of the way things are. One way or another, they were all definitely in democracy's current.

There were the young steelworkers in Pittsburgh who were trying to save their mill. I talked with working-class women from Louisiana's "Cancer Alley" who were going after the petrochemical industry that had poisoned their surroundings. I got to know Catholic nuns in Texas who practiced shrewd, tough politics on behalf of children, families, and communities. I remember a young Lakota Indian on a South Dakota reservation who had been through the fire of drugs and alcohol. He recovered his life by going back to the "old ways," helping to restore other troubled young Native Americans with his sacred vision of who they are. I also learned much from the retired corporate CEO in New Jersey who became a deeply informed crusader for company ownership by workers. It was the right thing to do for the country, he explained—the right thing for capitalism and for Christian morality. I will never forget the discontented autoworker in northeast Ohio who told me sorrowfully, "People don't understand that the ultimate power is in their hands."

One of the delights of roving around America as a reporter is learning about the country up close in small places. I witnessed the civil rights movement mostly in that way, dropping in on small towns where racial conflicts boiled over. In those settings, humble black people gave new meaning to the word "courage." Their movement changed all our lives. As Martin Luther King Jr. prophesied, white America was liberated, too.

Nearly forty years ago, I went to the small town of Summerton, South Carolina, and interviewed the aging black men and women who had started the fight that led to the hallmark Supreme Court decision in *Brown v. Board of Education,* which ended state-enforced racial segregation in public schools. The original complaint filed by the black folks in Summerton was a petition asking local officials to provide a school bus for the black children. Rejected, they went to court and their lawsuit asked for what the white kids got—free textbooks and a decent schoolhouse instead of a rural shack with a woodstove and no plumbing or lighting. Rejected again.[5]

The local banker, Charles Plowden, who pretty much ran things in Summerton, explained how white people justified the vicious inequalities. "The way we figured it at the time," he told me, "the white people paid the taxes and the white people had the better schools, no question about that. But most of the Nigras didn't go to school. They had to work in the fields to make a living."

Each time the black parents were turned down, they found themselves upping the ante. An NAACP lawyer from New York, Thurgood Marshall (the future Supreme Court justice), persuaded them to go all the way. Instead of demanding "separate but equal" schooling for their children, the lawsuit was amended to ask the Supreme Court to abolish racial segregation altogether. *Briggs v. Elliot* was one of five lawsuits eventually consolidated in the *Brown* decision.

"Our damper was up then," funeral director Billie Fleming, a local NAACP leader, said. "These Negroes had smelled freedom and they were hell-bent for it." But they were also putting themselves at grave risk. "It scared the fool out of us," a farmer named Joe Lemmon remembered.

Harry Briggs, whose son Harry Jr. was named as lead plaintiff on the lawsuit, lost his job at the filling station when white customers stopped going there. His wife was fired from the motel where she cleaned rooms. Briggs tried farming and taking odd jobs under an assumed name. He and his family were driven out of the county.

"I knew they were going to get me," Briggs said, "when they fired James Brown and Bo Stukes. I remember it was right before Christmas because, when he fired me, he give a Christmas present. A carton of cigarettes." The reprisals were intimate and effective. Small farmers discovered the local cotton gin would no longer take their cotton. Plowden's bank stopped making farm loans to anyone who had signed the petition. Someone from Olive's Café in the black part of town had to drive to Sumter or Columbia to get beer, soda pop, bread, and milk because the delivery trucks would no longer stop at Olive's.

"I think we had 120 sign that petition and they thrashed it down to 22," Briggs remembered. I found him living with his family in the South Bronx and working in a Manhattan parking garage. Harry Jr. was a truck driver, his mother made beds in a downtown hotel. The parents expressed pride that their younger children were going through New York City public schools with Italians, Jews, Puerto Ricans, and other African Americans.

Back in Summerton, some things had not changed. Charles Plowden was still running things and white people were still resisting. When I explained the situation to Harry Briggs, he laughed knowingly. "Maybe the Good Lord will call Mr. Charles away some day," he said. "That would be a stumbling block for him, wouldn't it."

The black people in Summerton paid a cruel price for demanding their rights and in 1970 their struggle still was not over—yet. Twenty years later, Briggs and his fellow agitators knew which side had won. It was not Mr. Charles. Their defiance had changed the nation.

"We was trying to get a little freedom for the kids, that's all," Harry Briggs told me. "It used to be, as long as you came under the white man's order, you was a good boy. But, as long as you speak for yourself, they call you nasty or smart. My grandfather would take what was give him. But that wouldn't do for me. I'm just as much as the next person."

Harry Briggs's eloquent clarity belongs somewhere in the archives of American politics: "I'm just as much as the next person." The conviction that motivated him is the founding idea of the nation, the promise that leads people to take great risks. It is what Goodwyn recognized in the democratic culture of the Populists and the quality that has driven other popular movements. It reminds me of an expression I heard along the way, though I do not remember where or when: "My people are as good as your people." Yes, that is the birthright. It is what Americans want to believe about themselves and their country, though the idea is not yet fulfilled.

Every good reporter harbors regrets about the questions he failed to ask. I wish I had asked Harry Briggs more about why he and his friends had stepped up when other people kept their heads down. Where did that come from—the confidence to throw off servility and refuse to be a "good boy"? Maybe it had been the recent experience of World War II, when black men had gone off to war to fight for American ideals that were denied to them back home. Maybe it was the memory of his grandfather's being compelled to bow low before white supremacy. Or something his parents had taught him about self-respect. Whatever the case, Briggs was looking forward. "We was trying to get a little freedom for the kids, that's all."

Some might argue that oppressed African Americans in the South rebelled because they had nothing to lose. But that wasn't the case. Marginalized as they were, these people had everything to lose, and some of them did lose their lives and livelihoods. What happened, I think, is that converging events presented them with a choice they had not expected to have—a rare opening to change their circumstances. Some of them decided to go for it.

For most Americans today, the choice looks very different. For starters, most of us are not impoverished and excluded. Indeed, the active risk now may be the fear of losing the security of a comfortable life. In that situation, it may be harder for many people to adopt a critical perspective and turn against the system that is identified with success. It seems smarter to keep your head down and remain a "good boy." The passivity is understandable, but as economic forces whittle away at the safe options, more people will see the logic of defiance.

★   ★   ★   ★   ★

We have reached a fracture point in our national story, one that changes the choices for nearly everyone. As this book has explained, the transformation is driven by the failures and misguided assumptions of those in governing circles, and also by large historical forces than cannot be avoided. The reckoning ahead does not doom the country to wrenching poverty, but it will profoundly alter American life, like it or not. I cannot predict precisely how these forces will play out, but I feel certain they have deeply unsettled the existing order. Painful and scary as that is, it is also a rare opening for a born-again democracy.

My hunch is that more and more Americans will pull away from the existing political order as they observe its lack of responsiveness to the broad society's deeper stresses and injuries. Passivity and resignation never change much. If people become anxious and angry, they are freed to think more independently about why our democracy isn't working. Some will switch sides and join the insurgents.

At that point, if Americans do find their voices and challenge the political order, the question of national maturity takes on an intriguing twist. Instead of deferring to the status quo, people may start asking, Who are the real grown-ups in American society? Are they the governing elites who are aligned with the past and committed to US presumptions to run the world? Or are they the aroused citizens who want America to come home and keep its promises?

To rehabilitate democracy and reclaim our role as citizens, Americans have to change the architecture of political power by creating a third front for popular sovereignty. The empty space between big government and the private sector's concentrated power could be filled by citizens in many new formations—groups large and small, local and national, that would speak independently and use their powers to persuade or punish the existing order. This is politics for the long run, obviously, but it is an approach that could lead to a fundamental rebirth of the democracy if people find the nerve and stamina to make it happen.

Think of these new formations not as political parties or organizations devoted to specific issues, but something in between. They could function more or less like political tribes or floating alliances of kindred spirits. Assemblies of like-minded citizens could represent the public concerns politicians don't dare touch (antimilitarism, for instance), mobilize the political power of neglected sectors (black Americans, the poor, home owners faced with foreclosure), or articulate fundamental new visions of what the country should become (having a family-first focus or hard-nosed morality in public life, for example). People in formations could carry the spear for whatever they see missing from politics and not worry about discomfiting incumbent politicians because, in fact, that would be their purpose.

The groups would be voluntary and loosely organized, serving as sounding boards where citizens could go with grievances and daydreams. These formations would necessarily be numerous, reflecting the rich variety of our differences. Indeed, some formations would be on opposite sides of important issues. But many would also collaborate openly to promote other large matters where they share mutual interests. Citizens could learn to negotiate power relationships with each other and then together bargain with those who hold power in official America.

These formations (or whatever people chose to call them) could also engage in electoral politics, but on their own terms, not as agents of the established parties. Most obviously, they could mobilize voters. But they could also sponsor selected insurgent candidates for office, challenging the old bulls and destabilizing the safe incumbency that protects the power of both major parties. Formations could also organize acts of nonviolent civil disobedience to purposefully interfere with unjust processes or defy laws designed to protect the powerful by limiting the rights of citizens. If government will not aid the millions of families losing their homes in the current economic crisis, assemblies of citizens could show up at foreclosures and advise the sheriff not to proceed. If the governing party hesitates to act, the formations must promise to punish them. These and other tactics for "thickening democracy" expand the opportunities for citizens to intrude on decision-making processes that are largely closed to them.

Think of the formations as islands of tough-minded people with convictions who are free to think for themselves because they have no permanent attachments to the existing parties and power structure. Think of them as bands of savvy guerillas roaming amid the aging mastodons of politics, looking for weak spots to attack them and leveraging change with lightning raids. Think of Americans rising up in surprising numbers to save democracy and, in the process, to liberate their elected representatives from the soul-deadening grip of the status quo. It is the politics of "organized people versus organized money," as IAF groups put it.

This could be fun. Democracy ought to be fun. It should also feel exalting and a little scary, what first-time parents feel when holding their newborn baby. Democratic engagement requires a spirit of playfulness. People put on a show in the hope that they will draw a crowd and get others to join them.

★　★　★　★　★

To organize their power as citizens, people have to begin with their own playful leap of faith—a willing suspension of cynicism in which they decide to believe what many of them know is not quite true: that they are citizens, in the full meaning of the term. They must believe that they actually possess the rights and responsibilities, the sovereign powers and duties granted to citizens by the founding documents. In the mystery of democracy, wishing something to be true can make it true. I have seen this happen many times. People who tell themselves they *are* "somebody" and act as if it is so discover that it is so.

This personal transaction was the ultimate source of power for the civil rights movement. Millions of people who were utterly powerless convinced themselves to believe otherwise. Historian Wesley C. Hogan described the process in *Many Minds, One Heart,* her intimate account of the Student Nonviolent Coordinating Committee (SNCC). The SNCC's organizers were mostly urban students from leading black colleges in the South. They went into very dangerous places like rural Mississippi to persuade the most vulnerable and oppressed black people to undertake defiant political actions, like registering to vote. The organizers' first challenge, Hogan explained, was learning to listen—truly listen—to the poor folks and accept the realities that these people described. Together, with patient conversation and learning, they developed a powerful way to overcome fear.[6]

"People learned how to act as if they were free to act as full citizens," Hogan wrote. Think of the courage that required, knowing it would provoke reprisals and violence. Most contemporary Americans are not so oppressed or threatened with violence, but they have to undergo a similar change of consciousness that involves rejecting the mass-market intimidation that teaches them to be passive and powerless.

As I mentioned in Chapter Nine, I borrowed the concept of formations from novelist Walter Mosley, author of the best-selling Easy Rawlins mysteries. In *Life Out of Context,* a provocative meditation on our dysfunctional democracy, Mosley proposed the formation of an independent black political party as a way for frustrated black Americans to aggregate their leverage and influence instead of waiting for the Democratic Party to address their problems. Other groups, he suggested, should do the same—farmers, women, "angry young white men," gays, even "true Republicans," whoever sees the need.[7]

"We could actually democratize America by taking power away from the two-party system and handing it over to the people," Mosley wrote. "Other special parties would arise, splintering off from the centrist attendants of the rich, once we show them the way." These groups could have great influence, he figured, even if they spoke for only 10 percent of their populations. Major parties would be forced to deal with them, if only in self-defense. Mosley envisions an American evolution that could "transform our two-party system into a kind of Virtual Parliament." In a parliamentary system, a major party can be brought down by the defection of any constituent part, so the parties cannot ignore any of them.

★ ★ ★ ★ ★

I was inspired by Mosley's thinking because it offers a rough blueprint for popular action that does not require the approval of the "authorities," laws, or formal organizations. These political assemblies would live or die according to the wishes of their adherents, which would be based on results, not rhetoric. They would not have to vet their agendas with political insiders or abandon big ideas and vital causes if the ruling order wasn't ready to consider them. Some big ideas need the sponsorship of citizens to give them visibility before the broader public is ready to take the issues seriously. In the nineteenth century, for example, American abolitionists campaigned for more than half a century before their cause prevailed. Given modern communications, it shouldn't take us that long to create comparable change.

The idea of independent formations—lots of them—is a potential nightmare for the system of two-party politics. Most incumbents, given their many advantages, would probably ignore the whole business at first, assuming these were simply more special interest groups making noise and demanding attention. But these unsanctioned formations wouldn't be empty front groups with fancy letterheads, they would be made up of real people. Multiple alliances of citizens mobilized as voters could target and punish indifferent politicians, picking off the supposedly safe incumbents of either party and even threatening to bring down a party's majority status in the House or Senate.

In my experience, nothing wakes up complacent senators and representatives like seeing a few of their colleagues cut down by new issues or a little-known challenger whom they did not take seriously. When power is made to feel insecure, it is less lazy and less prone to corruption. Citizens are not going to have power handed to them until they demonstrate that they already have some power and are using it for their own purposes. When independent citizens learn how to target smug incumbents and upset some of them, then a genuine democratic conversation can begin.

In fact, citizens have the potential to liberate regular politicians from the money-drenched politics that now confines them. A third front of mobilized citizens could force more complicated choices on the two parties, but also offer them a popular base as an alternative to relying on the concentrated wealth of corporations and special interest groups. Meanwhile, formations would open new space in politics for diverse views and principled dissent. Formations could protect conscientious representatives who stand alone on fundamental matters like civil liberties, war and peace, poverty, and injustice. Assemblies are vehicles for broadcasting these concerns to far larger audiences and forcing debates on taboo subjects.

Most important of all, a robust third front could liberate people from the confinements of the two-party system that have steadily weakened the people's role in the modern political system, now ruled by big government and mass communications. For ordinary people, the cost of being heard—not to mention of influencing a major party's agenda—is extremely high, and the potential for results is extremely uncertain. So the task of speaking to power has naturally shifted to larger players and major mediating institutions like organized labor, environmental organizations, and thousands of other civic-minded groups that can afford the investment. It is not just the cost of hiring well-connected lobbyists to persuade political incumbents that is prohibitive, but also the high cost of sustaining those insider relationships for the long haul, including campaign contributions at each election cycle.

This dependency sows another democratic dilemma. Major organizations that speak on behalf of broad constituencies are themselves confined by the power relationships in Washington. If they insist on promoting a controversial agenda that offends or frightens incumbent politicians, they may lose their access to the insiders. They cannot put this investment at risk casually because, for example, labor unions must defend their members from hostile political actions. So they count votes and decide it is unwise to pick fights with senators they may need in the future. Self-censorship seems logical and necessary, but it discourages rank-and-file members from expressing more radical ambitions. Farsighted political goals are sidetracked—or even silenced—so as not to disturb pragmatic politics.

In other words, big government and the two-party system have produced shrink-wrapped political debate that effectively shuts down free discussion and shuns ideas that arise from outside elite circles. In the party competition, both parties develop agendas premised on the same strategy—promoting themselves as the "less bad" alternative: You may not think much of what the Democrats are selling, but it's not as nearly as awful as what Republicans will do if they get power—or vice versa. The system exaggerates the differences between the two parties, strips the content from the party agendas, and suppresses dissent. In election seasons, party loyalists are told to stifle their complaints and pretend to be thrilled with the candidate, at least until the election is over.

The facade of a righteous two-party competition, however, has become less and less convincing to the public. The undeclared independents who spurn both parties are now roughly one-third of the voting population, equal in size to the Democrats and the Republicans. Nearly half of the voting-age population declines to participate at all, even in presidential elections.

Low voter participation makes the electorate more predictable and easier for incumbents to manage, but it represents a great opportunity for popular formations. Recruiting nonvoters is costly for the established parties because it requires house calls and patient conversations, not TV ads. But people know how to build long-term relationships among themselves in their own surroundings. They could literally destabilize the status quo by changing the shape of the electorate.

★　★　★　★　★

Among the rising costs of regular politics is the expense of finding out what the people think and what they want from politics by using elaborate marketing techniques like polling, focus groups, demographic analysis, and fanciful advertising. But these efforts are really directed at a different question: What do people think they want to see or hear from political candidates? Would you like to have a beer with him? Does she seem like a fighter? It costs a fortune to develop the answers and translate them into winning sales messages. It's an art form that is often empty and fraudulent.

"Life out of context," as Mosley put it, includes politics shorn of people. If the political parties, both leaders and followers, truly wish to know what the people think, then the people should tell them. But this information cannot pass through the elaborate filters erected by professional managers of the political competition. People have to speak for themselves, either collectively through numerous formations that they control or separately on soapboxes in parks. Let the politicians figure out how to listen to the gorgeous anarchy in Americans' voices and sort out the crackpots from the conscientious citizens. Let politicians find ways to incorporate what people have told them into the decision-making processes of government.

I was explaining some of this to a young friend who is an experienced organizer with a major labor union. "Who's going to organize it?" he asked. I gave him a lame answer: "The people." He did not seem impressed. Political organization does not happen by spontaneous combustion. I could invent a more convincing answer, but the truth is that I do not know exactly how these formations could arise from nothing more than conversations. Perhaps some "clubs for America" could start talking to other "clubs" and realize that they are thinking in very similar ways. Then they could go about building something larger together. Maybe churches would lend a hand. Maybe sympathetic organizations would show people the techniques of collective action without trying to control things.

Let a thousand flowers bloom. I am not a purist, but I know that one element is essential—the independence of the new formations. People have to "own" their organizations and be able to finance them. If a benefactor is an established institution with its own political agenda, the newcomers are likely to be influenced, if not ordered, to follow the wishes of the sponsor. If people cannot think freely for themselves, they are unlikely to reach far enough into new territory to get beyond the politics that already exists. It is another dilemma that citizens have to work through—how to cooperate with others without losing the integrity of their organizations.

From its earliest origins, the labor movement has always understood the importance of free trade unions that are independent of political parties and government and loyal only to their members. Labor's historically close relationship with the Democratic Party has become a mixed blessing, however, as unions have been weakened. Labor groups still put up lots of money and mobilize voters, but the Democrats have become less and less reliable allies. The Populist movement in the nineteenth century, Goodwyn explained, lost its focus when in frustration it aligned itself with the Democratic Party in the election of 1896. Its presidential candidate, William Jennings Bryan, thoroughly mangled the substance of what the Populists were trying to achieve and he lost anyway.

In this era, the Christian right is clearly the most successful political movement to arise from the ranks of ordinary citizens. Yet its close partnership with the Republican Party has resulted in regularly disappointed expectations. Evangelicals have loyally supplied the votes, but usually have been rewarded only with rhetoric, a relationship I once called "rancid populism."[8] Leading preachers gained celebrity, but the movement lost moral authority as its principles were compromised or ignored for short-term Republican gains. The question of who was using whom still lingers for conservative followers.

Along with independence, a popular formation must be able to communicate reliably with its members. In that regard, modern Americans have exciting advantages their forebearers lacked. Any new formation that arises outside of established politics cannot expect the news media to be helpful, since they will be indifferent or hostile to what citizens are attempting. In fact, members must learn to ignore the news media, especially at the outset. To grow and establish authenticity, the new organization must be able to regularly keep its members informed and to teach the content of the unsanctioned principles and policy ideas that are sure to be disparaged by conventional experts. The Populists, as

Goodwyn explained, learned to communicate despite many handicaps. They started their own newspapers, sent out traveling lecturers to spread the word, and organized massive, all-day rallies at which people learned the program and absorbed the principle of self-reliance.

But we have the Internet. The wondrous new technologies of the digital age could be the great allies of political insurgency. People around the world are learning how to use them. The Web is a place of mind-boggling anarchy, including everything from the sophisticated to the foul, from earnest discussions to half-baked anger and libelous conspiracy theories. We have already witnessed early uses of Internet communications as a potent organizing tool. The "meetups" organized for Howard Dean's upstart presidential campaign in 2004 got like-minded voters together in the same virtual room. MoveOn.org, with its targeted petitions and fund-raising, is like an ankle-biting kibitzer for the Democratic Party. The extraordinary surge of small donors supporting Barack Obama in the 2008 primary and election seasons suggests the presence of a new counterweight to big money. Internet technologies are an ideal fit for citizens organizing their own politics.

The advent of these technological and social changes "all add up to one big change: forming groups has gotten a lot easier," Clay Shirky, professor of telecommunications at New York University, explained. "To put it in economic terms, the costs incurred by creating a new group or joining an existing one have fallen in recent years, and not by just a little bit. They have collapsed."[9] People can now do it themselves without expending burdensome amounts of time and money or relying on existing institutions like political parties, companies, or governments.

In *Here Comes Everybody: The Power of Organizing Without Organizations*, Shirky explained the vast political implications. "The costs of all kinds of group activity—sharing, cooperation, and collective action—have fallen so far so fast that activities previously hidden beneath the floor are now coming to light," Shirky explained. "Prior to the current era, the alternative to institutional action was usually no action. Social tools provide a third alternative: action by loosely structured groups, operating without managerial direction and outside the profit motive."

"Organized money" has lost one of its big advantages. The long-standing issue in political debates—whether to put government or the private sector in charge—is now complicated by a third option: letting people assemble their own versions of governing responsibility through collective action. This does not mean government or business and finance will be stripped of power, but a powerful new countering force is now available to hold both of them to account. Independent formations are needed to make the case for citizens' direct engagement since we can assume that neither government nor business will speak reliably for them.

"Social tools don't create collective action," Shirky explained. "They merely remove the obstacles to it. The obstacles have been so significant and pervasive, however, that as they are being removed, the world is becoming a different place."

An early example he cites is Voice of the Faithful, a critical assembly of Catholic laity formed in response to the widespread abuses by priests. After the *Boston Globe* published a stunning series of revelations, people used the Internet to create and sustain a powerful community of protest. The Church was bewildered, having never encountered such a well-informed and persistent critical group based among laypeople rather than priests. Local formations like that group are likely to form first since people naturally focus more intently on their home communities. Uniting many local groups into nationwide voices is a much tougher challenge, but once again the technology is friendly. It leaps vast distances and differences.

New technologies are not utopia. They do not change human behavior so much as extend the reach of human beings and amplify the usual range of human qualities, both good and bad. The Internet cannot replace human conversation as the core of democracy. Still, this tool is an inviting breakthrough that provides an entirely different approach to reordering power. It awaits the ingenuity of young Americans who understand it and can show the rest of us how it might work.

Given our circumstances, Americans have a right to dream about a better future ahead. You might say we are obligated to do so. When I imagine that Americans will be awakened by difficult circumstances and set themselves in motion as citizens, it makes me feel hopeful for the country. People who are satisfied with the way politics functions may see the democratizing action as a formula for chaos that would splinter national unity and create more dissent in a system already unable to make big decisions. I think the opposite is likely. Once citizens of many different persuasions and perspectives have found their voices, they will see that they are united on many fundamental matters. When I spoke earlier about "fundamentalism," I meant that politics should be able to take up basic principles that are confined to neither the left nor right and are not defined by political parties.

These include some big questions those who uphold the status quo will not ask: When and how should the nation go to war? What defines (and limits) the role of government in using public resources to assist private enterprises? What essential rights and services ought to be available to anyone who is a citizen in this extraordinarily wealthy society?

A rich debate about fundamentals that includes citizens will produce a very different portrait of what Americans want for their country. As a people, we are both more generous and more realistic about these basic questions than the circumscribed political debate and distorted campaigns indicate.

I can see, for instance, a formation that would take on US militarism and lead a campaign to develop public support for a sane strategy for national defense. I can imagine military people, retired and active, joining with committed peace advocates to argue out the terms—hawks and doves at the same table. I imagine that an assembly advocating restoring integrity and honesty to both government and the private sector could unite the left and the right on fundamentals. At the very least, it would push members of Congress to face the waste and injustices inherent in the grand bazaar.

"Thickening democracy" is another fundamental objective that would unify most citizens despite differences on other matters. There are scores of reform proposals that elected politicians won't touch, mainly because they would empower citizens and insurgents at the expense of the established system. People with money, for example, are permitted tax deductions for philanthropic "gifts" that everyone knows really finance self-interested politics, such as think tanks and other supposedly nonpolitical front groups that "educate" Americans with artful propaganda.

Why not give a similar tax break to citizens—a tax credit of $200 or $400 a year for political contributions? But the people should be free to define their own "politics." They could contribute to candidates or parties if they choose, or give the money to their church, a charity, or an independent political formation—to whatever group they thought could improve the quality of our democracy.

Lots of other large possibilities for citizen intervention exist. We could rescue the ecological crisis from the stalling tactics of special interests, or jump-start the epic transition needed to create the post-petroleum economy. We could confront the nation's inventory of broken promises, including the scandal of poverty, and do something to make real change.

A lot of us know the situation. Official America is like a family member who is suffering from debilitating addictions. Our democracy is desperately in need of dramatic intervention by its sovereign citizens. We can do this. We can do it for ourselves, for our children and grandchildren, for the country. I don't claim to know for sure that we will succeed. I do believe that we will try.

ENDNOTES

CHAPTER ONE

1. The deterioration of US democracy has become a respectable subject since 1992, when I published *Who Will Tell People: The Betrayal of American Democracy* (Simon & Schuster, 1992). Foundations and universities devote research and study to the "problem," but neither major political party has yet acknowledged the failing system. Nor have US leaders stopped lecturing the rest of the world on the superior qualities of the American system.

2. James P. Young, *Reconsidering American Liberalism: The Troubled Odyssey of the Liberal Idea* (Boulder, CO: Westview, 1996).

CHAPTER THREE

1. David Barboza, "China Posts a Surplus Sure to Stir U.S. Alarm," *New York Times,* July 11, 2006], http://nytimes.com/2006/07/11/business/worldbusiness/11yuan.html.

2. The tragedy of New Orleans revealed many malignant dimensions at work, including racial bias, but one of the most devastating was the ineptitude of the federal government. See my article, "Apollo Now," in the *Nation,* January 2, 2006, http://www.thenation.com/doc/20060102/greider.

CHAPTER FOUR

1. Barack Obama, "The American Moment—April 23, 2007," April 23, 2007, http://www.thechicagocouncil.org/dynamic_page.php?id=64.

2. Tony Tassell, "European Bourses Eclipse US Markets by Value," *Financial Times,* April 3, 2007, http://www.ft.com/cms/s/0/f10e4dec-e17f-11db-bd73-000b5df10621.html.

3. Judy Mathewson and Todd Prince, "Gorbachev Says Bush Should Abandon 'Superpower' Perspective," Bloomberg.com, August 18, 2006, http://www.bloomberg.com/apps/news?pid=washingtonstory&sid=aBRVRJhIy87k.

4. The Reverend Martin Luther King's "Why I Am Opposed to the War in Vietnam" sermon (http://husseini.org/2007/01/martin-luther-king-jr-why-i-am.html), delivered at the Ebenezer Baptist Church in Atlanta on April 30, 1967, is particularly eerie when read against the backdrop of the war in Iraq.

CHAPTER FIVE

1. Jan Kregel, *Minsky's Cushions of Safety: Systemic Risk and the Crisis in the U.S. Subprime Mortgage Market*, Public Policy Brief No. 93, Annandale-on-Hudson, NY: Levy Economics Institute of Bard College, 2008, http://www.levy.org/pubs/ppb_93.pdf.

2. "The Financial System: What Went Wrong," *Economist,* March 19, 2008, http://www.economist.com/finance/displaystory.cfm?story_id=10881318.

3. William Greider, "The One-Eyed Chairman," *Nation,* September 19, 2005, http://www.thenation.com/doc/20050919/greider.

4. The warnings of a stock market bubble by Fed governors and Greenspan's response are from the minutes of Federal Open Market Committee closed-door meetings in 1996. Transcripts are not made public for five years, long after the public or politicians can usefully respond. For more information, see my article *"Il Maestro*'s Failed Magic" in the *Nation,* March 25, 2002, http://www.thenation.com/doc/20020325/greider.

5. Bob Woodward, in his adulatory book about Alan Greenspan—*Maestro: Greenspan's Fed and the American Boom* (Simon & Schuster, 2000)—reported on confidential interviews with the Fed chairman and assured readers that the tightening of credit in 1999 and 2000 was designed to pop the stock market bubble without announcing that intention. For a contrary view, see my article "Father Greenspan Loves Us All" in the *Nation,* January 1, 2001, http://www.thenation.com/doc/20010101/greider.

6. Office of the Comptroller of the Currency, Treasury Department, third quarter 2007.

7. The editors continued, "As for . . . Jamie Dimon, remind us to have him negotiate our next contract. He gets Bear's best assets, including a Manhattan building said to be worth $1.4 billion by itself. Meantime, he gets the Fed to backstop Bear's riskiest paper. We don't know the quality of that paper—and we hope the Fed has done its due diligence—but taxpayers are now on the hook for future losses." "Bear Naked Lenders," *Wall Street Journal*, March 18, 2008, http://online.wsj.com/public/article-print/SB102579841626143539.html [editorial].

CHAPTER SIX

1. For voluminous evidence on the devastating impact of lopsided US–China trade, see Robert E. Scott, *The China Trade Toll,* Economic Policy Institute Briefing Paper #219, Washington, DC: Economic Policy Institute; July 30, 2008, http://www.epi.org/content.cfm/bp219; and Charles W. McMillion, "China's Rapidly Changing Trade Flows," testimony before the US–China Economic and Security Review Commission, Washington, DC, July 16, 2008, http://www.uscc.gov/hearings/2008hearings/written_testimonies/08_07_16_wrts/08_07_16_mcmillion_statement.pdf.

2. "Attitudes Toward Trade and the Global Economy," Washington, DC: Lake Research Partners, March 16, 2007; and Pew Research Center for the People and the Press and Council on Foreign Relations, *America's Place in the World 2005: Opinion Leaders Turn Cautious, Public Looks Homeward,* Washington, DC: Pew Research Center for the People and the Press, November 2005, http://www.cfr.org/content/publications/attachments/Pew-Americas_Place_2005.pdf.

3. Charles W. McMillion, e-mail message to author.

4. Peter Morici, personal communication to author.

5. The research of the United States Business and Industrial Council provides an important counter to the more influential voices of the Business Roundtable and other trade associations that speak for the multinationals. See Alan Tonelson and Peter Kim, press release, December 5, 2006.

6. Deborah Solomon, "Foreign Investors Face New Hurdles Across the Globe," *Wall Street Journal,* July 6, 2007.

7. Peter Morici, "U.S. Records $60 Billion Trade Deficit in May," *Global Politician,* July 14, 2007, http://www.globalpolitician.com/23093-economics.

8. William Greider, "The Establishment Rethinks Globalization," *Nation,* April 30, 2007, http://www.thenation.com/doc/20070430/greider.

9. Nisha Agrawal, "Opening Remarks at the Launch of the Cambodia Equity Report 2007: Sharing Growth," Phnom Penh, Cambodia, June 12, 2007, http://web. worldbank.org/WBSITE/EXTERNAL/COUNTRIES/EASTASIAPACIFICEXT/ CAMBODIAEXTN/0,,contentMDK:21368954~menuPK:293861~ pagePK:2865066~piPK:2865079~theSitePK:293856,00.html.

10. William Greider, *One World, Ready or Not: The Manic Logic of Global Capitalism,* New York: Simon & Schuster, 1997.

11. Greider, *One World, Ready or Not.*

CHAPTER SEVEN

1. Roger C. Altman, Jason E. Bordoff, Peter R. Orszag, and Robert E. Rubin, *The Hamilton Project: An Economic Strategy to Advance Opportunity, Prosperity, and Growth,* Washington, DC: Brookings Institution, April 2006, http://www.brookings. edu/es/hamilton/THP_Strategy.pdf.

2. William Greider, "Born-Again Rubinomics," *Nation,* July 31, 2006, http://www. thenation.com/doc/20060731/greider. An edited transcript of my interview with Rubin, "A Conversation with Robert Rubin," can found at www.thenation.com/doc/20060731/ greiderweb.

3. Alan S. Blinder, "Offshoring: The Next Industrial Revolution?" *Foreign Affairs,* March/April 2006, http://www.foreignaffairs.org/20060301faessay85209/alan-s-blinder/offshoring-the-next-industrial-revolution.html. Blinder's remark on "irrelevant" economists is from his article "Free Trade's Great, but Offshoring Rattles Me," published in the *Washington Post* on May 6, 2007, http://www.washingtonpost.com/ wp-dyn/content/article/2007/05/04/AR2007050402555.html.

4. Lawrence Summers described the income inequities in two columns for the *Financial Times,* "The Global Middle Cries Out for Reassurance," October 30, 2006, http://blogs. ft.com/wolfforum/2006/10/the-global-middhtml; and "Only Fairness Will Assuage the Anxious Middle," December 11, 2006, http://blogs.ft.com/wolfforum/2006/12/ only-fairness-whtml.

5. Greider, "Born-Again Rubinomics."

6. Paul Krugman, "Divided Over Trade," *New York Times,* May 14, 2007, http://select. nytimes.com/2007/05/14/opinion/14krugman.html.

7. Jeff Faux, "Overhauling NAFTA," Economic Policy Institute Viewpoints, epi.org, February 29, 2008.

CHAPTER EIGHT

1. US Department of Defense, *Quadrennial Defense Review Report,* February 6, 2006, Report20060203.pdf, available at http://www.defenselink.mil/qdr.

2. James Traub, "Taunting the Bear," *New York Times,* August 9, 2008, http://www. nytimes.com/2008/08/10/weekinreview/10traub.html.

3. Albright's remark is quoted by retired army colonel Andrew J. Bacevich in *The New American Militarism: How Americans Are Seduced by War* (New York: Oxford University Press, 2005), a book that provides an excellent account of the years when US defense strategy shifted to all-purpose offense.

4. Condoleezza Rice, "Remarks at Town Hall Event at the University of Sydney's Conservatorium of Music," March 16, 2006, http://www.state.gov/secretary/rm/2006/63166.htm.

5. Cohen's original assertion appeared in 2005 and was updated in "The New American Cold War," *Nation,* July 10, 2006, http://www.thenation.com/doc/20060710/cohen.

6. Dana Priest, *The Mission: Waging War and Keeping Peace with America's Military,* New York: W. W. Norton, 2003.

7. Samantha Power, "The Democrats and National Security," *New York Review of Books,* August 14, 2008, http://www.nybooks.com/articles/21670.

8. Chalmers Johnson, *Blowback: The Costs and Consequences of American Empire,* New York: Metropolitan Books, 2000; *The Sorrows of Empire: Militarism, Secrecy, and the End of the Republic,* New York: Metropolitan Books, 2004; *Nemesis: The Last Days of the American Republic,* New York: Metropolitan Books, 2006.

9. My reporting led to a slender book, *Fortress America: The American Military and the Consequences of Peace* (New York: Public Affairs, 1998).

10. Michael T. Klare, "Containing China," TomDispatch.com, April 18, 2006, http://www.tomdispatch.com/post/78021/michael_klare_on_greeting_hu_with_a_21_gun_salute. See also Klare's "Revving Up the China Threat," *Nation,* October 24, 2005, http://www.thenation.com/doc/20051024/klare, and his book *Blood and Oil: The Dangers and Consequences of America's Growing Dependency on Imported Petroleum* (New York: Henry Holt, 2004).

11. Rhea Myerscough and Rachel Stohl, "U.S. Arms Exports and Military Assistance in the 'Global War on Terror,'" Washington, DC: Center for Defense Information, September 6, 2007, http://www.cdi.org/program/document.cfm?DocumentID=4080&from_page=../index.cfm.

12. Dilip Hiro, "The Sole Superpower in Decline," TomDispatch.com, August 20, 2007, http://www.tomdispatch.com/post/174830. Hiro's writing appears frequently in the *Nation* and Britain's the *Guardian.*

13. Stephen F. Cohen, "The New American Cold War," *Nation,* July 10, 2006, http://thenation.com/doc/20060710/cohen.

14. Robert D. Kaplan, *Imperial Grunts: The American Military on the Ground,* New York: Random House, 2005.

15. David Ignatius, "Ethiopia's Iraq," *Washington Post,* May 13, 2007, http://www.washingtonpost.com/wp-dyn/content/article/2007/05/11/AR2007051102114.html.

16. Oxfam International, "Somali Organizations Report of Bombings Targeting Innocent Civilians," Oxfam.org, January 12, 2007, http://www.oxfam.org/en/node/112 [press release].

17. Jeffrey Gettleman, "In Ethiopia, Fear and Cries of Army Brutality," *New York Times,* June 18, 2007, http://www.nytimes.com/2007/06/18/world/africa/18ethiopia.html.

18. Jeffrey Gettleman, "Ethiopia Holding 41 Suspects Who Fought with Somali Islamists, Officials Confirm," *New York Times,* April 11, 2007, http://www.nytimes.com/2007/04/11/world/africa/11ethiopia.html.

19. "Editor's Note: Somalia: Creating Another Iraq?" *AfricaFocus Bulletin,* January 16, 2007, http://www.africafocus.org/docs07/som0701a.php.

20. Issa G. Shivji, "Somalia: The Next Afghanistan + Iraq?" *Pambazuka News,* January 11, 2007, http://www.pambazuka.org/en/category/features/39142.

21. Salim Lone, "Destabilizing the Horn," TomPaine.com, January 8, 2007, http://www.tompaine.com/articles/2007/01/08/destabilizing_the_horn.php.

22. Danny Glover and Nicole C. Lee, "Say No to Africom," *Nation,* November 19, 2007, http://www.thenation.com/doc/20071119/glover_lee.
23. Ronan Farrow and Mia Farrow, "The 'Genocide Olympics,'" *Wall Street Journal,* March 28, 2007, http://www.miafarrow.org/ed_032307.html.
24. Jeffrey Gettleman, "As Somali Crisis Swells, Experts See a Void in Aid," *New York Times,* November 20, 2007, http://www.nytimes.com/2007/11/20/world/africa/20somalia.html.
25. Robert D. Kaplan, "Lost at Sea," *New York Times,* September 21, 2007, http://www.nytimes.com/2007/09/21/opinion/21kaplan.html.
26. Andrew J. Bacevich, *The New American Militarism: How Americans Are Seduced by War,* New York: Oxford University Press, 2005. Bacevich is a frequent commentator in newspapers and magazines; see, for instance, "The Semiwarriors," *Nation,* April 23, 2007, http://www.thenation.com/doc/20070423/bacevich.
27. Andrew J. Bacevich, "I Lost My Son to a War I Oppose. We Were Both Doing Our Duty," *Washington Post,* May 27, 2007, http://www.washingtonpost.com/wp-dyn/content/article/2007/05/25/AR2007052502032.html.
28. Cohen, "The New American Cold War."
29. Klare, "Revving Up the China Threat."
30. Klare, "Revving Up the China Threat."
31. Cohen, "The New American Cold War."
32. Hiro, "The Sole Superpower in Decline."
33. Alan Greenspan, *The Age of Turbulence: Adventures in a New World,* New York: Penguin, 2007.

CHAPTER NINE

1. Jeff Stein, "Can You Tell a Sunni from a Shiite?" *New York Times*, October 17, 2006, http://www.nytimes.com/2006/10/17/opinion/17stein.html.
2. Chalmers Johnson, *Blowback: The Costs and Consequences of American Empire,* New York: Metropolitan Books, 2000; *The Sorrows of Empire: Militarism, Secrecy, and the End of the Republic,* New York: Metropolitan Books, 2004; *Nemesis: The Last Days of the American Republic,* New York: Metropolitan Books, 2006.
3. Leaked documents that caused a sensation included White House and Justice Department "torture memos," the International Red Cross's confidential complaints about prisoner abuse at the prison at Guantánamo Bay, Cuba, and Defense Secretary Rumsfeld's authorization of holding "ghost prisoners" in violation of international law. See my article, "Embedded Patriots," *Nation,* July 12, 2004, http://www.thenation.com/doc/20040712/greider.
4. Richard J. Whalen, "Revolt of the Generals," *Nation,* October 16, 2006, http://www.thenation.com/doc/20061016/whalen.
5. Mosley begins *Life Out of Context* as a meditation on the cultural dislocation of African Americans. He ends with a vision of how politics can restore meaning to the lives of people who come together to act collectively as citizens. His book's provocative subtitle is *Which Includes a Proposal for the Non-Violent Takeover of the House of Representatives.*
6. Andrew J. Bacevich, *The New American Militarism: How Americans Are Seduced by War,* New York: Oxford University Press, 2005.

7. Michael T. Klare discusses the US reluctance to let go of Iraq and its oil in "Beyond the Age of Petroleum," *Nation*, November 12, 2007, http://www.thenation.com/doc/20071112/klare.
8. Statistics on worldwide defense spending are compiled annually by the Stockholm International Peace Research Institute (www.sipri.org). The data cited are available online.
9. Thom Shanker, "Joint Chiefs Chairman Looks Beyond Current Wars," *New York Times*, October 22, 2007, http://www.nytimes.com/2007/10/22/washington/22mullen.html.
10. George Wilson, a colleague and close friend since our days together at the *Washington Post*, has over the years been extraordinarily prescient in his understanding of the military institution. His article on the financial collision ahead is "Uncontrolled Pentagon Spending," *National Journal*, April 23, 2007.

CHAPTER TEN

1. Holly Sklar, "Billionaires Up, America Down," McClatchy-Tribune News Service, October 18, 2007, http://www.businessforafairminimumwage.org/node/71[opinion].
2. Charles W. McMillion, December 7, 2007, personal communication to author.
3. Greg Ip, "Income-Inequality Gap Widens," *Wall Street Journal*, October 12, 2007, http://online.wsj.com/public/article_print/SB119215822413557069.html.
4. William Greider, "The Education of David Stockman," *Atlantic*, December 1981, http://www.theatlantic.com/doc/198112/david-stockman. My series of interviews with David Stockman captured the chaos and confused realities that usually accompany intense political decision making, and these revelations angered Washington players with both of us. The budget director famously told me, "None of us really understands what's going on with all these numbers." My original account was expanded and published as *The Education of David Stockman and Other Americans*, New York: Dutton, 1982.
5. Ben Bernanke, c. 2004–2005
6. Ajay Kapur, Niall MacLeod, Narendra Singh, Priscilla Luk, Hao Hong, and Audrey Seybert. "Plutonomy: Buying Luxury, Explaining Global Imbalances," *Global Investigator*, October 14, 2005.
7. Ajay Kapur, Niall MacLeod, Narendra Singh, Priscilla Luk, Hao Hong, and Audrey Seybert. "Revisiting Plutonomy: The Rich Getting Richer," *Global Investigator*, March 5, 2006.
8. David L. Madland, "A Wink and a Handshake: Why the Collapse of the US Pension System Has Provoked Little Protest" (PhD dissertation, Georgetown University, 2007). Madland is now director of the American Worker Project at the Center for American Progress in Washington, DC.
9. John McClaughry, "Milton Friedman Responds," *Chemtech*, February 1974. For a more detailed exploration of how Milton Friedman's moral doctrine enabled business and finance to abandon the social contract and feed off others, see my book *The Soul of Capitalism: Opening Paths to a Moral Economy* (New York: Simon and Schuster, 2003).
10. Monica Langley, "Why $70 Million Wasn't Enough," *Wall Street Journal*, August 18, 2007, http://online.wsj.com/article/SB118740076313301636.html. The top 10 hedge fund managers in 2005 earned compensation ranging from $275 million to $1.5 billion, according to Jenny Anderson, "Atop Hedge Funds, Richest of the Rich Get Even More So," *New York Times*, May 26, 2006, http://nytimes.com/2006/05/26/business/26hedge.html.

11. Warren E. Buffett, "Memorandum to Berkshire Hathaway Managers," September 27, 2006, posted at http://www.ethicalleadershipgroup.com/blog/2006/10/warren_buffetts_memo_to_his_ma.html.

12. For a fuller account of usury and financial deregulation, see Chapter 5, "The Liberal Apology," in my book *Secrets of the Temple: How the Federal Reserve Runs the Country* (New York: Simon & Schuster, 1987).

13. James Buchan, *The Authentic Adam Smith: His Life and Ideas,* New York: W. W. Norton, 2006.

14. William Greider, "Friedman's Cruel Legacy," *Nation,* December 11, 2006, posted at http://www.zeitguy.com/wp-content/files/greider.htm.

15. The "peak oil" theory defines the critical point as the moment when half of the world's oil has already been pumped and consumed. Industry officials talk instead about the time when practical limitations will force oil production to a plateau well short of the peak and lead to the same profound economic disturbances. Russell Gold and Ann Davis, "Oil Officials See Limit Looming on Production," *Wall Street Journal,* November 19, 2007, posted at http://www.relocalize.net/oil_officials_see_limit_looming_on_production.

CHAPTER ELEVEN

1. I am inspired by the prophetic words economist John Maynard Keynes wrote nearly eighty years ago, as the Great Depression was enveloping the world. Eventually, Keynes explained, capitalism would produce such an abundance of capital that highly developed nations like the United States would be liberated from the ancient economic struggle for survival and could discard capitalism's brutish aspects, including greed and social destruction. "For the first time since his creation man will be faced with his real, his permanent problem—how to use his freedom from pressing economic cares, how to occupy the leisure, which science and compound interest will have won for him, *to live wisely and agreeably and well* [my italics]." Keynes's magnificent optimism is from the essay "Economic Possibilities for Our Grandchildren" in his *Essays in Persuasion* (New York: Harcourt, Brace, 1932).

2. For data on weakening conditions, see my article "Squeezing the Have-Nots," *Nation,* October 31, 2005, http://www.thenation.com/doc/20051031/greider.

3. Henry C. Wallich, "Zero Growth," *Newsweek,* January 24, 1972, quoted in Herman E. Daly, "A Catechism of Growth Fallacies," *Steady-State Economics,* Washington, DC: Island Press, 1991.

4. George Monbiot, "Bring On the Recession," *Guardian,* October 9, 2007, http://www.monbiot.com/archives/2007/10/09/bring-on-the-recession.

5. Among the controversial assumptions Daly made in constructing the Index of Sustainable Economic Welfare was that a measure of income inequality should be included. The premise was that society's well-being degrades as inequality increases, a point that only hard-right conservatives would dispute today. The book was revised and the index refined in a second edition published in 1994.

6. Lew Daly, e-mail message to author.

7. Daly's *Steady-State Economics* was first published in 1977 by W. H. Freeman, then expanded and reissued by Island Press in 1991. I first read it years ago and did not fully grasp the logic. When I reviewed the book recently and saw Daly's discussion of growth and maturity, it occurred to me that my use of the maturity metaphor might have been inspired by his work.

8. Wackernagel said in announcing the release of the *Living Planet Report 2006:*

"Humanity is living off its ecological credit card. While this can be done for a short while, overshoot ultimately leads to liquidation of the planet's ecological assets, and the depletion of resources, such as the forests, oceans and agricultural land upon which our economy depends." See Chris Hails, Jonathan Loh, and Steven Goldfinger, editors, *The Living Planet Report 2006,* WWF International, Institute of Zoology, and Global Footprint Network, October 24, 2006, http://www.footprintnetwork.org/newsletters/gfn_blast_0610.html.

9. In my last book, *The Soul of Capitalism: Opening Paths to a Moral Economy,* I explained many promising potential changes and described these reformers as pioneers.

10. The per capita income statistics are from the United Nations Human Development Index for 2007–2008 (available at http://hdr.undp.org/en/statistics/data) and based on purchasing power parity calculations. Other measures that include currency valuations produce somewhat different results and change from year to year based on economic conditions, but the general picture remains the same regardless of the measure used.

11. The children in poverty statistics are from UNICEF, *Child Poverty in Rich Countries, 2005,* Innocenti Report Card Number 6, http://unicef-icdc.org/publications/pdf/repcard6e.pdf. Income distribution was ranked by the World Bank in *World Development Indicators 2002,* available at http://go.worldbank.org/5VX9E9BNT0.

12. Janet C. Gornick, "Overworked, Time Poor, and Abandoned by Uncle Sam," *Dissent,* Summer 2005, http://www.dissentmagazine.org/article/?article=215. See also Janet C. Gornick, Alexandra Heron, and Ross Eisenbrey, *The Work-Family Balance,* Economic Policy Institute Briefing Paper #189, Washington, DC: Economic Policy Institue, May 24, 2007, http://www.sharedprosperity.org/bp189.html; and Janet C. Gornick and Marcia K. Meyers, *Families That Work: Policies for Reconciling Parenthood and Employment,* New York: Russell Sage Foundation, 2003.

CHAPTER TWELVE

1. I first compared modern corporations to the old big-city political machines in *Who Will Tell the People: The Betrayal of American Democracy* (New York: Simon & Schuster, 1992). The chapter entitled "Citizen GE" portrays General Electric's operation as an aggressive and ambidextrous political organization.

2. Robert S. McIntyre of Citizens for Tax Justice has been studying tax avoidance by major corporations for more than two decades, and his reports on profitable companies that arrange to be tax-free are always shocking. For the information in this and the following paragraphs, I have drawn upon a report by McIntyre and T. D. Coo Nguyen of the Institute on Taxation and Economic Policy, *Corporate Income Taxes in the Bush Years,* released in September 2004, as well as McIntyre's essay "Tax Cheats and Their Enablers," published in *Bridging the Tax Gap: Addressing the Crisis in Federal Tax Administration,* edited by Max Sawicky (Washington, DC: Economic Policy Institute, April 2006). Some historical comparisons are drawn from Joel Friedman's *The Decline of Corporate Income Tax Revenues,* Washington, DC: Center on Budget and Policy Priorities, October 24, 2003, http://www.cbpp.org/10-16-03tax.htm.

3. Andy Pasztor, "Boeing to Settle Federal Probes for $615 Million," *Wall Street Journal,* May 15, 2006; and CorporateWatch.org.

4. Jesse Drucker, "Wal-Mart Cuts Taxes By Paying Rent to Itself," *Wall Street Journal,* February 5, 2007, posted at http://www.realestatejournal.com/reits/20070205-drucker.html.

5. McIntyre and Nguyen, *Corporate Income Taxes in the Bush Years;* McIntyre, "Tax Cheats and Their Enablers," *Bridging the Tax Gap.*

6. "Backdating to the Future," *Wall Street Journal,* October 12, 2006 [editorial].

7. William Greider, "Election Matters: Kerry's Crucible," *Nation,* April 26, 2004, http://www.thenation.com/doc/20040426/greider.

8. Alex Berenson, "Tax Break Used by Drug Makers Failed to Add Jobs as Advertised," *New York Times,* July 24, 2007, http://www.nytimes.com/2007/07/24/business/24drugtax.html.

9. Timothy Aeppel, "Tax Break Brings Billions to U.S., but Impact on Hiring Is Unclear," *Wall Street Journal,* October 5, 2005.

10. "The State of Corporate Welfare," *Multinational Monitor,* September/October 2006, http://www.multinationalmonitor.org/mm2006/092006/editorial.html [editorial].

11. Aeppel, "Tax Break Brings Billions."

12. David Cay Johnston, "In Deregulation, Plants Turn into Blue Chips," *New York Times,* October 23, 2006, http://www.nytimes.com/2006/10/23/business/23utility.html; and Rebecca S. Smith, "A Brief History of Pricing Power," *Wall Street Journal,* January 16, 2007.

13. Johnston, "In Deregulation, Plants Turn Into Blue Chips"; and Smith, "A Brief History of Pricing Power."

14. Robert Weissman, "Big Business Is Even More Unpopular Than You Think," Editor's Blog, *Multinational Monitor,* January 15, 2008, http://www.multinationalmonitor.org/editorsblog/index.php?/archives/68-Big-Business-Is-Even-More-Unpopular-Than-You-Think.html.

15. "Oil, Pharmaceutical, Health Insurance, Managed Care, Utilities and Tobacco Top the List of Industries That Many People Think Need More Regulation," *Harris Poll* #107, November 1, 2007, http://www.harrisinteractive.com/harris_poll/index.asp?PID=825.

16. Anthony DePalma, "EPA Is Sued by 12 States Over Reports on Chemicals," *New York Times,* November 29, 2007, http://www.nytimes.com/2007/11/29/us/29EPA.html.

17. A fuller discussion of these insights appears in my book *The Soul of Capitalism: Opening Paths to a Moral Economy.* For examples of corporations having virtuous social values and behavior, see in particular the chapters "Imperious Capital" and "Command and Control."

18. My critique of the "grand bazaar" is not partisan or aimed exclusively at the spendthrift conservatives of today's politics. In fact, I first used the phrase in 1977 in an essay I wrote for a special section in the *Washington Post* commemorating the inauguration of Jimmy Carter. A *Post* editor liked the piece so much that he published it again four years later, in the inauguration issue for Ronald Reagan.

19. Doyle supervised GE's political operations during the 1980s. His remark, made at a conference of the Jerome Levy Institute held on April 28, 1995, was quoted previously in *The Soul of Capitalism.*

20. Rachel Nardin, "Obama's Health Plan, Dissected," *New York Times,* July 25, 2008, http://www.pnhp.org/news/2008/july/obamas_health_plan.php [letter to the editor].

21. David U. Himmelstein and Steffie Woolhandler, "I Am Not a Health Reform," *New York Times,* December 15, 2007, http://www.nytimes.com/2007/12/15/opinion/15woolhandler.html[opinion]; and "Health Policy Placebos," *Nation,* April 14, 2008, http://www.thenation.com/doc/20080414/himmelstein.

22. William Greider, "Riding Into the Sunset," *Nation*, June 27, 2005, http://www.thenation.com/doc/20050627/greider.

23. Greider, "Riding Into the Sunset." Teresa Ghilarducci, an economist and pension expert at the New School for Social Research, designed a comprehensive blueprint for a new national pension she calls a guaranteed retirement account. The plan can be found online at the Economic Policy Institute's Agenda for Shared Prosperity site, http://www.sharedprosperity.org/bp204.html.

24. Peter G. Peterson published his two-page ad in the *New York Times* on September 7, 2008. The alliance of sixteen economists propounded their strategy for cutting entitlements in *Taking Back Our Fiscal Future*, April 2008, http://www.brookings.edu/~/media/Files/rc/papers/2008/04_fiscal_future/04_fiscal_future.pdf.

25. William Greider, "Now That's a Patriot Act," TheNation.com, August 3, 2007, http://www.thenation.com/blogs/notion?pid=219923.

26. Deborah Groban Olson, personal memo to author, March 30, 2008. Information on fair exchange legislation is available at http://esoplaw.com/Fair%20Exchange.htm.

CHAPTER THIRTEEN

1. Many of my ideas for a jump-shift strategy to respond to the US trade debt and economic deterioration first appeared in my article "Debtor Nation," *Nation*, May 10, 2004, http://www.thenation.com/doc/20040510/greider.

2. Keynes predicted that technology and capitalist production would eventually solve the ancient problem of scarcity in a prescient essay, "Economic Possibilities for Our Grandchildren," published in *Essays in Persuasion* (Harcourt, Brace, 1932). Keynes wrote, "For the first time since his creation man will be faced with his real, his permanent problem—how to use his freedom from pressing economic cares, how to occupy the leisure, which science and compound interest will have won for him, to live wisely and agreeably and well."

CHAPTER FOURTEEN

1. For an account of the principles and practices of the faith-based community organizations nurtured by the Industrial Areas Foundation, read Edward T. Chambers, *Roots for Radicals: Organizing for Power, Action, and Justice* (Continuum, 2003). Chambers was a close colleague of Saul Alinsky, who pioneered community-organizing approaches and launched the Industrial Areas Foundation in 1940. Chambers took over after Alinsky's death in 1972 and developed a deeper understanding, grounded in the Gospels, of what people want and need to organize their own political power. Michelle Obama invoked the phrase "The world as it is, the world as it should be" in her speech at the 2008 Democratic National Convention that nominated Barack Obama for president. Years before, he'd learned the phrase as a community organizer.

2. The title of Wilkins's book—*Jefferson's Pillow: The Founding Fathers and the Dilemma of Black Patriotism* (Beacon Press, 2001)—refers to Thomas Jefferson's earliest childhood memory of being borne aloft on a big pillow by one of his family's slaves.

3. Anyone who reads Lawrence Goodwyn's book—*The Populist Moment: A Short History of the Agrarian Revolt in America* (Oxford University Press, 1978)—will recognize how much he has informed and influenced my understanding of democracy.

4. For the image of an underground river I am indebted to film director Terrence Malick,

who, upon hearing my description of people keeping the buried promise of democracy alive over years and generations, observed that it was "like an underground river."

5. My account of *Briggs v. Elliott* appeared in the *Washington Post* on September 3, 1970. Fifteen years after the Supreme Court had ordered school desegregation with "all deliberate speed," white authorities in places like Summerton were still resisting.

6. The compelling story of the SNCC explains the importance of grounding political action in nonviolent principles. See Wesley C. Hogan, *Many Minds, One Heart: SNCC's Dream for a New America* (University of North Carolina Press, 2007).

7. Walter Mosley, *Life Out of Context: Which Includes a Proposal for the Non-Violent Takeover of the House of Representatives,* New York: Nation Books, 2006.

8. William Greider, *Who Will Tell the People: The Betrayal of American Democracy,* New York: Simon & Schuster, 1992.

9. Clay Shirky, *Here Comes Everybody: How Digital Networks Transform Our Ability to Gather and Cooperate,* New York: Penguin Press, 2008.

ACKNOWLEDGMENTS

One of the random joys in life is encountering great teachers outside the classroom and learning from their wisdom, gratis. I have met many of these natural teachers over the years, as this book illustrates. I take this opportunity to thank them all.

In particular, this book's dedication honors Lawrence Goodwyn and Lee Halprin. Both are retired professors of history and deeply learned in the politics and culture of American society. Each generously played the role of friendly counselor and critic during the course of my work on this book—questioning, nudging, correcting, encouraging, frowning, and sometimes smiling. Our occasional conversations are a great luxury for me, like private tutorials. Talking with either is like a tonic that clears the mind and refreshes my spirit.

Larry Goodwyn, emeritus historian at Duke University, is author of *Democratic Promise*, the history of America's populist revolt I cited in Chapter 14. His understanding of social movements and the structure of political power has been a beacon of mine for many years. So is his relentless insistence on greater clarity in what I write.

Lee Halprin taught American studies for many years at the New England Conservatory of Music. He approaches the same terrain from a different angle— the deep interplay between culture and politics, the centrality of literature to political thought as writers and poets announce new values ahead of conventional political actors. Lee played a pivotal role in helping me get started by arranging the lecture series I delivered at Southern New Hampshire University's School of Community Economic Development. This was an opportunity to try out my scattered thoughts and develop more coherence. I suspect I got more from the experience than the audience did.

I owe a similar debt to *The Nation*, where I have written for the last 10 years and tried out early versions of some of the ideas in this book. I joined the magazine at the tail end of the Clinton years and was especially proud to be part of it during the reckless Bush regime. From the outset, *The Nation* was nearly alone as the brave voice confronting George W. Bush, his wrongful war in Iraq, and the many other malignancies of his presidency. Under Katrina vanden Heuvel, who succeeded Victor Navasky as editor and publisher, the magazine has become the country's largest political weekly (no others are close). *The Nation* operates on a simple formula—tough-minded reporting and human sympathy. Consistently out front in espousing a progressive vision for the country, *The Nation* does not wait for public approval or conventional politics. It opens new ground and invites others to follow.

At Rodale, my book was in very good hands—superb and attentive professionals at every level—and I thank them profusely for their smart, shrewd judgments. I am especially indebted to Shannon Welch as editor, copy editor Nancy E. Elgin, and senior project editor Nancy N. Bailey.

Finally, there is Linda Furry Greider who once again has endured the collateral costs of my obsessions. We have been married for 47 years and feel as though it is going to last. Twenty years ago, I dedicated my first big book, *Secrets of the Temple,* to Linda with these words: "Whose intellect and social sensibilities have informed this book." This is still true. And I still owe her.

INDEX

Stukes, Bo, 286
Sudan, 142, 163–64
Summers, Lawrence, 98
Sunni Muslims, 150–51
"Super bull market," 42, 47
Supply-side economics, 180
Sustainability, 194–95, 204, 255
Sweden, 215

Taiwan, 63–64
Tariffs, 104, 108–9
Taxes
  on capital gains, 256
  on consumption, 178–79
  corporate
    amnesty for, 223
    deforming of, 255–56
    incentives for, 220
    paid, 221–22
    penalties for, 106–9
    performance-based approach to, 241–42
  cuts in, 19, 177, 180–81
  flat rate, 179
  income, 179
  just taxation and, 256
  philanthropic gift credits, 298
  for political contributions, proposed, 298
  property, 256
  reform proposals, 179, 243–44, 256, 298
  on US multinational corporations, 106–9
Tax Justice Network, 222
Technological revolution and technology, 67, 69, 71
Terrorism, 19, 94, 118, 125
Terrorist attacks of 9/11, 15, 124–25, 137
Thrift Savings Plan, 239
TIAA-CREF pensions, 239
Trade deficits
  Buffet's warning about, 23–24
  cap on, proposal for, 103, 105–9
  China and US, 28, 63, 65
  dismissal of, 28
  globalization and, 17, 71
  governing elites and, evasion of discussing, 70
  impact of, 73–74
  Japan and, 105
Trade surplus, 71

Trade theory, orthodox, 76
Tragedy of American Diplomacy, The (Williams), 155
Triangle Waist Company fire (1911), 114
"Trickle down" economics, 179–80
Truth-telling, 1–2, 5, 149
Twain, Mark, 156
Two-party political system, 273–74, 291–93. *See also* Democrats; Republicans

Underground river of democratic promise, 283–84
Unemployment, 46, 49, 200–201
Unions, 88–89, 113–14, 217, 232, 295
United Nations, 26, 34
United States. *See also* Financial crisis (2008); *specific challenges facing*
  as adolescent, analogy of, 35, 206–7
  Africa and, 120, 140–43
  allies of, diminishing, 29
  arms race and, 19, 147
  arrogance of, 6, 28, 67
  budget deficits, 49, 177, 179–81, 252
  challenges facing
    democracy, decaying, 3–6, 22
    difference from past, 8–9
    ecological crisis, 20–21
    examining, 8–9
    free-market ideology, 19–20
    globalization, 16–18
    militarism and war, 18–19
    as turning point in history, 8
  China and
    containment strategy, 118, 144–45
    as creditor of, 17, 62–65
    military strategy, 18–19, 118–20, 134–35
    multinational corporations, 64–65, 72
    relationship between, 94, 134–35
    trade deficits, 28, 63, 65
  choices facing, 35–36
  cold war and, 26–27, 66, 123–24, 134, 147, 156
  "Come home, America" phrase, 9, 34–35
  communism and, 26–27, 66, 112, 152–53, 161
  debt, 16–18, 24, 62–65, 177, 179–81, 252

US multinational corporations (*cont.*)
  offshoring and, 64, 97, 106, 221–22
  taxing, 106–9
  think tank for, 71
USS *Arleigh Burke,* 133
US Steel, 232
US Supreme Court, 285
Usury, 190–91, 254. *See also* Borrowing;
  Debt

Venezuela, 29
Verizon, 220
Vietnam War, 34, 46, 129–32, 134,
  152–53, 160, 162
Vladek, Bruce, 22
Voice of the Faithful, 297
Volcker, Paul, 46–50

Wachovia, 221
Wackernagel, Mathis, 207
"Wage insurance," 98
Wages, 31, 63, 115, 176, 200. *See also*
  Incomes
Wallich, Henry, 202
Wall Street
  as debt industry, 54–55, 177
  deregulation and, 50–51
  Federal Reserve and, 49
  financial bailout for, 240–41
  financial crisis (2008) and, 23, 37,
    39–43
  greed and, 189
  Greenspan put and, 51
  hedge funds, 224
  megabanks and, 50
  power of, 58
  Shanghai (China) as next, 72
Wal-Mart, 80, 222
War. *See* Militarism and war; *specific
  name*
Washington, George, 165, 279
"Washington consensus," 68, 85–86, 94,
  124
Wealth accumulation, 261–62

Weapons of mass destruction. *See*
  Nuclear weapons
Weill, Sanford, 184
Weissman, Robert, 224–25
Welfare, corporate, 223
Welfare states, 31
Whalen, Richard J., 165
White supremacy, 139–40, 157, 159, 276,
  279–80
Who Will Tell the People (Greider), 3
Wilkins, Roger, 279
Williams, William Appleman, 155–56
Wilson, George C., 170–71
"Wink and a Handshake, A" (Madland's
  PhD dissertation), 188
"Winner's complex," 33, 122, 153
Woolhandler, Steffie, 236–37
Workers, industrial, 110–13. *See also*
  Labor unions
World as is and as it ought to be thinking,
  270, 273, 275
World Bank, 26, 29, 34, 66, 85–86
WorldCom, 189
World Trade Organization (WTO), 29,
  68, 94, 108–9, 115, 253
World War I, 26, 66
World War II
  borrowing money during, 251, 256
  economic policy during, 249–51
  facts of, complicated, 11
  Hitler and, 112, 159
  Japan in, 159
  meaning of war and, 159
  Pearl Harbor attack and, 249
  personal experience of, 10–11
  as possibility for transforming United
    States, 248–51, 257
  treaty after, 119
  triumph of, for United States, 25, 67
  years after, 26–27, 123
WTO, 29, 68, 94, 108–9, 115, 253

Yankelovich, Daniel, 69
Yeltsin, Boris, 123